ROUTLEDGE LIBRARY EDITIONS: DEVELOPMENT

SEAPORTS AND DEVELOPMENT

SEAPORTS AND DEVELOPMENT
The Experience of Kenya and Tanzania

B. S. HOYLE

Volume 69

Routledge
Taylor & Francis Group
LONDON AND NEW YORK

First published in 1983

This edition first published in 2011
by Routledge
2 Park Square, Milton Park, Abingdon, Oxon, OX14 4RN

Simultaneously published in the USA and Canada
by Routledge
711 Third Avenue, New York, NY 10017

Routledge is an imprint of the Taylor & Francis Group, an informa business

First issued in paperback 2013

British Library Cataloguing in Publication Data
A catalogue record for this book is available from the British Library

ISBN 13: 978-0-415-58414-2 (Set)
eISBN 13: 978-0-203-84035-1 (Set)
ISBN 13: 978-0-415-59502-5 (Volume 69 hbk)
eISBN 13: 978-0-203-83680-4 (Volume 69)
ISBN 13: 978-0-415-85050-6 (Volume 69 pbk)

Publisher's Note
The publisher has gone to great lengths to ensure the quality of this reprint but points out that some imperfections in the original copies may be apparent.

Disclaimer
The publisher has made every effort to trace copyright holders and welcomes correspondence from those they have been unable to contact.

SEAPORTS AND DEVELOPMENT

The Experience of Kenya and Tanzania

B. S. Hoyle
University of Southampton

GORDON AND BREACH SCIENCE PUBLISHERS
New York London Paris

Gordon and Breach, Science Publishers, Inc.
One Park Avenue
New York NY 10016

Gordon and Breach Science Publishers Ltd.
42 William IV Street
London WC2N 4DE

Gordon & Breach
58, rue Lhomond
75005 Paris

Library of Congress Cataloging in Publication Data

Hoyle, B. S.
Seaports and development.

(Transportation studies, ISSN 0278-3819 ; v. 3)
Includes bibliographical references and index.
1. Harbors–Kenya. 2. Harbors–Tanzania. 3. Underdeveloped areas–Harbors.
I. Title. II. Series.
HE559.K4H6 1982 387.1'09676'2 82-12128
ISBN 0-677-06030-0

Cover photograph shows the cityport of Mombasa, Kenya. (Courtesy of Kenya Ports Authority.)

Contents

List of Figures

Note: All maps are oriented with north at the top

List of Tables

List of Plates

Introduction to the Series

This broad-ranging series of books will cover many of the varied aspects of transportation. The subject area will be generally divided into two parts: the first, dealing with planning and technological aspects of transportation, the second with specialized transportation.

Within the context of this series, technology and planning will include the wide spectrum of various aspects of the design and planning of vehicles and infrastructure for the transport of freight and passengers, as well as operational and management considerations. The general aim of the planning and technology series is to provide readers with the state of the art and to summarize the status of transportation.

The second part of the series will seek to generate monographs dealing with improving the mobility of those groups in society increasingly characterized as the transportation disadvantaged, particularly, but not exclusively, the elderly, the disabled and families with low income. It is anticipated that the content of these books will be derived largely from research, policy analysis and documental field experience. The subject matter will include advances in relevant technology, service and methods demonstrations, improved planning and methodology, major or proposed changes in public policy and innovative proposals for system development or change.

Occasionally, more specific monographs will be published, presenting the results of individual studies into areas of special interest to planners and technologists.

As with any monograph series, the emphasis is on current information, and the material will be of interest to the transportation practitioner, the postgraduate student and academics working in the field.

NORMAN ASHFORD
WILLIAM G. BELL

Preface

The role of seaports in the development process in less-developed countries is vital but often unappreciated, and the object of this study is to demonstrate some aspects of this role and to underline its importance. Discussion is focused on the character of port activity within the interrelated contexts of transport systems and regional economic planning; the approach is essentially spatial, but the development of port systems over time is also considered. Throughout the study, general principles of port development are illustrated by detailed reference to one specific Third World port group – that of the Indian Ocean coasts of Kenya and Tanzania; the principal seaports of this area are analysed in relation to the space economy of the hinterlands they serve.

The research on which this book is based was begun in the early 1960s and has been continued at intervals over more than two decades. From my base at Makerere University, Uganda, I travelled on numerous occasions in the 1960s through Kenya and Tanzania; and I am grateful to Professor S.J.K. Baker and Professor J.H. Bird for stimulating and guiding my early interest in East African affairs and in problems of port development. More recently I have revisited East Africa from my home port of Southampton, and I acknowledge the financial support of the Nuffield Foundation which allowed me to undertake further work in Kenya and Tanzania in the mid-1970s and early 1980s. I also record my appreciation of the fact that research clearance was granted by the governments of Kenya and Tanzania.

Many members of the staff of the Kenya Ports Authority and of the Tanzania Harbours Authority were very helpful in providing access to published and unpublished information and in enabling me to make full use of the limited time available during recent research visits. At Mombasa, I am especially grateful for the continuing interest and assistance of Mr Jonathan D. Mturi (Managing Director, KPA), and I wish also to acknowledge the help given by Mr Samson Ondego (Public Relations

Officer), Mr Albert C. Mumba (Principal Planning Officer, Statistics) and numerous other members of the KPA staff. Similarly, at the Tanzanian ports, assistance given by many members of the staff of the THA was much appreciated: Mr Peter K. Macha (Executive Chairman), Mr D.A. Ndikumwami (Director of Planning), Mr Joseph J. Makiponya (Administrative Officer, Legal), Mr J.O. Mkinga (Senior Statistical Officer) and Mr A.S. Nandala (Port Manager, Tanga) all contributed substantially to the progress of the research. Interesting and useful discussions were held with many other people, too numerous to mention individually; but I wish to record the kind assistance of Captain P. Henrard (Technical Consultant, Kenya Cargo Handling Services Ltd.), Mr John D. Mettam (Bertlin and Partners), and members of the staff of the Kenya Railways Corporation and of the Tanzania Railways Corporation.

Parts of this book are based to a certain extent on an earlier study entitled *The seaports of East Africa* published in 1967 by the East African Publishing House, Nairobi. Some paragraphs in Chapter 1 are based on the introduction to my book *Transport and development* (Macmillan, 1973), and others are derived from my contribution to *La croissance urbaine en Afrique noire et à Madagascar* (Paris, CNRS, 1972, 708-718). Chapter 3 originated as a paper entitled 'Early port development in East Africa: the concept of changing port hierarchies' (published in *Tijdschrift voor Economische en Sociale Geografie* 58, 1967, 94-102), now rewritten and much extended in the light of more recent evidence. An earlier version of the *Anyport* discussion in Chapter 4 appeared in 1968 in the *Transactions of the Institute of British Geographers* (44, 163-183); and the East African version of the Taaffe, Morrill and Gould model (Chapter 1) first appeared in *Geographical essays in honour of K.C. Edwards* (Nottingham University, 1970, 163-183). The discussion in Chapter 8 on the proposal to develop a second deep-water port in Kenya is based on B.S. Hoyle and D.A. Pinder (eds.), *Cityport industrialization and regional development: spatial analysis and planning strategies* (Oxford, Pergamon Press, 1981, 297-301). I am grateful to the editors and publishers concerned for permission to adapt material in this way.

The maps and diagrams which form an integral part of the book have been drawn in the Cartographic Unit of the Department of Geography at Southampton University, under the supervision of the Principal Experimental Officer, Mr A.S. Burn. To him and his staff, and to our Departmental Secretary Mrs Renée Flint, I extend my sincere thanks for their skill and patience. Additional typing assistance was provided by Miss Helen Boby and Mrs Sally Johnson.

A survey of a port complex within such a relatively brief compass inevitably contains errors of fact or emphasis, and some parts of this book will date quickly as port development and research continue. A number of colleagues and friends have been kind enough to read through parts of the text and have helped to clarify many points; I acknowledge in this context the advice of Dr Bashir Datoo, Captain P. Henrard, Mr Peter Macha, Mr John Mettam, Mr Jonathan Mturi and Dr Francis Ojany. The responsibility for remaining errors is nevertheless my own, and views expressed do not necessarily reflect those of the port authorities. I fully realise that many of those who sail the ships, work the cargoes and administer the ports know far more about shipping and port development than I do, but I nevertheless hope that anyone involved in problems of seaport systems or of regional development planning who may chance to read these pages will find in them something of value in the form of reference material or new viewpoints on familiar scenes.

B.S. HOYLE
University of Southampton

1 Transport Systems and Seaport Development

A seaport is fundamentally a central place of economic and cultural interchange; more specifically, it is a place where the mode of transportation changes from land to water-borne systems. Such a place originates and grows as its functions develop in response to demands from a wide variety of sources and as a reflection of interrelationships that extend over a wide area on various scales (Alexandersson and Norstrom, 1963; Bird, 1973). As a modern node in a multimodal system, the essential function of a seaport is transport integration; but in the performance of this function, and for other reasons, a seaport may also become a major urban centre, an important source of employment, and an influential factor in regional and national development. It is unwise, therefore, to consider the problems and characteristics of seaports in isolation; to be understood, any seaport or seaport system must be looked at in regional, national and international terms, and in relation to the various factors that influence its development and operation. Increased understanding of the role of seaports in relation to the economies and societies they serve will not necessarily lead to the solution of any of the problems with which seaports are associated; but it should provide part of the essential background against which such problems can be realistically assessed.

The problems of seaports and their interrelationships with the processes of socioeconomic change are nowhere more critical than in the less-developed countries (LDCs) of the so-called Third World. In many countries of Latin America, Africa and Asia the role of the seaport in the development process is at once vital yet little understood. In this book an attempt is made to underline the importance of seaports in the development process by using information from a specific region of the less-developed world: the seaports of Kenya and Tanzania, which serve an East African hinterland that transcends the boundaries of these two coastal countries, illustrate in a variety of ways problems that are common to the Third World as a whole. Each specific aspect of the East African port system that is discussed here, therefore, is set within a broader appreciation of port problems and is used to illustrate ways in which those problems may be approached and analysed. In this introductory chapter an attempt is made to place the study of seaports within the broader context of transport systems and their relationships with development, to introduce the general pattern of tropical African seaport systems, to outline some of the major factors that affect seaport development and to look at ways in which the study of port development may be approached.

Transport and Development

The complex interrelationships between transport systems and the development process provide a subject of considerable theoretical interest and practical importance, and one that has occupied a good deal of attention in both advanced and less-developed countries (Hoyle, 1973). The interaction between the level and pattern of transport resources and the average standard of living of the population of an area is a critical factor affecting economic and social progress, and should be taken into account at all stages of national and regional development planning. In the currently advanced countries, a good deal of attention was paid to transport innovation during the formative years of industrial growth; today, new strategies of economic planning require the modification and renewal of inherited transport systems. In the less-developed countries there is widespread concern for transport in the context of the desire to promote rapid economic development. Today, the spectrum of transport modes available in the Third World ranges from head porterage to jumbo jets and from simple canoes to international containers, although in many localities the degree of intermodal choice is often severely restricted. Yet "there is no escape from transport" (Munby, 1968, 7); even in the most remote and least developed parts of the Third World, transport in some form is a fundamental part of the daily rhythm of life.

The study of transport is not, of course, the unique prerogative of any one academic discipline, but is shared by and requires the cooperation of several interrelated disciplines. Each subject offers its own range of techniques and viewpoints relevant to the study of development and to the formulation of development plans. Economists are concerned particularly with the assessment of the demand for transport and with the problems of the cost of overcoming distance (Fromm, 1965; Prest, 1969); the costs of investment in the transport sector are weighed objectively against the benefits likely to accrue, and against the potential feedback from investment in alternative sectors. For the geographer the chief importance of transport arises from its role as one of the principal factors affecting the location and distribution of economic and social activities. Geographers are concerned with the changing spatial structure of transport networks in relation to other aspects of the landscape, and with factors affecting changing patterns of traffic flow (Vigarié, 1968 and 1979; Taaffe and Gauthier, 1973).

Ideas concerning the nature of the relationship between transport and development have changed considerably over time. Transport is clearly a factor of fundamental importance in all economic activity, and the cost of transport is one of the most significant variables affecting the market price of any commodity. But beyond the basic level of infrastructural provision, where transport – like labour, capital, markets, land and power supplies – is a *sine qua non* for modern economic growth, it quickly becomes a matter for debate and enquiry whether, as development proceeds, it is advantageous to extend or otherwise improve transport facilities, or whether limited capital resources available for investment might be used more efficiently and beneficially in other ways. This is a matter of vital concern to planners in the less-developed countries, and it is important to maintain an awareness of the multidimensional nature of the problem: the economic, social, political and spatial dimensions of transport are all significant and in some senses are complementary – although it may perhaps be argued that it is frequently the political dimension in which situations and problems involving transport decisions are most often predominantly viewed.

A widespread belief in the overriding importance of transport, and in the efficiency of transport improvements as accelerators in the development process, is revealed in much of the relevant literature within the fields of transport economics and transport geography. Probably the most extreme claim for transport in the context of development was that made by the colonial administrator Lord Lugard, who wrote many years ago that "the material development of Africa may be summed up in the one word – transport" (Lugard, 1922, 5); a United Nations study claimed in the 1960s that transport is "the formative power of economic growth, and the differentiating process" (Voigt, 1967); today it is sometimes suggested that transport systems are really a result, rather than a cause, of economic development. Such statements are, of course, gross oversimplifications. The transport/development relationship is essentially an interaction process, and the results of the interaction depend upon the types of economy involved and upon the levels of development at which transport improvements are introduced. At a given stage of economic development, a region may be said to require a certain level of transport provision in order to maximise its development potential; theoretically, there is an optimum transport capacity for a given level of development. The existence of an unsatisfied demand for transport is likely, over time, to have serious adverse effects on the economy; conversely, the results of over-capitalisation in the transport sector may be serious if too much is spent on transport provision and improvement in anticipation of demand which never materialises.

Many useful studies have been made by economists and geographers in the field of transport; in recent years there has been an increased awareness on the part of economists of the importance of spatial and ecological variables in development situations, and geographers have appreciated more fully the value of economic models. Both disciplines have moved away from the unquestioning assumption that transport improvements automatically promote development; they have recognised that transport provides one element in the varied infrastructure necessary for economic growth, no more and no less important than other elements; and have accepted the view that transport does not provide, necessarily, the positive stimulus previously assumed. Emphasis on the permissive element in transport provision has led to the view that transport investment may sometimes have a negative impact on economic growth, in that the creation or expansion of transport capacity may absorb scarce resources which could be employed more productively in other ways (Gauthier, 1970). The critical role of the seaport in the development process has received some attention from geographers (Hoyle and Hilling, 1970; Hoyle and Pinder, 1981); a seaport in a less-developed country, through which almost all the external trade of that country (and sometimes that of its landlocked neighbours) passes, is well placed to act either as a growth pole or as a restrictive influence upon development. Which of these alternatives becomes the dominant trend depends partly upon the range, level and efficiency of the port services available, partly upon the policies of the relevant government and parastatal organisations involved, and partly upon the attitudes and practices of the multifarious range of port users. An absence of adequate port facilities can become a major deterrent to national and regional economic growth, whilst the provision of modern port services may positively assist development by removing the inhibiting factor of low-level port facilities. Less-developed countries today are dependent – for a variety of historical, geographical and economic reasons – upon overseas trade, often with far distant countries; the expansion of trade (and the amelioration of trading terms) is an essential concomitant of modern economic growth. As a result, there if often a close relationship between the stage of economic development reached in a given country or port hinterland and the level and efficiency of port facilities available. The efficiency of port services in the Third World is, however, often seriously affected by three important factors: the inheritance of transport infrastructures and economic systems from the colonial period; the continuing predominance of primary tropical products in national trade structures; and the need to establish modern port systems at a time of rapidly changing world trading patterns and far-reaching changes in cargo-handling techniques. The basic dilemma of port authorities in less-developed countries today is therefore the problem of balancing national systems, opportunities and goals against international trends in commodity flow, transport technology, and economic cooperation.

Tropical African Cityport Systems

The history of port development is often an epitome of changing economic, political and technological circumstances on various scales and over varying periods of time. In the past, traders from overseas often found tropical African coasts a barrier to commercial activity rather than a natural link with the interior of a continent that remained for so long largely unknown to the rest of the world; but many of the transforming influences that have affected the modern development of tropical Africa have come by sea and have entered through the ports. The independent countries of tropical Africa are today very deeply concerned with the improvement of the international economic and political relationships that affect national development strategies; overseas trade is vital in this context, and tropical African economies remain strongly oriented towards distant overseas markets. It follows that the characteristics of tropical African port systems, and the role played by seaports in the development process throughout this region, deserve close attention (Morgan, 1973; O'Connor, 1971 and 1978; Ojany and Ogendo, 1973). A basic feature of the economic geography of tropical Africa is the very uneven density and distribution of modern transport media. This has helped to produce, and is now helping to intensify, what Hance (1967) termed the "islandic pattern of economic activity" which characterizes the entire region. Relatively small areas of population concentration and economic production for export are separated by wide zones of sparse population density and little significance in the cash economy. An associated problem is that of the very uneven distribution of access to the sea, which depends of course upon both distance and transport development. Inland states such as Niger or Uganda are dependent upon transport facilities through neighbouring countries to foreign coastal ports, and inland regions in coastal states seldom have a choice of outlet to the sea. This pattern arises partly from the political circumstances of tropical Africa's formative period and partly from the scarcity of good harbour sites. Together, these and other factors have encouraged the growth of large cityports at a limited number of specific favoured locations; and, once established, the process of urban and port concentration is hard to reverse.

The number of major seaports serving tropical Africa is relatively small; many are primate in a national context, and few countries can claim a national hierarchy of seaports (Fig. 1.1). There is a tendency, too, for primate ports to increase their dominance in modern trading and technological conditions, and for smaller places in seaport hierarchies to decline in relative significance. The association between major seaports and primary development zones and points is close, and is partly a function of historical and economic factors as well as of environmental conditions. The major seaports of tropical Africa are usually also important as urban centres (Hoyle, 1972); with few exceptions – of which Mombasa (Kenya) is perhaps the most notable example – a seaport is the primate city in most tropical African coastal states. The primate *cityport* thus fulfils a dominant role in the urban and the transport geography of the region, although there is generally no direct correlation between the size of the urban population and the throughput of the port. The association between port throughout and city size, however, highlights the contrasts between

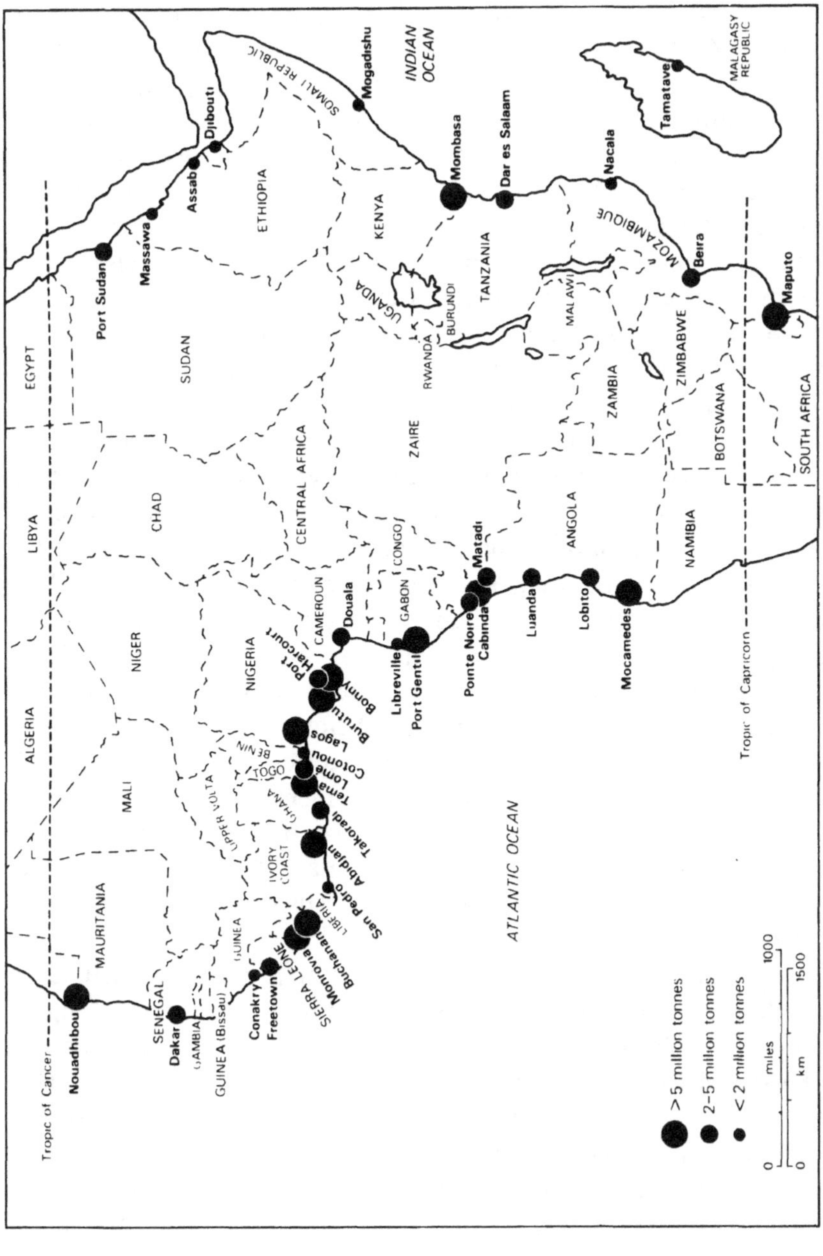

FIGURE 1.1 Comparative cargo throughput at major tropical African seaports, 1980. (*Sources of data: United Nations statistical yearbook*, and port authorities.)

several distinctive types of tropical African seaport; the unifunctional exporters of crude oil, such as Bonny (Nigeria), or of iron ore, such as Nouadhibou (Mauritania), are of little general importance as ports or urban centres, although their export traffic flows are very high; in contrast, a wide variety of urban activities has been attracted to the numerous locations that have developed as small or medium-sized multifunctional ports (such as Freetown, Dar es Salaam, Takoradi), and this group includes a number of new ports as well as long-established centres; thirdly, the general cargo giants of tropical Africa (Abidjan, Dakar, Lagos and Mombasa) are distinctive in that the concentration of urban populations and cargo throughput in these locations represents a higher and more complex level of cityport activities and functions than is found elsewhere in the urban and seaport hierarchies of tropical Africa.

Cityport complexes are well placed to act either as growth poles or as restrictive influences upon economic development. Growth of overseas trade is a basic factor involved in the expansion of the money economy, stimulating the increase of urban populations, the growth of local markets, the modernization of agricultural systems and the growth of industry. The development of modern port facilities is an essential precondition for economic growth in tropical African countries, especially in view of the excessive trade dependence of these countries upon distant overseas markets, which arises both from geographical similarities in their patterns of resource endowment and from common historical patterns of colonial dependence. The stage of economic development reached in a given tropical African country is often closely related to the capacity and efficiency of the port facilities available, and in a wider sense reflects the capacity of the cityport region as a whole to absorb and transform external benefits.

The present-day cityport hierarchy of tropical Africa thus includes a small number of major multifunctional centres of international significance and a much larger number of port towns whose role is mainly within the regional economic structures of their respective countries. The multifunctional cityports are obviously amongst the region's major centres of transport and trade, industry, political and cultural life, innovation and modernization. As seaports, they fulfill a critical role in the development process; as cities they provide some of the main locations for the operation of the transforming influences involved in the modernization process. Interrelations between port and city in functional and physical terms, and especially in relation to employment and industrial expansion, require more thorough investigation than they have hitherto received if the role of the cityport in the development process is to be maximized. Present-day levels and patterns of cityport industrialization in tropical Africa are not, however, necessarily an indication of an approach towards economic take-off; rather, they frequently seem to provide a further indication of under-development.

Factors Affecting Seaport Development

The growth of cityports is fundamentally affected by four separate sets of factors: the *land situation* and the *water situation*, and the *land site* and the *water site*. Of these, the water site (i.e., the physical conditions of the harbour) often provides the initial stimulus to development, but unless conditions in the other three categories are favourable, the settlement is unlikely to prosper. The level of port development, measured in terms of cargo-handling capacity or the volume and value of commodity flow, is chiefly a reflection of land situation – the extent and pattern of economic development in the hinterland, including transport development – rather than of land or water site. Nevertheless, the land site constitutes a direct control over the pattern of urban growth, and where factors in all four categories are broadly favourable (as at Dakar, Mombasa and Lagos) there tends to be some degree of correlation between the level of port development and the extent of associated urban growth. In all cases, however, the port function lies at the root of the physical expansion of the port-town in terms of location, layout and size.

Numerous environmental problems are associated with the growth of tropical African cityports. From a navigational standpoint the surf-beaten coast of West Africa and the coral reefs of the East African coast present considerable dangers. In terms of urban settlement and port development a major difficulty is the lack of good natural harbours, a characteristic which was often cited in the past as an important local disincentive to external penetration of the continent. Today it is no longer possible to contend, in most areas, that a lack of harbours impedes economic progress; as development has proceeded the pattern of cityport location has been adjusted, partly by the continued growth of some established port-towns (Dakar, Lagos, Mombasa) and the decline of others (St. Louis,

Calabar, Zanzibar); and also by the construction of artificial harbours (Tema, Cotonou, Lomé) in locations where port facilities are essential but natural harbours are not available.

The utilisation of a limited number of good natural harbours of various physical types, such as the drowned river valleys at Mombasa and Dar es Salaam, the lagoons at Lagos and Abidjan, or the sheltered bay at Dakar, has involved urban development on a considerable scale. In these cases the physical form of the harbour has exerted a strong measure of control not only over the layout of port facilities but also over the form and pattern of the associated urban development. Unfortunately the physical site conditions which encouraged the establishment of some of tropical Africa's ports in the past, and which still today encourage continued port expansion, do not necessarily also favour urban development. A site with defensive attributes important in medieval times, for example, does not always lend itself particularly well to modern urban or port growth. In East Africa a comparison of Lamu, Mombasa and Kilwa demonstrates this point effectively. Elsewhere, sites selected by Europeans during the initial phases of colonial activity have not always proved very successful in the long term. Freetown (Sierra Leone), founded in 1781 on the shores of one of the world's most capacious deep-water harbours, has not reached a high level of development either as a seaport, because its hinterland is areally restricted and not richly endowed, or as a city, since its growth level reflects severe physical site problems on the hilly Freetown peninsula as well as the realities of Sierra Leone's economic situation.

The capacity of a given site to absorb not only expanding port development but also rapid urban growth is essentially limited in most cases, especially if the site has been inherited from an era when urban centres and transport systems operated on a much more restricted scale. The problem of adaptation of expanding cityports to restricted sites becomes especially acute where the cityport is also the national political and economic capital. In such circumstances serious problems of physical congestion and economic and social dislocation may occur and are likely to require close attention from planning authorities in both port and town; in extreme circumstances a stage of gross overurbanization and urban hypertrophy may be reached, coupled with very serious congestion in the port. These conditions may all too readily act as a very real brake on the development of both the cityport complex itself and of the wider areas served (Vennetier, 1969). The extent to which these points apply to the two larger East African seaports is discussed in later chapters; but it may be noted here that Mombasa has experienced not only traffic congestion in the port but also urban problems on its original island site, and the spread to the mainland has introduced transport problems that are proving difficult and expensive to resolve. Dar es Salaam also suffers from congestion in the port, and in urban terms has traditionally combined in one location the political, economic and cultural functions that in Kenya are divided between Mombasa and Nairobi. The establishment of a new, more centrally-located political capital city at Dodoma may possibly remove some of the pressures upon urban growth at Dar es Salaam and may also help to resolve some of the inter-regional and interurban disparities in development levels that now characterise modern Tanzania.

The growth and development of a seaport is due "not to the direct influence of any inherent qualities of land and water sites, but to the way in which such sites were assessed by the founders" (Bird, 1972, 24), and to the combined effect over time of a range of factors operating on a comparative basis: environmental, technological, political and economic. In this context the growth of tropical African urban and port systems are closely interlinked, and the modern seaport and cityport hierarchies owe much to their historical antecedents. The extent of pre-European urbanisation in tropical Africa was essentially limited, except in Nigeria, but in those areas where towns developed they frequently arose within the context of transport systems linking tropical Africa with other areas by land or sea routes. In East Africa, pre-European urbanization was largely confined to the coastlands, a zone of trading contact between the interior of East Africa and the trading circulations of the Indian Ocean from at least the first century A.D. In this zone, towns such as Lamu, Mombasa and Kilwa were established as flourishing port-towns at an early date, and of these Mombasa has survived as a modern cityport because of its relations with the hinterland and its site advantages. In West Africa, pre-European urbanization emphasized the transitional Sahel and Sudan zones in the north, where desert-margin 'ports' developed (Kano, Gao, Timbuktu), and the forest margins of the south (Kumasi, Oyo, Ibadan) rather than the Guinea coastlands; but European contact along the coast, dating from the fifteenth-century Portuguese explorations, involved the establishment of coastal trading settlements. European contact brought a scatter of small trading forts and posts along the coasts of tropical (especially West) Africa; most of these early settlements have decayed, and only those few favoured by outstanding attributes of situation or site have been able to survive the selection process involved in changing physical, economic and political conditions. These survivors, together with more recent foundations, form the contemporary cityport hierarchy of tropical Africa.

The early growth of the modern cityports of tropical Africa was an expression of the economic power and aims of the European nations which established themselves in the region in the nineteenth century. During the prelude to the European partition of tropical Africa the coastal port-towns were the obvious points of political, economic and cultural contact between colonizer and colonized. The port-towns provided the main routeways through which intensifying contact developed, the chief filters through which the new transforming foreign influences passes, and they logically became at least initially the main foci of European administration. The selection and use of coastal ports as political capitals has been the common experience of many parts of the world that have received the tide of European expansionism. But the convenience of the colonial administrators and traders in maintaining close contact with their homelands whilst exploiting and developing the new hinterlands has, in many cases, become the inconvenience of modern planners, because the multifunctional character of the favoured port sites has created excessive demands on the limited potential which these sites provide. The colonial system of port-city capitals is, of course, extremely difficult to change once well established, as the experience of Australia and Brazil has shown. In thirteen out of twenty-four coastal states of tropical Africa, the capital city and the major port-city share the same location. Tropical Africa provides only two examples of coastal capitals which no longer function as seaports, although both were founded as such: Accra (Ghana) and Porto Novo (Benin). Five states (Ethiopia, Cameroun, Kenya, the Malagasy Republic and Sudan) have long possessed an inland capital located fairly centrally within the state and at some distance from the major port. Suggestions have been made, as in Tanzania, that in the interests of economic and political development capitals should be reestablished in interior locations, but generally such changes seem unlikely on grounds of cost alone.

The modern seaports of tropical Africa form part of a transport infrastructure designed to serve the area during the formative period of colonial rule, and subsequently modified to meet the requirements of independent Africa. The emergence of an outline system of surface transport in tropical Africa was initially deeply affected by the political relationships between Europe and Africa in the later nineteenth century, and the development of the system has been circumscribed by a variety of more recent political influences. The initial colonisation and partition of tropical Africa involved the superimposition of European rule and the suppression or incorporation within the new units of the precolonial political entities at the coast and inland. The foundation of many of tropical Africa's modern seaports was closely related to the nineteenth-century political partition of the continent which created an economic as well as a political framework for African development that still persists.

Political changes since independence in many tropical African states have involved, *inter alia*, an increasing emphasis on national-scale development and some attempts to foster interstate cooperation in transport on a regional basis, of which the recent history of Zambia provides the best-known example. In response to the increasing demands of the developing economies they serve, the major seaports of tropical Africa have experienced accelerated growth in recent years; there has been some adjustment in the pattern of their cargo throughput and in the structure of their hinterland and foreland relationships. These points underline the significance of the dynamic elements in port geography; modern port hierarchies, like their predecessors, change in response to a wide range of factors. Increasing concentration of port activity in the larger seaports is the dominant trend at present, although there are signs in many tropical African countries that the dangers inherent in these trends are clearly perceived and that attempts are being made to modify or decelerate them.

Approaches to the Study of Seaport Systems

Anyone who works in or who attempts to study a seaport realises quickly the complexity of the factors that affect the way in which a port fulfills its essential functions. What happens today at the quayside depends upon a wide range of circumstances – some local, others national or international; some economic or technological, others social or political; some contemporary, others historical. A seaport is an element in a global transport system, a servant of an international economic order, and a gateway to and from a national or regional hinterland. Geography is concerned with spatial systems and with relationships in area, and a geographical approach to seaport study must focus on the essential port function: the development of an effective node in an international transport system, linking together several interdependent transport modes and integrating efficiently a range of transport networks. A comprehensive analysis of a modern seaport would reflect both this essential focus and the wide range of controls within which it is set; such an analysis would require the combined efforts of economists, historians, engineers, geomorphologists, geographers, and a large number of government and port officials. It follows that any study attempted by an individual writer is unlikely to survey more than a small part of the whole; selected aspects of East African seaports dealt with in this book include the environmental setting, growth and development, installations and operation, throughput and hinterland structure. Many related and important aspects are largely ignored, including some vital questions of port management, engineering, finance, and ship operation (Couper, 1972; Nagorski, 1972). The remaining agenda seems quite wide enough, particularly in view of the need to maintain interport comparisons and the attempt to preserve both a chronological and a spatial viewpoint.

Many writers have discussed the growth and significance of tropical African transport and port systems (e.g. Van Dongen, 1954 and 1963; Hofmeier, 1973), but relatively few have attempted to postulate models of transport development in the Third World or to relate changes in the transport sector to the wider processes and patterns of economic development and social progress. The most well known attempt to analyse transport/development relationships in terms of a diachronic model remains the ideal-typical sequence of transport network development in a less-developed country, postulated by Taaffe, Morrill and Gould (1963) and based on West African material (Fig. 1.2a). This study provided a basis for later work in other less-developed areas (e.g. Rimmer, 1967; Stanley, 1970), and Wiese (1981) has related the model to the experience of South Africa. Efforts to identify factors helping to explain spatial variations in transport network densities are important as pointers towards a model simulating the economic growth process and allowing the evaluation of alternative transport development strategies. There is an important distinction between the development impact of *initial transport provision* in the earliest stages of economic development, and the anticipated effects when *transport elaboration* is undertaken at a later stage. In the initial stages of economic growth, the introduction of modern transport makes a wide variety of new economic opportunities available simultaneously,

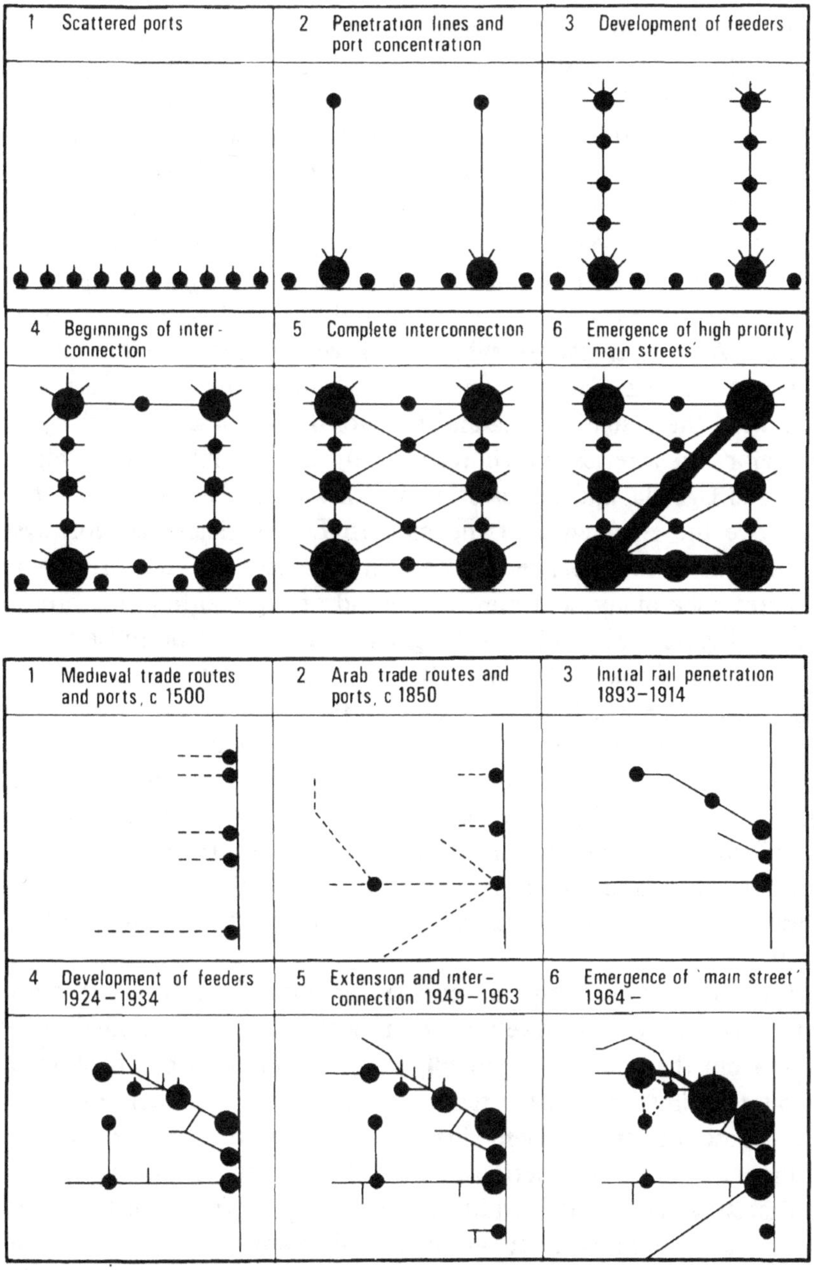

FIGURE 1.2. Transport network development in less-developed countries: (a) an ideal-typical sequence, after Taaffe *et al.* (1963); (b) the evolution of the modern East African surface transport network.

and is therefore likely positively to encourage economic growth and spatial diffusion of development; in more advanced stages, transport is but one of several sectors in which productive investment may be channelled, and the observed effects of initial transport provision should not be falsely projected as likely results of modern transport elaborations.

East Africa provides an example of an area where road, rail, air and maritime transport systems are all reasonably well developed, in terms of both internal and external linkages, and where changes in the network structure have been a subject of close political and economic attention. The East African transport system as a whole links together the three countries of Kenya, Tanzania and Uganda, and connects the East African region with the rest of Africa and the world; it is based essentially upon two major rail arteries which respectively link Mombasa with highland Kenya and Uganda, and Dar es Salaam with western Tanzania. In historical perspective the emergence of the modern East African transport system may be seen as the most recent stage in a process of transport evolution that dates back many centuries. A method of representing this process is shown in Figure 1.2b, which is designed as an application to East African circumstances of the Taaffe, Morrill and Gould model to which reference has been made above. In its original form the purpose of the model was to indicate in hypothetical terms the way in which a transport system evolves from a scatter of small, unconnected ports through various intervening stages to become a fully integrated network closely attuned to a mature stage of economic development. In its modified form the model retains the diachronic style and the terminology of the original, but refers to the experience of a specific area rather than to less-developed countries in general.

Within the East African transport system ports have operated as fundamental elements in the development process, and the principal railways leading from them have traditionally provided an economic backbone for the countries involved. The three upper stages of the model represent the broad phase of development identified as *initial transport provision*, culminating in the construction of an outline system of modern transport. The first stage represents conditions over a period from the first century A.D. to the early nineteenth century; the diagram shows a scatter of small ports, largely isolated from one another and linked more firmly with the maritime trading circulations of the Indian Ocean than with those parts of the interior from which slaves, ivory and other items of trade were regularly extracted. Few of the ports or routes represented in stage 1 of the model continued to develop in later periods, but the pattern represents the historical precedents of the modern system. In contrast to West Africa, medieval trading ports along the East African coast were mainly Arab rather than European in origin and affiliation. Stage 2 represents the zenith of Arab trading activity in East Africa, focused in the mid-nineteenth century upon the Arab-controlled island emporium of Zanzibar; from a series of outports along the mainland coast (of which Bagamoyo is perhaps the best known) trade routes radiated inland as far as western Tanzania and Uganda and indeed well beyond the confines of present-day East Africa. The concentration of East African transport routes upon Zanzibar at this time reflected the predominant role of the port in the economic and political life of the entire area, and involved a sharp decline in the fortunes and number of trading centres on the mainland coast. The central Tanzanian transport axis initiated in stage 2 by the Bagamoyo-Tabora slave route is re-emphasised in stage 3 by the Dar es Salaam-Kigoma railway, the equivalent of which in Kenya was the Mombasa-Kisumu line. These two rail arteries, together with the less successful Tanga-Moshi line in northern Tanzania, date from a relatively brief period (1890-1919) when coastal East Africa was divided between two colonial powers, Britain and Germany; since all three lines were initially based upon political rather than economic motivations, it is interesting to speculate upon the possible patterns of East African economic geography that might have emerged if the colonial partition of East Africa had been differently arranged and if the railways had been differently located. The basic rail arteries have influenced profoundly the pattern of economic development and subsequent transport provision in East Africa, particularly in the areas of mineral exploitation, cash crop development and intensive rural and urban settlement.

A second broad phase of East African transport development, represented by the three lower diagrams in Figure 1.2b may be termed *transport elaboration.* During this phase, the basic infrastructure provided by the pre-First World War rail arteries has been extended, and its efficiency improved. Stage 4 indicates the elaboration of the three original railway lines by branch and feeder lines designed to serve areas of increasing settlement and cash crop production, especially parts of highland Kenya which in the 1920s and 1930s were an important focus of European immigration and settlement. Major extensions to Kampala, Arusha and Mwanza were also completed during this phase. Stage 5 is marked by the brief appearance of a railway designed to serve the newly-opened deep-water port of Mtwara, in south-east Tanzania, and by the interlinkage of the Tanga and central Tanzanian lines in the coastal zone, thus creating a physically unified rail system in the East African area. Two major extensions of the rail system, to the west and north of Uganda respectively, also date from this period. The final stage 6 of the model represents the present-day situation and emphasises particularly the Kampala-Nairobi-Mombasa axis, which has clearly emerged as East Africa's 'main street.' The extension of the East African transport system to include the first extra-East African rail link, the TAZARA line from Dar es Salaam to the Zambian copperbelt, is also shown.

Initial transport provision in East Africa thus involved the construction of an outline system of surface communications which permitted economic growth and development to a certain level, and indeed in the early stages of the modern era may well have stimulated development simply by introducing a wide range of hitherto unknown possibilities. Beyond a certain point, however, the restrictive influence of an infrastructure of this kind becomes apparent; in the second broad phase of *transport elaboration*, therefore, transport improvements permit further economic expansion but are not the direct stimulus to development that many have assumed. The Mtwara railway, for example, was designed to evacuate anticipated groundnut crops from south-eastern Tanzania, but failed in this objective (and was lifted in 1963) partly because the new port initially supplemented the old lighterage port of Lindi to the north, and road hauliers were able to use the new railway to absorb peak loads rather than to carry the bulk of the output. The Ugandan extensions, built respectively to transport copper from the west and cotton from the north of the country, do not appear to have attracted a significant volume of additional traffic; they seem initially to have had only limited developmental impact upon the areas served (O'Connor, 1965), although more recent evidence suggests that some more widespread beneficial effects had become apparent by the later 1970s. These case histories provide an important body of evidence for the argument that transport elaboration within an established economic system is very unlikely rapidly to accelerate development unless further steps are taken to utilise more fully the facilities provided, and to encourage the spatial coincidence of development effort, investment and projects in a variety of economic sectors.

Some attempt has been made to recognise this situation in the context of the TAZARA line through southern Tanzania. The decision to construct a railway designed to link the Zambian copperbelt with the Tanzanian port of Dar es Salaam was taken in 1969 in the context of Zambia's efforts to reorientate her economy away from southern and towards eastern Africa. Construction, based upon Chinese surveys, loans and labour, was completed in 1975. Although the primary initial objectives of this new artery of transportation were clearly related to Zambia's economic needs and political circumstances, the Tanzanian authorities have shown considerable interest in the promotion of agricultural development, coal and iron ore mining, and hydroelectric power production in hitherto neglected parts of the southern highlands. The Dar es Salaam-Zambia and Mombasa-Kampala routes both illustrate a current tendency towards *axial multiplication* in African transport development: both routes are already served by improved roads, air services, oil pipelines and modern telegraphic communication. The economic viability of individual transport modes in situations such as these is sometimes open to question.

In a chronological and in a spatial sense, therefore, a close relationship exists between the broad pattern of East Africa's transport system and several other aspects of the economic geography of the area, and such relationships are not untypical of the Third World as a whole. In the pre-railway stages East African trade was channelled into limited routeways linked, in some cases rather tenuously, with the Indian Ocean. Other traffic was local in origin and destination. These early stages provided, prior to the period of European colonialism, established modes of access and movement, and influenced considerably the initial foundation and alignment of the pioneer elements in the colonial transport infrastructure. These elements – seaports, rail arteries, and major roads – provided a foundation for later elaboration and a basis upon which the modern economy of the area has at least in part been developed. The specific location of the various nodes and links in the transport network (particularly the rail network) serving East Africa has very strongly influenced the location and economic growth of those areas that are today most heavily involved in the cash economy. Rail access was an important factor in the location and development of major cash crops (coffee, cotton, sisal) and in the exploitation of minerals (copper, soda ash). Today road feeder lines are increasing in importance, road-rail competition for transport to the ports is intensifying, and some important cash crop zones (notably tea in western Kenya) do not have rail access; yet the basic areal association between the cash economy and the transport infrastructure remains. Parts of East Africa without reasonable access to modern road or rail communication, yet with considerable economic potential, have tended to lag behind other areas more favoured in transport terms and have not emerged as core areas of export production either during the colonial period or subsequently. Such an area is southern Tanzania. In the context of the distinction suggested above between *initial transport provision* and *transport elaboration*, it does not follow that contemporary transport improvements will encourage the emergence of new zones of economic advancement, but if an attempt is made to preserve a reasonable degree of intersectoral and inter-regional investment balance the range of opportunities provided for development should be considerably increased.

A rather more specific aspect of seaport development, and one that is more often directly subject to quantification, involves the measurement of the port in terms of its facilities, functions and activities. This may be done in a chronological or a spatial sense, and a full understanding of port operations requires analysis in both dimensions. In one sense, "the essential task . . . is to trace the development of those areas where the function of transhipment is carried out" (Bird, 1947, 14); in another sense, a distinction must be made between the sea *port* or gateway through which multidirectional traffic flows are channelled, and the sea *terminal* designed to facilitate the reception and processing of imported bulk cargoes (Bird, 1971, 13-15). The facilities with which the port is equipped for the handling of goods and passengers provide a rough but useful indication of the extent and significance of the activity of a port; beyond this, the most essential aspect of port study concerns port operation and throughput – the analysis of patterns of commodity flow through a port and the efficiency with which these flows are achieved. The nature of the goods handled and the direction of their movement give a clear indication of the character of a port, whilst value and tonnage statistics help to form an estimate of the relative significance of the port compared to others elsewhere. It is of course essential to distinguish between different categories and types of cargo, especially between bulk cargoes that are relatively easily handled and require little labour, and break-bulk cargoes which are more varied and need individual handling.

A port cannot realistically be considered in isolation, and measurement of the facilities and activities of the port area must therefore be placed within a much wider setting, involving the hinterland on the landward side and the sea routes and the foreland on the maritime side. In this aspect of port study lie the explanations underlying the features of the port itself, and indeed the reasons for the very existence of the port. An item of immediate interest in this context is the provenance of the principal export and import commodities that the port handles. A study of exports sets the port very firmly in its regional and national context, in relation to the economy of the country within which it lies and the areas that it serves. Exports originating within the immediate environment of the port town may be distinguished from those derived from various parts of the country in which the port is situated, and from goods passing through the port from sources beyond the national boundaries. In dealing with imports it is also sometimes possible to distinguish between goods destined for local, national or extranational consumption, and it is of interest whenever possible to examine the relative significance of various parts of the maritime foreland in terms of the sources of imported commodities.

A different question, but one closely related to the movement of goods, concerns means of transportation. This question is concerned not only with the different types of ships using the port, but also with the road, rail and inland waterway systems serving the port on the landward side. The various types of ocean carriers are chiefly of geographical interest insofar as they affect the development of port facilities, although, as will be made clear in Chapter 4, the evolution of shipping in terms of size and manoeuvrability has profoundly influenced the very sites of ports. Specialized shipping, for example oil tankers, needs special facilities and creates special problems. Very often a vital question is whether dredging to a given depth is economically feasible in relation to actual or potential traffic flow through the port (Weigend, 1958). The problem of the hinterland of the port is thus analysed in terms of land transport routeways, sources of export commodities and destination of imports, that is in terms of the land area the port serves and the means by which it does so. This creates a complex geographical pattern, and there is a sense in which it is more accurate to speak of many individual hinterlands (for example, the coffee hinterland of Mombasa, or the sisal hinterland of Tanga) rather than of one composite hinterland. Few ports can claim an exclusive hinterland; there is almost invariably a considerable degree of overlap between the hinterlands of one port and those of another.

The role of cityports within national and international economic systems is especially important, for in addition to the dominant position which they occupy in the transport network and in the provision of standard urban services (including markets and employment), cityports are likely to develop a major industrial sector within the urban economic base. In the cash sector of the LDC economy the cityport is particularly well placed to act as a control point for cash crop and mineral production, involving both intermediary head-office administration and transport control of commodity flow between producing areas and overseas markets. In the reverse direction the cityport acts as a primary distribution point for a wide variety of imported manufactured goods and raw materials, a high proportion of which may be absorbed within the immediate market of the cityport itself, especially if it is also the primate capital and chief industrial centre.

The industrialisation of port regions in the less-developed countries is one of the most important spheres in which the interaction of port functions and urban processes may be observed, as part of a much wider system involving relationships between hinterland production and market areas, port facilities and efficiency, land and sea transport systems and overseas markets. Port industrialisation is not merely a secondary function of port transit trade; port industries are themselves major importers and exporters, creators of employment and users of urban space, and thereby active agents of urbanisation in a physical, economic and social sense. Three main types of industry are commonly represented in LDC cityports. Most basic are those industrial port activities based on bulk raw materials – oil refining, steel production, aluminium and chemicals – where for economic reasons transport between quayside and plant is reduced to a minimum. Second, there are general port industries which take advantage of the port location as a break of bulk point but which do not require specialized port facilities or, in most cases, a very large volume of raw materials. This large and varied group includes those industries processing local primary products destined for export and others transforming imported goods for the domestic market. A third group of industries, not directly dependent upon the port, is strongly oriented towards the growing urban market; such industries frequently derive considerable advantages from interindustry linkages within the cityport complex.

These various economic problems link together the port and urban systems and bring with them problems of location, distribution and planning. In social terms a basic reason for the indivisibility of port and urban phenomena is the fact that a port creates employment not only through the primary port functions of the navigation and servicing of vessels and the handling of cargo and passenger flows, but also through the development of port-oriented industries in both the secondary and tertiary sectors. Within the economic infrastructure of any LDC cityport, the urban issues of employment, underemployment and unemployment are paramount. The drift of population to the towns, and particularly to the coastal ports in many countries, is commonly out of all proportion to the range and number of employment opportunities available, and this leads not only to the familiar range of urban social problems but also to serious problems of land neglect in rural areas. The social problems of cityports in the less-developed countries turn mainly on the question of employment opportunities, but in another sense they arise from the social and economic juxtaposition of different tribes and races as a result of the multifunctional economic role of the cityport areas. These problems are often accentuated because cityports are frequently the largest urban settlements, presenting the most varied economic systems and employment opportunities, and because they are perhaps more open to external as well as national influences and trends. Whilst the cityport acts as an entry point for a wide range of influences including some of the powerful agents of social change and modernisation, the rapidity of change which characterises the cityport environment can at the same time seriously exacerbate intertribal and interracial rivalry and friction.

This book is based primarily upon data derived from a study of the major Indian Ocean ports of Kenya and Tanzania in which the ports are regarded as a factor in the development of the East African countries and as an illustration of general principles of transport geography. The approach is partly chronological but essentially spatial, in the sense that although the development of the port system is viewed over time, the main emphasis is on present-day patterns, functions and relationships. Relatively little information is widely available on East African ports, or indeed on seaports in the less-developed world in general; and although such ports are frequently a subject of economic and political attention their role is often unappreciated and their importance underestimated. Modern seaports are seen in one perspective as the successors to earlier port hierarchies that have served trade requirements in the past; and in another perspective the growth, layout, throughout and spatial relationships of the ports are examined on a comparative basis. The two major East

African deep-water ports of Mombasa and Dar es Salaam provide the main points of reference and the most useful general illustrations. Three other Tanzanian seaports are also discussed in some detail: the lighterage port of Tanga in the north, the deep-water port of Mtwara in the south, and the island port of Zanzibar. There are of course numerous smaller seaports on the East African coast – Lindi, Kilwa, Malindi and Lamu are examples – which handle coastal traffic and some overseas trade; these ports are of considerable historical interest but their commercial significance today is very limited.

In the analyses of environmental influences, port growth, installations, operation and throughput, and in the discussion of hinterlands and forelands, an attempt is made to structure the discussion in the context of the methods of analysis used in port studies in general, with special reference to relationships between port systems in the less-developed countries and the processes and patterns of socio-economic modernization now being experienced throughout the Third World. East Africa is used throughout as an area of reference from which information and materials are drawn to illustrate general principles. Although the study is concerned primarily with present conditions, focusing essentially upon the analysis and interpretation of what happens at the quayside today, some attention must inevitably be devoted to the past. Chapters 3 and 4 provide the historical background essential to an understanding of modern patterns; these chapters do not claim to add new facts to our knowledge of the history of East Africa, but their inclusion in the work seems justified because of the need to examine present geographical phenomena in a chronological as well as a spatial context, and by the need to emphasize the long-established continuity of trade relations on the East African coast. The reader should bear in mind, however, that the objectives of this study are not merely to illustrate or explain the specific character of a particular group of ports, but to demonstrate the broad principle that seaports occupy and fulfill a crucial role in the development process as a whole.

REFERENCES

Alexandersson, G., and G. Norstrom (1963), *World shipping: an economic geography of ports and seaborne trade* (London & New York, Wiley).

Bird, J.H. (1947), *The geography of the port of London* (London, Hutchinson).

Bird, J.H. (1971), *Seaports and seaport terminals* (London, Hutchinson).

Bird, J.H. (1973), 'Of central places, cities and seaports', *Geography* 58, 105-118.

Couper, A.D. (1972), *The geography of sea transport* (London, Hutchinson).

Fromm, G. (ed.) (1965), *Transport investment and economic development* (Washington, Brookings Institution).

Gauthier, H.L. (1970), 'Geography, transportation and regional development', *Economic Geography* 46, 612-619.

Goss, R.O. (ed.) (1977), *Advances in maritime economics* (Cambridge, Cambridge University Press).

Hance, W.A. (1967), *African economic development* (New York, Praeger).

Hofmeier, R. (1973), *Transport and economic development in Tanzania* (Munich, Weltforum Verlag, for the Ifo-Institut for Economic Research, African Studies 78).

Holye, B.S. (1967), *The seaports of East Africa* (Nairobi, East African Publishing House, for the Makerere Institute of Social Research).

Hoyle, B.S. (1972), 'The port function in the urban development of tropical Africa', *La croissance urbaine en Afrique Noire et à Madagascar* (Paris, Centre National de la Recherche Scientifique), 705-718.

Hoyle, B.S. (ed.) (1973), *Transport and development* (London, Macmillan).

Hoyle, B.S. and D. Hilling (eds.) (1970), *Seaports and development in tropical Africa* (London, Macmillan).

Hoyle, B.S. and D.A. Pinder (eds.) (1981), *Cityport industrialization and regional development: spatial analysis and planning strategies* (Oxford, Pergamon Press, Urban and Regional Planning Series, Vol. 24).

Lugard, Sir F.D. (1922), *The dual mandate in British tropical Africa* (Edinburgh, Blackwood).

Morgan, W.T.W. (1973), *East Africa* (London, Longman).

Munby, D.L. (1968), *Transport* (Harmondsworth, Penguin Books).

Nagorski, B. (1972), *Port problems in developing countries* (Tokyo, International Association of Ports and Harbours).

O'Connor, A.M. (1965), 'New railway construction and the pattern of economic development in Uganda', *Transactions of the Institute of British Geographers* 36, 21-30.

O'Connor, A.M. (1971), *An economic geography of East Africa* (London, Bell, 2nd edn.).

O'Connor, A.M. (1978), *Geography of tropical African development* (Oxford, Pergamon Press, 2nd edn.).

Ojany, F.F. and R.B. Ogendo (1973), *Kenya, a study in physical and human geography* (Nairobi, Longman).

Ports of the world yearbook (London, Benn Publications, annually).

Prest, A.R. (1969), *Transport economics in developing countries* (London, Weidenfeld and Nicholson).

Rimmer, P.J. (1967), 'The search for spatial regularities in the development of Australian seaports, 1861-1961/2,' *Geografiska Annaler* 49b, 42-54.

Shipping statistics yearbook (Bremen, Institute of Shipping Economics, annually).

Stanley, W.R. (1970), 'Transport expansion in Liberia', *Geographical Review* 60, 1970, 529-547.

Taaffe, E.J., R.L. Morrill and P.R. Gould (1963), 'Transport expansion in underdeveloped countries: a comparative analysis', *Geographical Review* 53, 503-529.

Taaffe, E.J. and H.L. Gauthier (1973), *Geography of transportation* (Englewood Cliffs, Prentice Hall).

Van Dongen, I.S. (1954), *The British East African transport complex* (Department of Geography, University of Chicago, Research Paper 38).

Van Dongen, I.S. (1963), 'Mombasa in the land and sea exchanges of East Africa', *Erdkunde* 17, 16-38.

Vennetier, P. (1969), 'Le développement urbain en Afrique tropicale', *Etudes de géographie tropicale* 1.

Vigarié, A. (1968), *Géographie de la circulation, vol. II, la circulation maritime* (Paris, Editions Genin).

Vigarié, A. (1979), *Ports de commerce at vie littorale* (Paris, Hachette).

Voigt, F. (1967), *The importance of the transport system for economic development processes* (Addis Ababa, United Nations Economic Commission for Africa), E/CN. 14/CAP/39.

Weigend, G.G. (1958), 'Some elements in the study of port geography', *Geographical Review* 48, 185-200.

Wiese, B. (1981), *Seaports and port cities of southern Africa* (Wiesbaden, Franz Steiner Verlag GMBH: Kölner Geographische Arbeiten 11).

2 Environmental Influences on Seaport Growth

The relative success of a port, measured in terms of its commercial importance as a modern transport node, is influenced by several groups of factors: the trade potential of the hinterland; the land transport system; relationships with the foreland, including the pattern of sea transport links; and the institutional framework at the level of port administration and at the level of national and intergovernmental organisation. These factors operate in several dimensions – physical, economic, political, technological – on differing scales and over varying time periods. They do not include, however, the physical conditions within the immediate port area, which influence the *pattern* rather than the *level* of port growth. This chapter seeks to clarify some of the physical and human environmental factors affecting the general level of port activity in an area, and more particularly to explain the local factors influencing the pattern of port development at individual locations. The East African case-study area is used throughout to illustrate points of general principle.

Port location invariably represents a compromise between the influence of numerous factors, and to understand some of the complexities involved it is useful to borrow the bifocal vision of the urban geographer. The terms *situation* and *site* have long been used to distinguish the broader, 'horizontal' components involved in urban growth, and the more immediate 'vertical' elements. Applied to port geography, the concept is extended to include factors from the seaward as well as from the landward side. The situation is the geographical position of the port in a broad sense: the physical, human and especially economic environment within which the port lies (the *land situation*); and the relationships of the port to world sealanes and to other important seaports and terminals (the *water situation*). The site, in contrast, is the area of land and associated waters on which the port and port town are actually developed: the configuration of the harbour and the conditions of area, depth, temperature and movement of the waters within the harbour and its approaches (the *water site*); and the details of the topography, drainage, stability and aspect of the site of the port town (the *land site*). These two distinct aspects, the broader and the closer view, are necessarily complementary and form an essential basis to the study of the geography of any seaport. Clearly, the development of a seaport is normally governed to a far greater extent by the general situation than by conditions of the immediate site; "however magnificent a site may be for the approach and accommodation of shipping in a sheltered harbour, it cannot create a port unless the situation allows the development of the all-important relations with the hinterland" (Smailes, 1953, 57). There are many examples of splendid 'natural' harbours within which only limited port development has taken place, and some have remained unutilised; Freetown provides an apt West African illustration of a harbour the physical potential of which vastly exceeds the relatively modest level of port development so far experienced (McKay, 1970). In East Africa the small, but in a limited sense excellent, 'natural' harbours at Dar es Salaam and Mtwara were little used until modern times. Conversely, physical configuration, patterns of economic development, and the concentration of routeways upon particular stretches of coast, sometimes make necessary the development of seaports in areas where 'natural' harbour facilities are entirely absent; probably the best African example of this situation is provided by the Ghanaian port of Tema (Hilling, 1966 and 1970). In spite of the greater general significance of situation factors, however, the details of site conditions exert a marked control over the pattern of development both at an individual port and in the broader sense that the utilisation of a 'natural' harbour may be both easier and cheaper than a new beginning on a basically unsuitable or neutral site.

Historical factors also affect an evaluation of the relative significance of situation and site factors in port development. In East Africa, as in many former colonial areas, it was essentially from the seaward rather than the landward side that seaports were initially developed. In the case of Mombasa, the only East African seaport of major significance in both medieval and modern times, the existence of a defensive island site for the town and of a harbour offering in past times adequate shelter for sailing craft and in modern times the availability of considerable stretches of deep water has encouraged continued activity and development. The penetration of the interior by the railway, coupled with the economic growth of

Kenya and Uganda in the present century, has involved the development of a hinterland focused upon one particular outlet. This contrasts markedly with conditions in Europe or North America where an area is often in a position to choose amongst various potential port outlets. In some interior parts of Africa – Zambia and Zimbabwe are examples – the available options in transport terms have been strongly influenced by political factors in both colonial and postcolonial times. Each of the major East African ports was initially selected as a good harbour and port site in modern times by Arab or European traders or administrators; each became the starting point of a railway to the interior, and each has been able to build up a relatively extensive and largely exclusive hinterland focused upon a single seaport gateway.

When analysing the physical conditions that have influenced the growth of a port, it is often useful to maintain the traditional distinction between the harbour, which is the sheltered area of water within which a port is located, and the port installations where the transhipment of cargo and passengers takes place. Some degree of shelter, natural or artificial, is essential for port development, and an important factor in the classification of port facilities is the extent of the sheltered deep-water area. The conditions of the harbour, in its natural or improved state, and the level of development of port facilities within the harbour, thus present two distinct sets of factors, the relationships between which are very variable. A harbour in its natural state is frequently quite inadequate for more than elementary port development, but because traffic is concentrated at a particular point extensive artificial additions must be undertaken. On the other hand, excellent 'natural' harbours sometimes remain for long periods relatively or even completely unfrequented by commercial traffic, since the particular stretches of coast on which they lie are not important in terms of the land and sea exchanges of their region. Thus the correlation between the fortuitous distribution of 'natural' harbours and the spatial structure of modern port and transport systems is never close, but the pattern of port growth is nevertheless conditioned by the characteristics of the harbours within which it takes place.

Situation Factors: the East African Seaport System

A basic factor in the situation of the East African port group is the relationship of the group to the pattern of trade routes in the Indian Ocean. Until the earlier nineteenth century, the East African coastlands were, for trading purposes, essentially part of the western shore of the Indian Ocean rather than a maritime facade of a continental area; they comprised an important if rather peripheral element within the widespread network of trading towns and ports stretching in medieval times through south-western Asia to China. Although trade with India is still significant, and that with China, Japan and Hong Kong is increasing, the coastwise routes towards the Cape and towards Europe have generally been more important in modern times. Traffic through the north-western part of the Indian Ocean and the Red Sea to the Mediterranean and north-west Europe owes its modern development, of course, to the opening of the Suez Canal in 1869; the existence of this canal has been a vital factor in the development of East African trade, and the closure of the canal in 1967 seriously affected the seaports of the western Indian Ocean; the increased use of the Cape route to Europe which was thereby enforced involved considerably increased costs and the rearrangement of shipping schedules. The reopening of the canal in 1975, however, did not bring extensive commercial benefits to East Africa, although the increased flexibility offered by an additional routeway was generally welcomed, and trade with southern Europe increased to some extent.

On the landward side, the principal factor involved in the situation of the seaports of East Africa is the hinterland transport system (Fig. 2.1). The relationship between the growth of the modern seaports and the East African railway network is especially important; it was from selected port sites that pioneer railways were built westwards to serve the interior, and these routes and gateways have been of very great importance in the emergence of the modern economies of the East African countries. Since there are no major river transport routes penetrating the East African interior, the hinterlands of the major seaports are largely defined by political boundaries and by the extent of rail and road services. The port of Tanga illustrates particularly well the fact that port development closely reflects the extent of hinterland communication systems; although it was the first East African mainland seaport to be initiated in modern times, Tanga is now overshadowed by both Mombasa and Dar es Salaam not only because their harbour conditions and port facilities are superior but also because their hinterland communication systems penetrate much further into the interior. The modern port hierarchy still reflects, in some

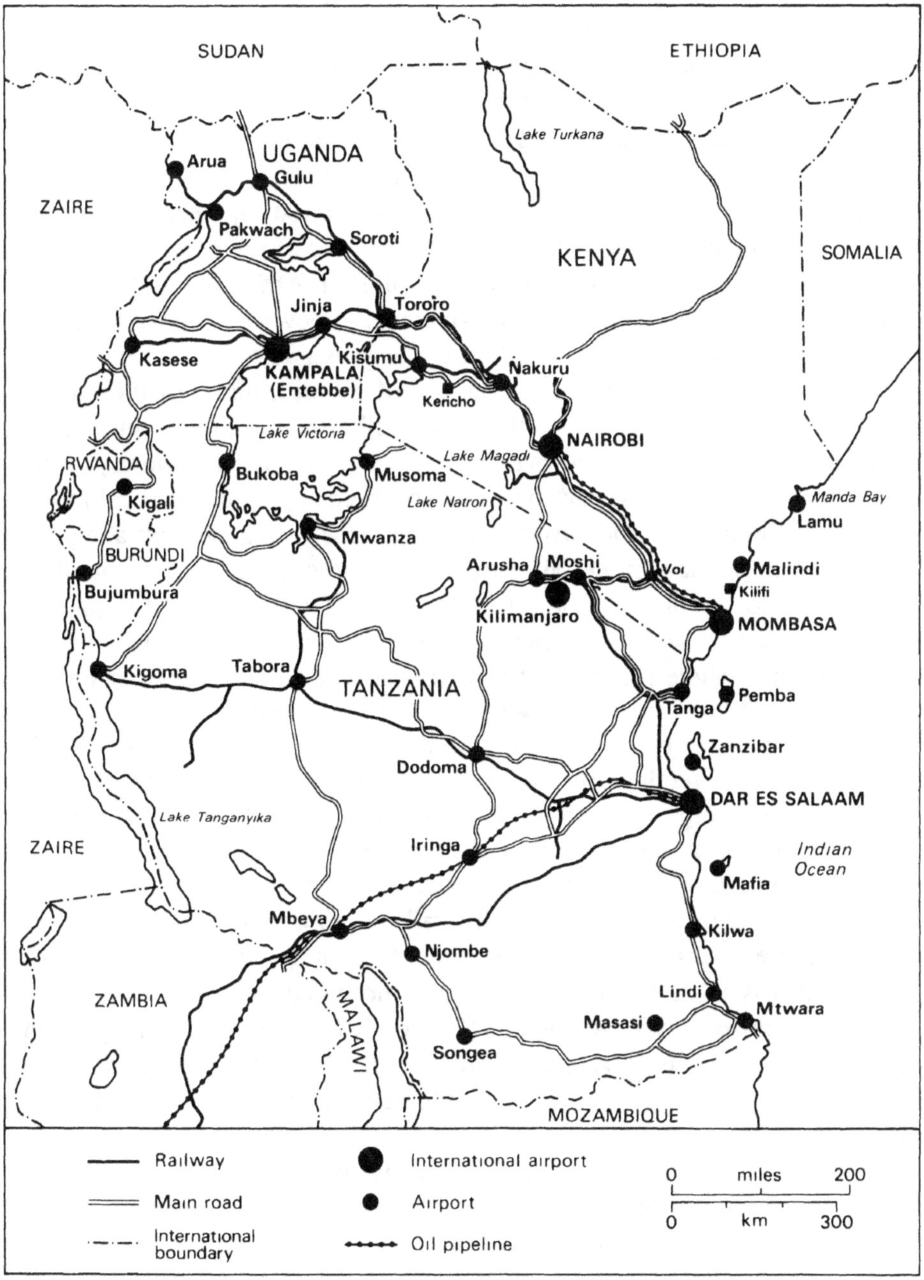

FIGURE 2.1. The pattern of transport services in East Africa.

measure, the situation during the period 1905-23 when the three principal mainland seaports were served by three geographically independent railways; the interconnections established between the Uganda Railway at Voi and the Tanga line at Moshi (1924), and between the Tanga line at Mnyusi and the Tanzanian central line at Ruvu (1963), have not materially affected the hierarchy established at the turn of the century.

In present-day East Africa there is a close relationship between areas of relatively advanced economic activity, major lines of rail communications, and ocean ports. The economic history of East Africa has not involved areas of marked potential wealth experiencing development and finding convenient routes to suitable outlets at the coast. The seaports have, it is true, grown in response to the expansion of the economies of the various countries, but the sequence of events has rather been in the reverse direction. Port sites were selected, within good natural harbours; railways were built inland, their length and direction governed largely by political rather than by economic considerations; and the areas thus served by adequate communications have in certain cases, where other factors are favourable, been able to reach quite a high standard of economic development. Southern Uganda and the highlands of Kenya and northern Tanzania are cases in point where modern development in a favourable area was initially made possible by rail communication with port outlets. Once the basic pattern of port, railway and potential development area was established, such areas have tended to develop more rapidly in proportion to their resources in comparison with other areas. The southern highlands of Tanzania, for example, are relatively undeveloped today partly because adequate lines of communication with major seaports have only recently become available. A proliferation of rail extensions in an economically advanced area does not necessarily promote commensurate development; but the provision of basic arteries for the movement of goods is of course a prerequisite for any development (Hoyle, 1973). The functional pattern of the seaports of East Africa is closely related to the pattern of these arteries and to the patterns of economic activity in the areas which they serve.

The foundation of the modern seaports of East Africa was closely related to the political partition of the area between British and German spheres of influence towards the end of the nineteenth century. The mathematical line of demarcation which today forms, unaltered, the Kenya-Tanzania boundary, exerted a strong influence upon the direction of railway building from the coast, and for a time the various port-railway-hinterland systems of East Africa existed in parallel isolation. Uganda, of course, situated some 1300 km from the coast, is largely dependent upon the railway link with Mombasa, through Kenya, for her external traffic, since the northward routeway via the Nile system has never been fully developed and the routes to Tanga and Dar es Salaam via Lake Victoria are inconvenient. The western frontiers of East Africa generally follow physiographic divides, separating the higher and relatively more productive plateaulands from the lower areas of Zambia, Zaire and Sudan. The hinterlands of Mombasa and Dar es Salaam extend, however, beyond these frontiers: traffic from Zaire has long been significant, and Zambian traffic increased substantially from the later 1960s. Very little commercial traffic, however, moves across the Tanzania/Mozambique or Kenya/Ethiopia boundaries.

A problem of political geography that affected East African seaports in the recent past was that of the coastal strip, and the situation of Mombasa within the Kenya section of the strip added point to the need to find a solution to the problem prior to Kenya's independence in 1963. The East African coastal strip was defined as the zone lying approximately within ten miles of the coast; in Kenya, separated from the interior by the semi-desert scrublands more effectively than from Asia by the ocean, the strip represents a minor East African parallel with the relationship of the Maghreb to the Sahara and to Europe. For centuries the coastlands and offshore islands of East Africa were largely controlled by immigrant Arab traders, and there existed for long a considerable degree of geographical unity, physical and human, reflected in historical circumstances and population conditions. With the coming of the Europeans to East Africa in larger numbers during the later nineteenth century, the Tanzania section of the strip was ceded by the Sultan of Zanzibar to Germany in 1890, and thus became part of Tanganyika in 1919; the Kenya section, however, administered by Britain, remained technically under the authority of the Sultan until 1963 (Melamid, 1963). A commission of inquiry, set up in 1961, reported that a majority of the inhabitants of the strip favoured union with Kenya (Robertson, 1961). The *de jure* Arab rule of the coastal strip was thus brought to a peaceful end; but this was quickly followed early in 1964, a few weeks after Zanzibar's independence, by a revolution which ended the *de facto* Arab rule in the offshore islands. The safeguarding of the traffic of Mombasa was clearly one of the most vital aspects of these political developments.

Several of the factors that have influenced the growth of the mainland seaports of East Africa have also been involved in the general situation of the port of Zanzibar; but, because of Zanzibar's insular location, some of the factors outlined above have been significant in rather different ways. First, the fortunes of Zanzibar have been more closely geared to the wind regime of the western Indian Ocean than have those of the mainland ports; the nineteenth century period of Zanzibar's predominance was a period when most of the shipping using the port still moved under sail, whereas the twentieth century growth of the mainland seaports had taken place within the era of steam propulsion. Second, in relation to communications in the interior of East Africa, Zanzibar occupied a fortunate position in the nineteenth century; utilising small mainland outports, principally Bagamoyo, Zanzibar stood for a time as the eastern terminus and control point of a series of inland trade routes, at least one of which is perpetuated by present-day railway lines. With the coming of the railways, however, Zanzibar was placed at a distinct disadvantage and was no longer able to maintain its dominant position. The economic development of the interior has further tended to emphasise the growth of the mainland ports, so that Zanzibar, with its comparatively minute hinterland, has shown a steady relative decline in the present century. The political subdivision of mainland East Africa furthermore reduced the spheres of economic influence of the Arab sultans to nothing more than the offshore islands, so that after the 1964 revolution political union with Tanganyika remained the only logical course. The circumstances of situation which so favoured Zanzibar in the nineteenth century no longer apply; the predominance of the port at that time was a result of Seyyid Said's aptitude in taking advantage of a transitional period that was by its nature bound to be short-lived. Many of the circumstances which actively encouraged the growth of Zanzibar in the nineteenth century now actively discourage it, the most important of all being the virtual restriction of the formerly extensive hinterland to the offshore islands.

Present day circumstances of situation thus militate more strongly against the growth of Zanzibar than against any other major East African seaport, with the possible exception of Mtwara. In the eras prior to the development of railways on the East African mainland, Zanzibar profited from a water situation that was as good as that of any mainland port, and took full advantage of it politically. The coming of the railways linking the mainland seaports with extensive hinterlands enhanced the land situation of these developing terminals, and nullified the advantages of the water situation at Zanzibar. The only redeeming feature of the situation of Zanzibar today lies in its considerable strategic value in relation to East Africa as a whole, a factor that has not escaped the attention of those foreign powers interested in the area.

Site Conditions at East African Seaports

The Pre-Cambrian Basement System which constitutes the essential foundation of the geology of much of Africa is widely exposed in eastern Kenya and Tanzania, but the immediate coastal area is fringed mainly by sediments of Tertiary and Quaternary age. Successive marine transgressions along the coast have been a notable feature of the post-Jurassic era in East Africa; Lower Tertiary deposits are infrequent, but the Miocene and Pliocene periods are represented by widespread sandstones, clays and limestones mainly of marine origin but sometimes originating in deltas or estuaries (Saggerson, 1969). In southern Tanzania, the sandstones known as the Mikindani beds reach a maximum thickness of 91 m, and similar formations are found along many parts of the coast and on the offshore islands (Stockley, 1937). During the Quaternary era positive and negative eustatic changes of sea level continued along the coast, and the Pleistocene period is represented chiefly by raised coral reefs, by drowned river estuaries, and by sandstones, sands and dunes, the latter apparently eroded and wind-transported from Tertiary rocks inland. Most of these sediments dip at a low angle towards the coast. Faults are not much in evidence in the coastal area, but a feature of some interest is a line of falls and rapids marking most of the smaller rivers a few miles island from the coast and coinciding with a north-east to south-west fault running from the vicinity of Tanga to the Rovuma river.

The most interesting geomorphological feature on the coast of Kenya and Tanzania, and the one most significant from the standpoint of port development, is the existence of a series of drowned valleys or *rias* resulting from Pleistocene changes in the relative sea level; these were first noted by Maufe (1908) and discussed by Sikes (1930). A number of tidal creeks occur on the East African coast; they vary considerably in size, their rock floors are considerably below present sea level, and it is clear that they represent land valleys carved by river erosion and subsequently drowned. The subaerial erosion which produced these valleys probably took place subsequent to the formation of the Pleistocene raised coral reefs which form much of the existing coastline. There is considerable similarity of form between Port Reitz and Port Tudor at Mombasa and the harbour of Dar es Salaam (Figs. 5.1, 5.2). These inlets are characterized by narrow, winding deep-water channels, partly blocked by submarine shelves of recent coral growth where they pass through the fringing reefs. During the Pleistocene period, when the sea level was at one stage relatively much lower than at present, the creeks were formed as deep river valleys on the seaward slope of the land, and their rapid erosion was evidently accentuated by a contemporaneous pluvial epoch. Subsequently the advancing sea flooded the creeks and caused the gradual aggradation of the channels resulting in their present flat-bottomed form. Small examples of creeks of this nature are to be found along many parts of the East African coast; Kilifi Creek, a short distance north of Mombasa, is a well-known instance since it interrupts the main Mombasa-Malindi road and is crossed by ferry.

The larger examples mentioned above are those that have been utilised for port development. The incidence and length of these drowned valleys is not, perhaps, sufficiently pronounced to justify the classification of this coastline as a *ria* coastline (comparable with that of, for example, south-western Ireland), but they are nevertheless locally important. In the Dar es Salaam area, associated features include a series of low-lying steps, which appear to be raised beaches and old cliff lines and seem to owe their origin to pauses in the retreat of sealevel during the later Pleistocene period (Threlfall, 1950; Temple, 1970). In general, therefore, the present detail of the coastline of East Africa has been brought about by discontinuous alterations of ocean level during Pleistocene and more recent times, alterations which appear to be still in progress. Another point of interest is that until late Pleistocene times the island of Zanzibar was a promontory joined to the mainland by a coral-fringed sandbank, whereas Pemba was severed from the mainland by faulting in Miocene times; this is reflected in the differences between the living fauna of Pemba on the one hand and that of Zanzibar and the mainland on the other.

The immediate environs of Mombasa provide ample evidence of coastal submergence (Fig. 5.1). The area now occupied by the open waters of Port Reitz and Port Tudor represents the drowned mouths of the rivers Kombeni, Cha Simba and Mwachi, and the present deep channel of Kilindini

Harbour marks the line of the outlet to the sea of a former major river. A somewhat complex ria thus forms the most fundamental aspect of the site of Mombasa; its formation was considerably aided by the easily erodable Jurassic shales that occur in the area. The widespread development of coral offshore is subsequent to the formation of the major creeks; silt carried in the waters of the numerous streams entering Mombasa and Kilindini Harbours has prevented coral growth across the entrance, since the coral polyp can survive only in clear water at a temperature of at least 70°F (21°C). The break between the Leven and Andromache reefs which flank the harbour entrance is vital for the navigation of vessels entering and leaving the harbour. Mombasa Island on which the town and most of the port facilities are sited, lies between Mombasa and Kilindini harbours and is separated from the mainland on the northern and north-western sides by Port Tudor, Makupa Creek and Port Reitz. The southern two-thirds of the island, and the corresponding mainland areas on either side, are composed of coral reef and coral breccia, thicknesses of 24 m being exposed above low-water level (Caswell, 1953). Pleistocene beds known as the Kilindini Sands, probably contemporaneous with the coral, form the remainder of the island. Shales and limestones, through which the Mwachi river cut deeply in the past, are present on the adjacent mainland. Borings near the head of Port Reitz have shown that the rock floor is 21-24 m below low-water level. Raised coral reefs of early Pleistocene age are horizontally bedded and similar in type on either side of the various creeks, and appear therefore to have been formerly more continuous and to antedate the river erosion that produced the harbours.

Each of the two major arms of the ria system has been developed for commercial purposes, though in entirely different ways. The fact that Mombasa has been a seaport of significance in both medieval and modern times is largely attributable to the geographical juxtaposition on this site of two harbours contrasted in area, depth and capacity; these conditions have enabled the port to adapt itself successfully to functional and navigational changes over time. Mombasa Harbour, generally known as the Old Harbour, lies on the eastern side of the island between Ras Serani and Nyali Bridge. Overlooked by Fort Jesus and the older parts of Mombasa town, this small harbour provided excellent shelter for early sailing craft; but neither the entrance channel, which involves a rock bar, nor the harbour itself is sufficiently wide or deep for large modern vessels. Due to physical constriction Mombasa Harbour largely retains the form and

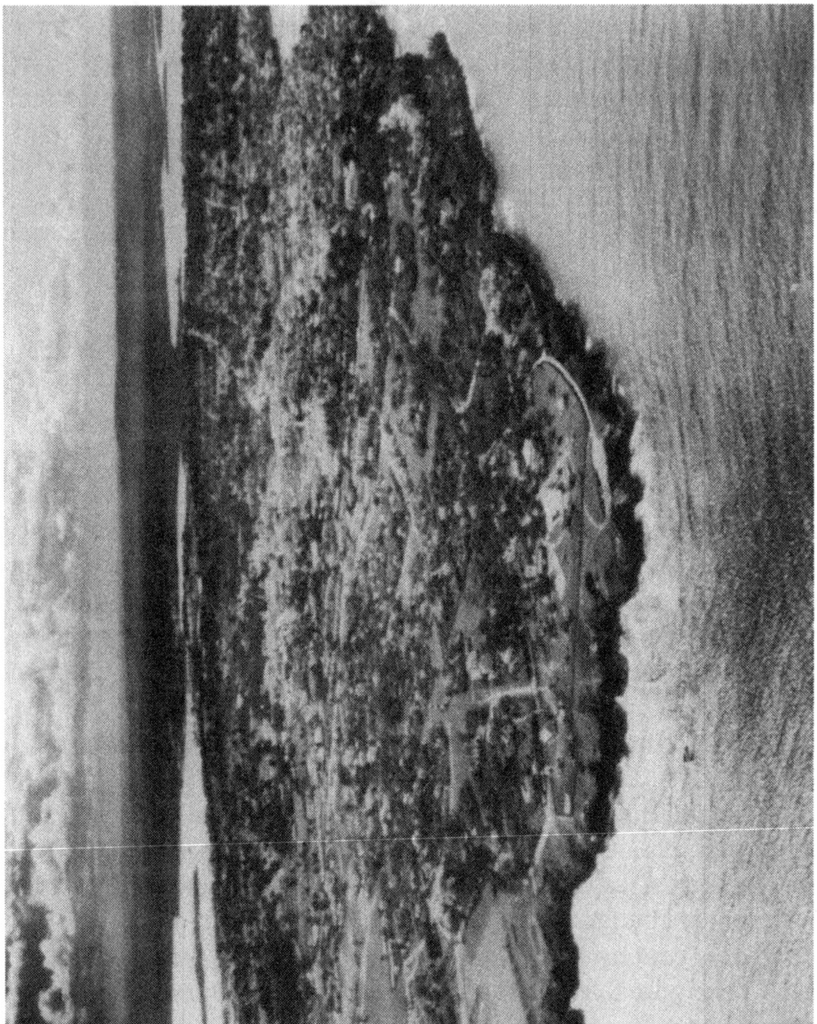

PLATE 2.1. Mombasa Island: an aerial view from the southeast. The island, on which the city centre is located, separates Mombasa Harbour (right, overlooked by the old town) from Kilindini Harbour and Port Reitz (top left). Links with the mainland are provided by the Makupa and Kipevu causeways (top centre). (*Source:* Kenya Railways Corporation, Nairobi.)

functions it acquired in the later Middle Ages. It is still used by traditional dhows, which now come in relatively small numbers each year on the north-east monsoon; but modern port facilities are very limited. If this small creek were all that Mombasa possessed as a harbour, the modern development of the seaport would have been very restricted.

Kilindini Harbour, on the south-western side of the island, is much wider and deeper than Mombasa Harbour, and is clearly much better fitted from the standpoint of physical geography to become the focus of modern shipping at Mombasa. The entrance from the sea, which of course also serves Mombasa Harbour, is a channel some 274 m wide at its narrowest point between the 9-m lines, and is flanked by coral reefs on either side. The depth of the channel varies considerably: the maximum depth is about 46 m, and for many years the minimum was maintained at 10 m; this permitted the entry of vessels of up to 45,000 dwt and 244 m in length. In 1966, however, the building of an oil refinery necessitated the deepening of the entrance channel to allow the entry of large tankers up to 13.4 m draught, and in 1980 the channel was widened at Ras Mzimle and at Ras Kilindini to allow vessels of up to 300 m in length to enter the harbour. The maximum depth in the entrance channel is now 9.75 m and the maximum permissible draught is 13.4 m; this allows for about 2.3 m underwater clearance for wave and sea rolling. The tidal range in the harbour varies from 0.9 m to 4 m during the year. An important advantage of Kilindini Harbour is that deep water is available close inshore at several points. Over 3000 m of deep-water quay length is now available, and the maximum permissible draught varies between 9.45 m at berths 1-5 to 10.97 m at berths 16-18 and at the Mbaraki cement wharf. At the Kipevu oil terminal the maximum permissible draught is 13.4 m. There are also several important navigational disadvantages: the entrance channel is wide enough to permit the passage of only one vessel at a time, and the fringing reefs are dangerous; inside the harbour, the lying-off space available for vessels awaiting a berth or being worked in midstream is limited, so that great care is required by pilots controlling shipping movements.

The port and town of Tanga (Fig. 5.3) are located on the southern shore of Tanga Bay, a considerable indentation along a stretch of the East African coast otherwise characterised by mangrove swamps and by muddy or sandy estuarine flats. The bay, roughly circular in shape, represents the drowned mouths of the rivers Sigi and Mkulumuzi; these small streams merge into the open waters of the bay through a maze of mangrove

PLATE 2.2. The site of Mombasa: an aerial view from the northwest. The Kipevu berths 11 and 12 (foreground) are linked to the deep-water berths on Mombasa Island by the Kipevu causeway. The entrance to Kilindini Harbour from the sea is visible (top right), and beyond the island is Mombasa Harbour (top left). (*Source*: Kenya Railways Corporation, Nairobi.)

swamps fringing the western shores. The harbour is sheltered from the south-east monsoon which blows in strongly, setting up a sea; outer reefs, however, protect the harbour from a heavy swell. Toten Island provides further protection for the inner harbour. The town of Tanga stands on a raised coral platform about 15 m above low water level. The port facilities are grouped on a small area of land, partly of artificial construction, at the base of the 15-m cliff. Ships approaching the harbour must pass through the ship channel, a gap in the outer reefs about 10 km from Ras Kazone, and the inner harbour is entered through a channel between the reefs lying off Ras Kazone and Toten Island; the width of this channel is about 500 m. The tidal stream in the harbour is virtually negligible, and shipping movements are limited only by the depth of water available at the various berths and moorings. Depth of water close inshore is the chief physical obstacle restricting the development of Tanga as a seaport; within the inner harbour, less than one square kilometre is available with a depth of more than 5 m, and a similar but shallower area is available for smaller craft. With these restrictions, Tanga was able to develop only as a lighterage port until the multipurpose jetty extending into deep water off Ras Kazone was opened in 1972. There are five anchorages for ocean-going vessels of up to 20,000 dwt within the inner harbour, where the maximum length of vessels that can be accommodated varies between 150 and 180 m, and the maximum draught between 6 and 8 m. There is also an anchorage situated to the north north-east of Toten Island, suitable for vessels of up to 9 m draught, but during the north-east monsoon weather conditions frequently make this berth unsuitable for working cargo. Several other anchorages are available for small craft. Except at the multipurpose jetty, vessels using the port of Tanga are worked at anchor in the inner harbour. Cargoes are transported between vessels and quays by lighters, a rather unsatisfactory procedure which involves the double transhipment of goods and thereby increases the risk of damage.

Many of the physical features noted in the case of Mombasa are also characteristic of the harbour at Dar es Salaam (Fig. 5.2). The tidal harbour basin and its extension known as Southern Creek together represent another example of a drowned river valley. Three small streams now drain into the mangrove swamps at the head of Southern Creek. From a navigational standpoint, Dar es Salaam is in some respects the most difficult of the East African harbours receiving ocean-going ships, for in spite of its deep-water facilities the harbour itself is small and the entrance is con-

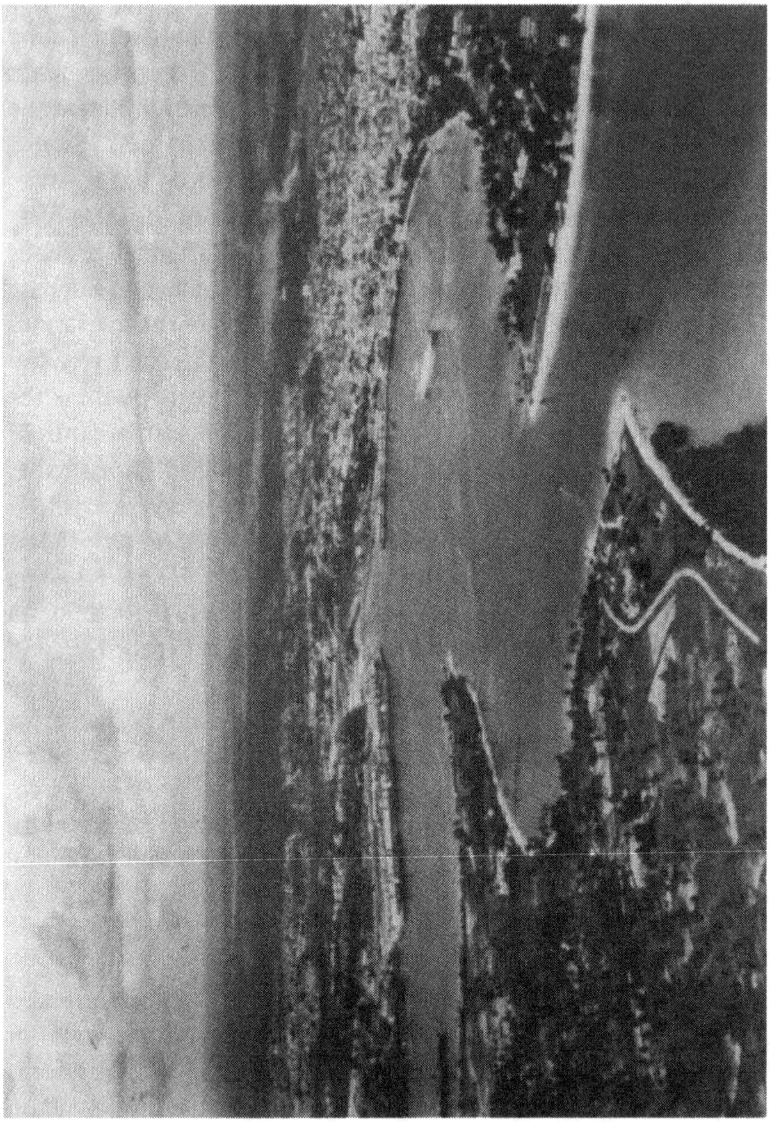

PLATE 2.3. Dar es Salaam: an aerial view over the harbour and city. The city centre lies to the north (right) of the harbour. Opposite the constricted harbour entrance, Kurasini Creek separates the lighterage quays from the deep-water berths (left); additional deep-water berths have been built since this photograph was taken (see Figure 5.2). (*Source*: Kenya Railways Corporation, Nairobi.)

stricted. At the north-eastern end of the main basin, the entrance channel is narrow and angular, and is obstructed by coral growth. The maximum tidal range is 3.7 m. Shipping movements in and out of the basin are subject to restrictions depending on draught and the state of the tide, especially the spring tides. Normally vessels of up to 180 m in length are permitted to enter the harbour, and the maximum permissible draught at various tides varies between 6 and 9 m. However, few ships entering the harbour exceed 7.6 m draught. Ship manoeuvres, for which pilotage is compulsory at all times, are limited as far as possible to the hours of daylight. An important obstacle to navigation at Dar es Salaam is that vessels must stem the tide when entering or leaving the harbour, especially during the spring tides. The picturesque inner harbour, sometimes incorrectly described as a lagoon, is well concealed from the sea; Captain Owen, when making his hydrographic survey of the East African coast for the Admiralty in 1824-26, completely failed to realise its existence (Owen, 1833). In addition to the deep-water berths, partly constructed on reclaimed land, and the lighterage berths, several additional anchorages are provided within the main basin. A small creek in the south-western corner of the basin, known as Kurasini Creek, is too shallow to be of much use. More important is Southern Creek, the main arm of the ria, which is navigable for about 2.4 km for ships drawing up to 9 m of water. Although deep water close inshore is lacking, Southern Creek is a major extension of the main basin and has provided the site of major deep-water port extensions in recent years.

Mtwara Harbour is the larger of two almost landlocked stretches of water in the inner reaches of Mikindani Bay, a considerable indentation on the coast of southern Tanzania near the Mozambique border (Fig. 5.4). Mtwara and Mikindani Harbours, together with Mikindani Bay of which they form a part, constitute an extensive ria system comparable to those noted at the more northerly seaports of East Africa. However, whereas Mikindani Harbour is small and relatively shallow, Mtwara Harbour provides a spacious area of some 11.7 km^2 of deep and well-sheltered water, and it is on this fact that its modern development as a seaport is based. Within the harbour there is ample room for ship manoeuvres and numerous anchorages are available in depths up to 33 m. A limiting factor is the entrance to the harbour, which is a dog-leg not unlike that at Dar es Salaam and involving an awkward turn. Vessels entering Mtwara Harbour from Mikindani Bay must negotiate a narrow channel, some 24 m deep

PLATE 2.4. Dar es Salaam: a cargo vessel negotiating the narrow entrance channel. (*Source*: Kenya Railways Corporation, Nairobi.)

PLATE 2.5. The site of Dar es Salaam. The narrow entrance from the sea (bottom left) leads to the lighterage and deep-water quays and to Southern Creek (top left) where additional berths have been built (see Figure 5.2). (*Source*: Kenya Railways Corporation, Nairobi.)

at its shallowest point, between Mwamba Ribunda and Mwamba Shangani, two stretches of low coral reef exposed only at low tide. Abreast a low sandspit known as Msemo Spit, the entrance channel is only 270 m wide, and it is at this point that a 90-degree turn is involved. A deep-water quay is situated on the south side of the harbour, developed partly on artificial ground, and the minimum depth at the quayside is 10 m.

At the port of Zanzibar, the general pattern of nineteenth century suitability and twentieth century unsuitability in terms of the geographical situation is unfortunately repeated in terms of site conditions. The port and town lie on the western side of Zanzibar Island which is more varied geologically and physiographically than the eastern side and, like the western coast of Pemba Island, is more sheltered and better equipped with natural harbours and safe anchorages. Both islands have a core of sedimentary rocks of Miocene-Pliocene age, closely related to similar rocks on the mainland and surrounded by recent reefal limestone which in the case of Zanzibar occupies the whole of the eastern and southern half of the island. Pemba is separated from the mainland by a deep, faulted trough, but the Zanzibar Channel is comparatively shallow (Stockley, 1928). Zanzibar Harbour consists of an area of water sheltered by a number of small islands rising from coastal coral reefs; these form a semicircle and ensure that the waters of the harbour are almost always fairly calm. Ships approaching Zanzibar from the north use the English Pass between Chapani Island and the coast of the main island near Mtoni. From the south entry is made via the broader Southern Pass, and thence through a narrow gap in the reefs south-west of Ras Mbweni. Vessels may also enter through the Western Pass. The navigation of these passes, which are well buoyed and lighted, is not difficult, although pilotage is compulsory.

The principal feature of the land site of the port of Zanzibar is a triangular promontory culminating in Ras Shangani (Figs. 2.2, 4.2). In the early nineteenth century the tip of this promontory was virtually an island, separated from the more easterly parts of the peninsula by a shallow creek but connected at the southern end by a sand bank. This situation is clearly portrayed on a French map, dated 1846, in the Zanzibar Museum. A road across the southern end of the creek was built by Bishop Steere (Bishop of Zanzibar, 1874-82), and a German map dated 1882 (also in the Zanzibar Museum) shows a certain amount of infilling at the southern end of the creek. The creek was described in 1928 as "an ill-defined stretch of mud flats only covered with water at high tide,

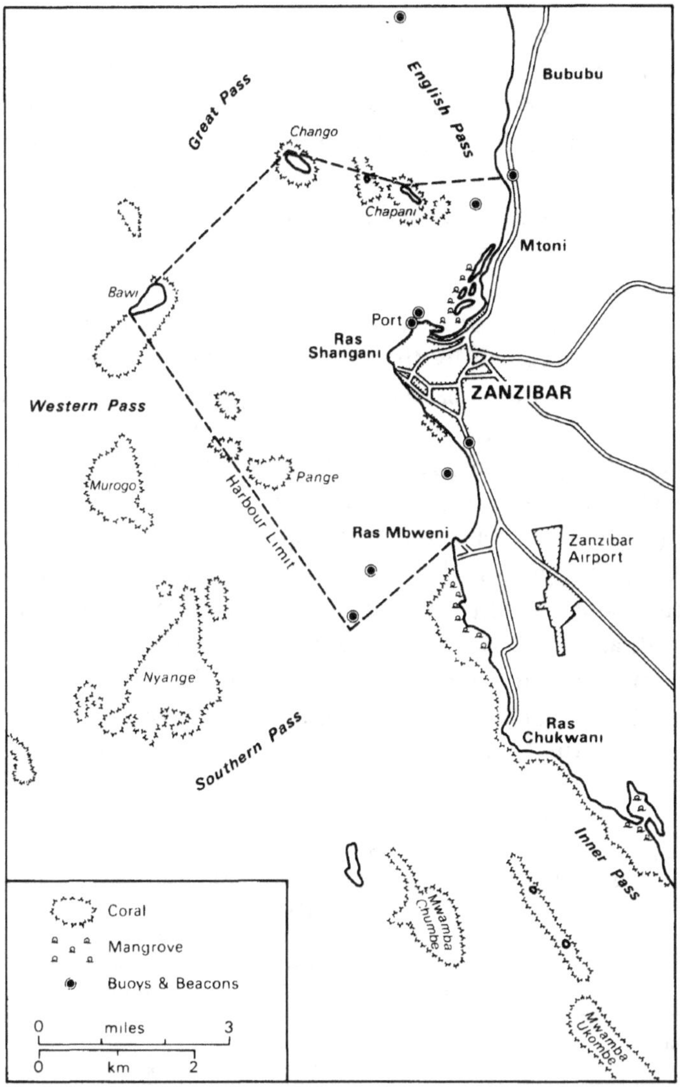

FIGURE 2.2. Zanzibar harbour. (*Source of data:* Admiralty Chart 665.)

and . . . the receptacle for every kind of filth pertaining to an Eastern town" (Zanzibar Protectorate, 1929, 10). In the 1930s the creek was canalised as far north as Darajani Bridge and it was filled in during the 1950s so that only a relatively small area, known as Funguni Creek, is now covered by water at high tide. The area of the former creek, largely unsuitable for building purposes, still remains an open space effectively separating the former Arab 'stone town' on the tip of the peninsula from the remainder of the township which was originally constructed of less substantial materials; the area is known as Ng'ambo ('the other side') and is characterised by single-storey houses roofed with coconut palm (*makuti*) or old petrol tins, partly replaced in recent years by multi-storey blocks of flats constructed as part of the government's extensive and ambitious housing programme.

From the standpoint of navigation and port activity the significance of the promontory occupied by the town is chiefly to be seen in relation to the wind regime of the Indian Ocean. During the *Kaskasi* (north-east monsoon, November-March), the waters off the exposed north-western shore of the promontory become rough, and the sheltered waters south of Ras Shangani were therefore formerly used at this period. Conversely, during the *Kusi* (south-west monsoon, April-September) the area of water north of Ras Shangani, lying in the lee of the peninsula, is the more sheltered. During the rainy seasons that occur between the monsoons (*Masika*, March-April; and *Vuli*, October-November) the sea is generally fairly calm. At most times of year, therefore, some part of Zanzibar harbour is able to provide sheltered anchorage. An attempt was made to perpetuate these advantageous natural circumstances in the construction of modern port facilities.

TABLE 2.1
PARTICULAR AND RELATIVE DEFECTS IN THE LOCATION OF EACH EAST AFRICAN SEAPORT*

	Water Situation	Water Site	Land Situation	Land Site
Mombasa				
Tanga		x	x	
Dar es Salaam		x		
Mtwara			x	
Zanzibar		x	x	x

*x represents a defect.

Table 2.1 summarises the general position by indicating in very simplified terms certain particular and relative defects of the mainland seaports of East Africa in terms of situation and site conditions. It is at once obvious that Mombasa is unique among the seaports of East Africa, having no major defect of situation or site. Although the water situation of all East African seaports is broadly the same and is reasonably favourable, Mombasa clearly possesses the most advantageous water site and the best land situation in terms of an extensive and comparatively well-developed hinterland. These facts clearly go some way towards explaining the predominance of Mombasa as East Africa's principal seaport. Dar es Salaam, in comparison, does not share the same advantages, having a comparatively restricted water site and a less-developed (although still very extensive) hinterland. The shallowness of the inshore waters within the harbour at Tanga, and the disadvantageous land situation between the two larger ports (so that hinterland growth has been restricted) help to explain the comparatively low level of development at that port. The only major defect in the location of Mtwara, in contrast, is in the land situation: with relatively little development in the hinterland, and with no railway, Mtwara remains a port of potential rather than actual development. At Zanzibar, the land situation of the port on an offshore island is obviously a major disadvantage in terms of modern transport systems, and the water site is not conducive to the development of modern deep-water port facilities.

REFERENCES

Caswell, P.V. (1953), *Geology of the Mombasa – Kwale area*, Report 24, degree sheet 69 (Nairobi, Government Printer, for the Geological Survey of Kenya).

Hilling, D. (1966), 'Tema, the geography of a new port,' *Geography* 51, 111-125.

Hilling, D. (1970), 'Port development and economic growth: the case of Ghana,' in B.S. Hoyle and D. Hilling (eds.), *Seaports and development in tropical Africa* (London, Macmillan), 127-145.

Hoyle, B.S. (ed.) (1973), *Transport and development* (London, Macmillan).

McKay, J. (1970), 'Physical potential and economic reality: the underdevelopment of the port of Freetown', in B.S. Hoyle and D. Hilling (eds.), *Seaports and development in tropical Africa* (London, Macmillan), 57-73.

Maufe, H.B. (1908), *Geology of the East Africa Protectorate* (London, Col. Rep. Misc. 45, Cd. 3828).

Melamid, A. (1963), 'The Kenya coastal strip', *Geographical Review* 53, 457-459.

Morgan, W.T.W. (ed.) (1969), *East Africa: its peoples and resources* (Nairobi, Oxford University Press, 2nd edn.).

Owen, W.F.W. (1833), *Narrative of voyages to explore the shores of Africa, Arabia and Madagascar* (London, 2 vols., Bentley; repr. 1968, Gregg International Publishers, Farnborough).

Robertson, J.W. (1961), *The Kenya coastal strip: report of the Commissioner* (London, HMSO, Cmnd. 1585).

Saggerson, E.P. (1969), 'Geology', in W.T.W. Morgan (ed.), *East Africa: its peoples and resources* (Nairobi, Oxford University Press, 2nd edn.), 67-94.

Sikes, H.L. (1930), 'The drowned valleys on the coast of Kenya', *Journal of the East Africa and Uganda Natural History Society* 38, 1-9.

Smailes, A.E. (1953), *The geography of towns* (London, Hutchinson).

Stockley, G.M. (1937), 'Geological notes on the coastal region of Tanganyika', *Tanganyika Notes and Records* 3, 82-86.

Stockley, G.M. (1928), *Report on the geology of the Zanzibar Protectorate* (Zanzibar, Government Printer).

Temple, P.H. (1970), 'Aspects of the geomorphology of the Dar es Salaam area', *Tanzania Notes and Records* 71, 21-54.

Threlfall, H.R. (1950), 'Some physical features of the Dar es Salaam district', *Tanganyika Notes and Records* 29, 68-72.

Zanzibar Protectorate (1920 *et seq.), Report on the Public Works Department for the year 1920, et seq*. (Zanzibar, Government Printer).

3 Seaport Hierarchies

An important principle underlying several aspects of this study is that it is generally more profitable to consider seaports in terms of their interrelationships within port groups rather than to analyse the characteristics of a specific port in isolation; in other words, the competitive position of a port in relation to other ports is the criterion which most profoundly influences its fortunes in the longer run. In reality, no port is an isolated phenomenon, but belongs to a *port complex*, a group of ports which are functionally interrelated on a local, national or international scale. Viewed from the maritime side, ports linked functionally to the same forelands are related together in this sense; on the landward side, ports serving a series of continuous or overlapping hinterlands are related. Thus the relationships between ports may be complementary or competitive, and a given port may belong to several port complexes. Ports in Canada, West Africa, Australia and elsewhere which export iron ore to the Japanese foreland constitute one type of port complex; West Africa may be said to comprise a single port complex stretching from the Niger delta to Mauritania, but with smaller-scale port complexes in Nigeria, Ivory Coast, Liberia etc. In East Africa an interstate port complex serves both coastal and inland countries.

In this chapter the principles of port interrelationships and interport competition are extended to include not only the spatial dimension but also the temporal framework; for a port is essentially a dynamic phenomenon, changing in its morphology, functions and status in relation to other ports as circumstances vary over time. The various ports which comprise a port complex are obviously of unequal significance at any given point in time, whatever the criteria of measurement that may be adopted, and where adequate data are available ports may therefore be ordered into a hierarchy. The character and functions of the various ports in a hierarchy change in various ways over time, as a result of the differential impact of factors influencing port growth. At a given point in time a port may be of increasing or decreasing relative significance, vis-à-vis other ports in the complex; thus the ranking of ports within a complex changes, as does the composite character of the complex as a whole. Ogundana suggested that the composite pattern of a port complex, over time, may take one of two basic forms – *port concentration* or *port diffusion*: "*Port concentration* implies that a few of the many ports in a complex are of disproportionate significance, and this structure emerges as a result of the increasing relative significance, over a period, of certain ports as compared to others which either gain more modestly or decline in absolute terms. *Port concentration* results initially in a relative decline but may lead to an absolute decrease in the number of ports operating. *Port diffusion* occurs when higher-order ports decline, leading to the increasing significance of new or previously smaller ports, and involves an absolute or relative increase in the number of functioning ports" (Ogundana, 1970, 169).

Clearly, each era of *port concentration* or *port diffusion* may be said to possess its own hierarchy. If a hierarchy undergoes frequent and considerable change, the complex may be said to possess an *unstabilised port structure*. On the other hand, a port which maintains its leadership within a complex over a lengthy period of time may be described as a centre of *sustained port dominance*. In the twentieth century the factors affecting port development have generally favoured the process of spatial consolidation, involving the increasing concentration of port traffic at the larger terminals. This process was noted in 1938 by Sargent, who observed that "the tendency of modern sea traffic is to concentrate so that the number of effective ports grows less" (Sargent, 1938, 2). Today the economics of maritime transportation require ever-increasing specialization of port installations: "If specialisation means concentration, the throughput of cargo via a small port must either increase to justify modern port installations, or the cargo will be concentrated at one of a series of small ports, to the others' disadvantage which may be mortal" (Bird, 1971, 74). Over much longer time periods, however, it is possible to recognise alternating periods of concentration and diffusion in the evolution of a port complex. In some areas, the interpretation may be that a long-term trend towards concentration has been periodically interrupted to yield a cyclical evolutionary sequence in which concentration alternates with some form of diffusion. Elsewhere a flexible system of diffusion of port activity may be the norm over many centuries, yielding to a form of concentration only when investment in modern facilities requires the stabilisation of a formerly fluid pattern.

The Case of East Africa

The application of these general principles of port development to a specific area of the less-developed world, where the present-day port system is the successor to a series of earlier port hierarchies, serves to illustrate the variety of factors and processes involved. The growth of port activity on the East African coast may be divided into two broad periods of very unequal length, the first stretching from the first millennium A.D. to the mid-nineteenth century, and the second from the later nineteenth century to the present day. The use of Zanzibar as the principal maritime trading centre in East Africa in the mid-nineteenth century represents a crucial transitional era in the evolution of port activity in this part of the continent. The patterns and levels of development of East African seaport hierarchies, in the past and today, are in part a reflection of contemporary relationships between maritime forelands and interior hinterlands; but they also express the changing nature of these relationships over time.

The East African coastlands today constitute the maritime facade of a rapidly developing region of considerable economic potential, and form a vital, outward-looking link with the rest of the world. This orientation is largely a product of the last two hundred years, for during all the long preceding centuries the coastlands of East Africa were for trading purposes little more than part of the western shore of the Indian Ocean (Lucas, 1922, 9). They presented a relatively productive and not inhospitable environment to early traders and invaders from the sea, but were for long largely ignored by traders from the land; within this coastal environment successive generations of men built up widely differing hierarchies of seaports (Datoo and Sheriff, 1971). These contrasted port hierarchies illustrate the need to view land and sea influences upon port development in the context of man's technological achievements in a given period, and in the context of his perception of the value and trade potential of particular sites. "The location of ports is due not the direct influence of any inherent qualities of land and water sites, but to the way in which such sites were assessed by the founders" (Bird, 1971, 24).

The various trading settlements developed along the coast by early Asiatic traders from the north and east, and later by Europeans approaching from the south, were to a large extent cut off from what are now the hinterlands of the modern seaports by the *nyika*, the dry thorny savanna across which there were relatively few reliable routeways before the railway era. Apart from physical difficulties, hostile tribes often discouraged inland penetration by coastal traders; and there was little positive encouragement to inland exploration since slaves, ivory and other trade goods were generally available within the coastal region and after about 1800 were brought to the coast, first by African and later by Arab traders. In the nineteenth century slaves and ivory were the chief economic products of East Africa, although the idea that they sometimes reached the coast as joint products when the slaves provided the transport for the ivory is largely a myth (Smith, 1963, 268-9; Beachey, 1967). Then, as now, the range of commodities that could withstand the heavy cost of transport to the sea from the further reaches of East Africa was essentially limited. On the maritime side, pre-twentieth century trading patterns in the western Indian Ocean were essentially related to monsoonal influences. The seasonal wind reversals, sufficiently strong to be matched by a reversal of currents, were an essential geographical basis of the trade circulations of the north-western Indian Ocean in the days of sailing ships. From November to March the north-east monsoon is the prevailing influence; for centuries past this has brought dhows to East African waters from ports in south and south-west Asia, to which they returned with the aid of the south-west monsoon which blows from April to September but which is too strong for sailing vessels between mid-May and mid-August. Provided that commercial transactions were completed in time, most dhows preferred in the past, as today, to leave East Africa during the 'build-up' of the southwest monsoon in April, thus avoiding the need to spend four idle months 'wintering' in East Africa (Datoo, 1970a).

Documentary or archaeological evidence of early trading patterns on the East African coast is still generally slight, though increasing. The nineteenth century, essentially a period of development and transition, is reasonably well documented, and presents a clear and striking contrast with present-day circumstances of traffic and trade. For earlier periods the material is much more scanty, but it is possible to envisage (although at times somewhat dimly) the character and extent of East African trade at certain periods and the distribution and activities of the ports through which that trade passed. No attempt is made here to paraphrase the long and complex history of the East African coastlands or to elaborate early port hierarchies in detail; Sutton (1966) and Chittick (1968) provide useful starting points in the exploration of this field; Datoo (1975) offers a comprehensive and scholarly analysis of port development from the ninth to the sixteenth centuries; and numerous other references are listed at the end of this chapter (e.g. Freeman-Grenville, 1963; Mathew, 1963). Instead, a brief discussion of four contrasted eras of East African port development is offered, with special reference to the nineteenth century conditions from which the modern hierarchy has emerged.

The Pre-Islamic Period

The earliest maritime links between East Africa and other lands are obscure. For the period before the fifteenth century the main key to the past is the trowel of the archaeologist. It appears that the coastlands were rather sparsely populated at this time by Galla and Somali peoples migrating from the north-east, by Bantu-speaking tribes moving northwards along the coast, and by Arabs who came by sea, initially from Yemen and the Hadramaut. Information on the geographical location of ports and towns during this early period is vague, and commercial activity seems to have been a tentative offshoot of the more active circulations of the Red Sea and the north-west corner of the Indian Ocean. The earliest surviving description of the external trade relations of East Africa is to be found in the *Periplus of the Erythraean Sea* (Huntingford, 1976), a guide to the commerce of the Red Sea and the Indian Ocean written at some time during the late first or early second centuries A.D. by a Greek trader of the Roman Empire living in Alexandria. The book describes a voyage along the coast of East Africa, then known as Azania, and mentions the Pyralaean Islands (the Lamu archipelago), Menuthias (Pemba, Zanzibar or possibly Mafia), and the trading port of Rhapta which was subsequently described as a 'metropolis' in Ptolemy's *Geographia* (Stevenson, 1932). The site of Rhapta, East Africa's first seaport, has not yet been satisfactorily identified, although Pangani has been suggested as a possible location (Baxter, 1944). Datoo (1970b) has reviewed the topographical clues against a background of meteorological conditions in the western

Indian Ocean, and has suggested that it is not possible to identify a site but merely to delimit a locality between the mouths of the Pangani and Rufiji rivers, more probably in the northern section of this stretch of coast. Rhapta may have been an important link in the cinnamon route which extended from the Far East to the Red Sea via East Africa (Miller, 1969) or the port may have owed its economic importance to the growth in demand for ivory in the Mediterranean world from the latter part of the first century B.C. (Datoo, 1970b). It is clear, however, that whatever its precise location or economic function, Rhapta occupied only a peripheral position in the commercial system of the western Indian Ocean, although it may have been pre-eminent in an East African context.

The *Periplus* appears to indicate an established trade pattern of some regularity in East Africa, based upon a scatter of small ports along the coast. These were places to which Arab traders from western India probably brought grain, sugar, cotton, porcelain, knives and cloth in exchange for slaves, ivory, rhinoceros horn, hides and copper. Some of the exports despatched in this early period eventually withstood, remarkably, almost two thousand years of exploitation. Imports were for the most part of trifling value but considerable practical use both in daily life and trade; they included, however, several important food crops now widespread in Africa which are thought to have originated in south-eastern Asia – coconuts and bananas are examples (McMaster, 1962). Indonesian influences may have reached East Africa in the early centuries A.D. either directly along the south equatorial current, via Madagascar (where a considerable proportion of the population has been shown on physical and linguistic grounds to be of Indonesian descent), or by stages around the coasts of India and Arabia. It is possible that Indonesian merchants were pioneer traders along the East African coast at the time of the *Periplus;* much later, in the eighth century, the Hindu kingdom of Sri Vijaya centred on Sumatra became an important mercantile power in the Indian Ocean (Sutton, 1966, 8), but links with East Africa are dubious. By the early Middle Ages, however, the trade circulations of the western part of the Ocean were dominated by the Arabs who, following upon the early growth of Islam in the seventh and eighth centuries, gradually incorporated the coastlands of East Africa within the Muslim world.

The Twelfth, Thirteenth and Fourteenth Centuries

Writing in the twelfth century the Arab geographer Al Idrisi refers to the importance of the ports of Malindi, Manrisa (probably Mombasa) and Kilwa (Ferrand, 1913). These and other early medieval trading ports, such as Manda on the north Kenya coast (Chittick, 1967 and 1969; Martin, 1973), probably dominated in turn from their defensive island sites varying areas of coast and hinterland, their fluctuating comparative importance reflecting their varying fortunes in trade and in warfare. For long the number of Arab colonists was small, their settlements poor and their trade negligible. Trade may perhaps have been continuous from the first to the eleventh century, but a more important point is that by the early Middle Ages trade between East Africa and south Arabia had become a major element within the wider commercial circulations of the Indian Ocean.

The later Middle Ages were marked by a much fuller development of Islamic civilisation in East Africa, revealed in recent years by systematic archaeological investigation. The fourteenth century, in particular, shows a considerable expansion and diversification of material culture in the East African coastlands; rapid urban expansion and trade development at this time may have been associated with increasing agricultural production and better security conditions in the now dry semidesert lands of northern Kenya (Kirkman, 1956). Political disturbances in north-east Africa may have accelerated southward Galla migrations, and may also have diverted some traffic from Red Sea ports to those of East Africa. In a wider context, Mathew has pointed out that the fifteenth century climax of Indian Ocean trade (Fig 3.1) fell between the eclipse of the overland routes from the Far East to the West and the discovery of the sea route to India via the Cape (Mathew, 1963, 120). Most of the ruined monuments – mosques, tombs, houses and palaces – that dot the coast of East Africa (Kirkman, 1964) date from the period 1200-1500. Each settlement had periods of relative prosperity and relative decline, but a general level of prosperity was maintained. Several settlements of this period have been excavated. One of the best preserved is Gedi, the remains of which occupy a 45-acre site some 13 km south of Malindi. Gedi was not a seaport, but illustrates the character of the Arab colonial towns at the height of their prosperity. Gedi was founded in the late thirteenth or early fourteenth century, reached its apogee in the mid-fifteenth century and was finally abandoned

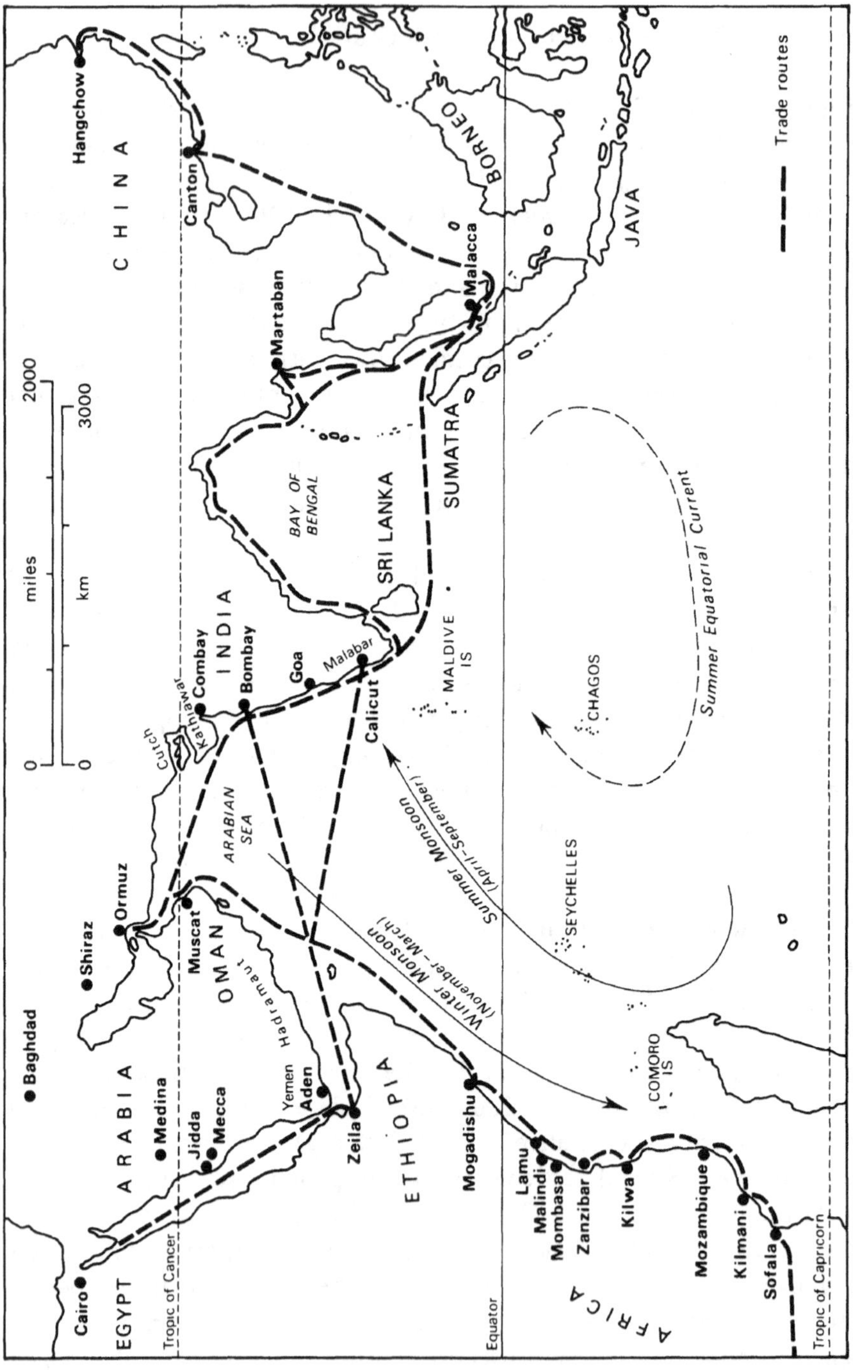

FIGURE 3.1. Medieval trade routes of the Indian Ocean. (Based in part on Oliver and Mathew, 1963, p. 109.)

in the early seventeenth century. Little is known of the reasons for the foundation of the town or of its commercial role, but archaeological evidence suggests that it had a large and relatively prosperous population. A tomb dated A.H. 802 (A.D. 1399), a palace, a mosque, and a number of houses have been excavated (Kirkman, 1954, 1960a and b).

Evidence of the remarkable prosperity of East African commerce in the fourteenth century is also provide by the wealthy island merchant city of Kilwa (Freeman-Grenville, 1962a and b; Chittick, 1963 and 1965). Probably founded by Shirazi colonists who migrated along the East African coast in the twelfth century, Kilwa was described by the Arab geographer Ibn Battuta in 1332 as "one of the most beautiful and best-constructed towns" (Freeman-Grenville, 1955). The emergence of Kilwa as a major medieval seaport, exerting a powerful influence upon trade along the entire East African coast from Malindi to Mozambique, was probably due to two principal factors: the defensive island site of the town; and the control exerted over the supplies of gold reaching the tributary port of Sofala by head porterage and by canoe from what are now Zimbabwe and South Africa. Kilwa derived large revenues from this trade during the fourteenth and fifteenth centuries, and her entrepôt function was supported by an advanced commercial organisation. In addition to gold, she exported ivory and rhinoceros horn from the interior, pearls, tortoiseshell and ambergris from the neighbouring coasts; foodstuffs were imported from the adjoining mainland, pottery from China and Persia, calico, silks and beads from India, carpets, coffee and dates from Persia and Arabia. The seasonal reversal of winds in the Indian Ocean, in addition to facilitating the general trade of the coast, helps also to explain the particular thallasocracy developed by Kilwa. Dhows can sail as far south as Kilwa and still make the return northward journey in April, provided that they sail past Zanzibar by the end of January (before the northeast monsoon begins to retreat northwards) and provided that they do not stay too long in the harbour of destination (Datoo, 1970a). The tributary port of Sofala, lying much further south, was too far away to be visited by traders hoping to return to Asia without 'wintering' in eastern Africa for several relatively idle months. The prosperity of Kilwa also emphasizes the fact that medieval trade in East Africa was chiefly carried on between the coast of present-day Tanzania and the areas lying to the southwest; the thinly populated, inhospitable *nyika* scrubland effectively prevented extensive trade relations between the coast of present-day Kenya and the uplands of

Kenya and Uganda at this time.

A significant proportion of the trade of the medieval seaports of East Africa was with China (Wheatley, 1964). Chinese porcelain is found at various levels and in considerable quantities in coastal archaeological sites, at times in association with local earthenware pottery, glazed Arab pottery, and trade wind beads providing evidence of imports from India. There is evidence that Chinese vessels visited East African seaports in 1417 and 1422 (Duyvendak, 1949), but normally Chinese trade with East Africa was indirect, transhipment of goods taking place at intermediary entrepôts in south and south-west Asia. Indian merchants of Kutch and Kathiawar brought goods from China to sell to Arabs from Oman and the Persian Gulf, who in turn sold to the Arab sea captains who sailed to East Africa on the north-east monsoon. The prosperity of the entrepôts may have depended to a considerable extent upon the East African trade. Always the principal item of export from East African ports was ivory, most general in provenance and least subject to fluctuations in supply or demand due to political conditions; slaves were sent to many Asian destinations including China itself

PLATE 3.1. Dhow traffic at Mombasa: cargoes for the Persian Gulf being loaded in the old harbour. (*Source:* Author.)

The activities of the medieval seaports of East Africa thus represent an intensification of a pattern of commercial activity the roots of which can be seen in the *Periplus*. The temporary stability and relative prosperity of the thirteenth, fourteenth and fifteenth centuries did not reflect the development of new East African resources but depended essentially upon external influences – the products of other parts of Africa and the trade requirements of non-African areas linked with East African seaports through the medieval mercantile circulations of the Indian Ocean. The somewhat parasitic prosperity of the East African coast at this time turned essentially upon the location of the seaports; as Sutton explains, "whether on island or on mainland the Muslim traders and townsfolk built almost without exception against the seashore, facing a harbour or reasonably calm roadstead, or sometimes hidden behind the mangroves. They were maritime settlements looking out to the wider world. The power and wealth of each town . . . rested on the merchandise that entered and left her harbours. Dues were exacted on cargoes, and foreign merchants had to observe harbour regulations . . ." (Sutton, 1966, 19). Thus the bulk of Indian Ocean trade passed into Arab hands, a development which introduced greater unity and prosperity into the system as a whole.

Figure 3.2a shows the distribution of relatively major and relatively minor seaports along the East African coast at the end of the fifteenth century; based upon a range of sources, the map seeks to indicate the general position at a point in time rather than to delineate a more detailed hierarchy; an attempt to differentiate entrepôts, major ports and minor feeder ports has been made for various periods by Datoo and Sheriff (1971). The full development of the Arab settlements and of their trade and culture immediately preceded a gradual decline in the commercial prosperity of the coastlands. Kilwa lost her pre-eminence in the late fourteenth century, and during the fifteenth century Mombasa emerged as the chief seaport on the coast; and at the end of the fifteenth century "the restless energy of western Europe intruded upon . . . the East African coast like an unseasonable monsoon for which the inhabitants were totally unprepared" (Ingham, 1962, 6).

The Portuguese Period

"Further on . . .," wrote Duarte Barbosa in c.1517, "there is an isle hard by the mainland, on which is a town called Mombaça. It is a very fair place, with lofty stone and mortar houses, well aligned in streets (after the fashion of Quiloa) . . . This is a place of great traffic, and has a good harbour, in which are always moored craft of many kinds and also great ships . . ." (Dames, 1918, 1921). Europe was first brought into direct contact with the eastern coasts of Africa by the long continued Portuguese programme of coastal exploration which culminated in the rounding of the Cape of Good Hope by Bartholomew Diaz in 1486 and in Vasco da Gama's celebrated voyage to India in 1497-99. The site and trade of Mombasa impressed da Gama, but he received a warmer welcome at Malindi; there the explorer erected a stone cross which still stands as a record of his visit and found a pilot to guide him to Calicut, utilising the south-west monsoon (Datoo, 1970a, 2-3).

The chief aim of the Portuguese seafarers was to gain control of the maritime trade of the Indian Ocean; in the western part of the Ocean they were mainly interested in the reports of gold, silver and other metals reaching the East African coast from the interior. Early in the sixteenth century Portugal became the principal naval power in the Indian Ocean, as a result of her possession of superior vessels, naval techniques and firearms; the strategic location of Goa, headquarters of Portuguese activities in India, enabled the newcomers to sever the sea routes linking the Arabian Sea with south-east Asia. Throughout the Indian Ocean the Portuguese attempted to obtain control of important trade centres and to curtail or prohibit trade in non-Portuguese ships.

The seaports of the western shore of the Indian Ocean were amongst the first to experience the impact of Portuguese competition. Kilwa came under their control in 1502, and other ports were swiftly subjugated, a process facilitated by their "inability . . . to compose their rivalries and jealousies even when faced by a greater and more dangerous enemy" (Ingham, 1962, 8). This accomplished, the chief effect of Portuguese rule in East Africa was negative, in that the prosperous and well-established trade system of the preceding centuries declined and partially disintegrated under their impact. Some relatively prosperous ports, such as Kilwa, fell partially into decay; elsewhere, where the new order was more submissively accepted (as at Malindi) life and commerce continued for a time much as before. No attempt was made to establish widespread administration, and inland settlements were few and precarious. The only positive Portuguese interest in the interior of eastern Africa was in the gold and other metals of the Zambezi region, which still reached the coast at Sofala; some gold may have reached Europe via Mozambique and the Cape, but most was used for the purchase of spices in India. The regular export of ivory from East Africa continued, however, and manufactured cloth from India was still a staple import commodity. Gradually the economic life of the coast became more and more bleak, increasingly fragmented and confined to local exchange rather than overseas trade, and commercial links with India and the East became once more very indirect (Gray, 1947a; Mathew, 1956). Mombasa often maintained an attitude of open revolt against Portuguese authority from the time of da Gama's first arrival in 1497 until the final withdrawal to the south at the beginning of the eighteenth century. In 1505 and again in 1528 Mombasa was sacked by the Portuguese; the ruins of the formidable Fort Jesus on Mombasa Island stand now as the only substantial physical monument to Portuguese rule north of Cape Delgado (Boxer and Azevedo, 1960; Kirkman, 1974).

Although the impact of Portuguese rule on the societies and economies of the East African coast was predominantly negative, the claim that "it had no lasting influence whatsoever on the country, and East Africa today would appear the same even if there had been no Portuguese period in her past" (Strandes, 1968, 320) cannot be justified. In cultural terms, Portuguese influence upon the Swahili language was not inconsiderable, and the design of local sailing craft was improved. In an economic context, the Portuguese introduced into East Africa a variety of new agricultural and horticultural commodities including maize, cassava, cashew nuts, avocados, guavas, and possibly tobacco and pineapples. In trading terms Alpers (1969) suggests that the deflection of the Sofala mineral trade away from Kilwa appears to have stimulated the development of a new pattern of trade between Kilwa and its more immediate hinterland, involving the movement to the coast of the Yao people of northern Mozambique who traded in iron, ivory, beeswax, rhinoceros horn and animal skins. Alpers describes "the linking up of two independently evolved regional trading networks. One centred on the hinterland of the Kilwa coast, and seems to have been catalyzed into existence by the new commercial orientation of Kilwa away from the ocean and towards the continent as a direct result of Portuguese economic policy in East Africa after 1505. The other arose in Yaoland as a result of the internal demands of the Yao economy for iron hoes . . . The integration of these two regional trading systems was brought about by the desire of the Yao to trade directly for foreign

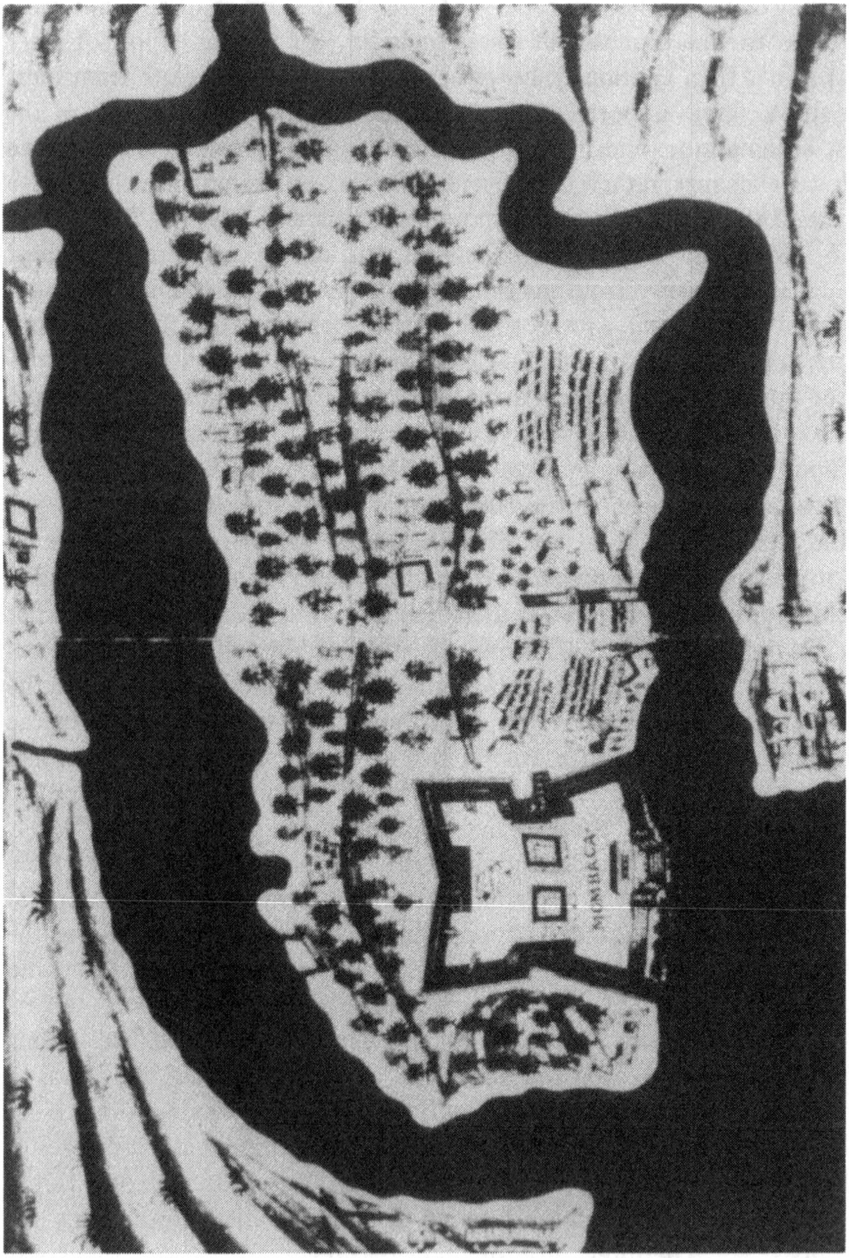

PLATE 3.2. A plan of Mombasa dated 1636, from Boccaro Rezende's *Livro da Estado da India*. (*Source*: reproduced from the original held in the British Museum, London, by kind permission of the trustees.)

goods . . . imported at Kilwa" (Alpers, 1969, 43-44).

The gradual decline of the ports of the East African coast in the sixteenth century was not entirely a result of the impact of the Portuguese, although the suppression of a good deal of trade (especially the gold trade originating in the Zambezi region) was clearly fundamental. A contributory cause of commercial decline was the continued southward migration of the Galla which in the seventeenth century caused the northern frontier of the Bantu speakers to be pushed back to the vicinity of Kilifi; together with the raiding activities of the coastal and some interior tribes (notably the Zimba who attacked Kilwa in 1587), this process hastened the abandonment of many mainland coastal settlements, including Gedi and, for a time, Malindi; trading interests were concentrated in the more easily defended island ports of Mombasa, Lamu and Pate. From these ports trading links with India and the Far East became again very indirect. During the seventeenth century the influence of the Portuguese was increasingly confined to the western side of the Indian Ocean, as Dutch, French and English traders appeared on the scene and as Arab trade revived. Omani Arabs captured Muscat in 1650, thereafter challenged Portuguese supremacy in the western Indian Ocean and brought about the fall of Fort Jesus in 1698, after a three year siege. The eighteenth century was thus a transitional period in which the Omani sultanate gradually attempted to establish control over the East African coastlands, trade with Arabia and India became more free, and in particular the exploitation of the East African interior for slaves and ivory was intensified.

The Omani Period and the Rise of Zanzibar

The complex historical processes of the nineteenth century in East Africa produced an important change in the geographical relationships of the seaboard with the interior and with the rest of the world. In the early years of the century the interior of East Africa was still a relatively undeveloped area, and the sea a source of raiders and unscrupulous merchants. By the end of the century East Africa lay open to the outside world, the broader aspects of her geography revealed, and the seaports of the coast linked with the sealanes of the world.

Three main trends may be discerned in the history of nineteenth century East Africa; all had important geographical implications. One was a marked expansion of indigenous African trading activity and a strengthening of trading connections between the northern *Mrima* coast and the interior. Lamphear has written that "the initiative for, and the exploitation of, the interior trade during the first half of the century lay not with the coastal Swahili, but with indigenous peoples of the interior. Mombasa . . . depended . . . upon the commercial systems of the Nyika and the Kamba peoples of its hinterland for the vast majority of its trade items throughout the earlier decades of the century . . . Direct Swahili caravan penetration . . . was not so much a spontaneous explosion of Swahili commercial activity as a more gradual response to the decline of the indigenous commercial systems . . . " (Lamphear, 1970, 75).

Similarly, Alpers has pointed to the importance of a major interior trade network in central Tanzania in the late eighteenth and early nineteenth centuries, linking the southern *Mrima* coast with the interior. This trade, which was largely controlled by the Nyamwezi, dealt chiefly in ivory, iron, salt and copper; there may have been additional outlets on the *Mwera* coast (Alpers, 1969, 51-52). Another trend was a strong recrudescence of Arab activity; gradually the Arabs of Oman filled the coastal trade gap left by the Portuguese withdrawal, and expanded East African overseas trade far beyond its previous level. In addition a further important development was the reappearance of Europeans in considerable numbers upon the East African scene; traders appeared at the coast during the earlier years of the century, and were followed by missionaries and explorers, many of whom were chiefly stimulated by the antislavery movement. Penetration of the interior of East Africa by explorers and missionaries led to a deeper commercial penetration and to the political 'scramble' and the establishment of European rule towards the end of the century.

Much of the history of the commercial exploitation and development of the East African coastlands in the nineteenth century turns on the character and activities of Seyyid Said, ruler of Oman from 1806 to 1856, who greatly augmented the power and wealth of Oman itself and, by gradually extending his dominion southwards, brought East Africa once more into close touch with the life and commerce of the world at large. In 1840, staking his future on a new Omani domain in East Africa, Said finally transferred his court and capital from Muscat to Zanzibar, bringing with him a considerable influx of Omani settlers and Asian financiers; at Zanzibar he developed a new port and town as the principal entrepôt and outlet for East African trade. With its valuable strategic and commercial situation and the best fresh water supply on the East African coast, Zanzibar was able to retain this position until it was undermined at the end of the century by the establishment of railway links between the mainland seaports and the interior. The advantages which the deep, sheltered harbour of Mombasa holds today over the less spacious and more open port of Zanzibar were not important in 1840. More significant was the occupation of the hinterland of Mombasa by tribes from whose territory ivory then reached the coast only in relatively small quantities. The commercial opportunities of Zanzibar were much better; situated further south, where on the mainland the fertile coastal belt is broader, Zanzibar lay opposite to the easiest routes of access to the interior. Zanzibar thus became the outstanding emporium of East African trade in the mid-nineteenth century; and, as Zanzibar flourished, so many of the older mainland seaports fell increasingly into decay. Mogadishu, Barawa, Pate, Malindi and

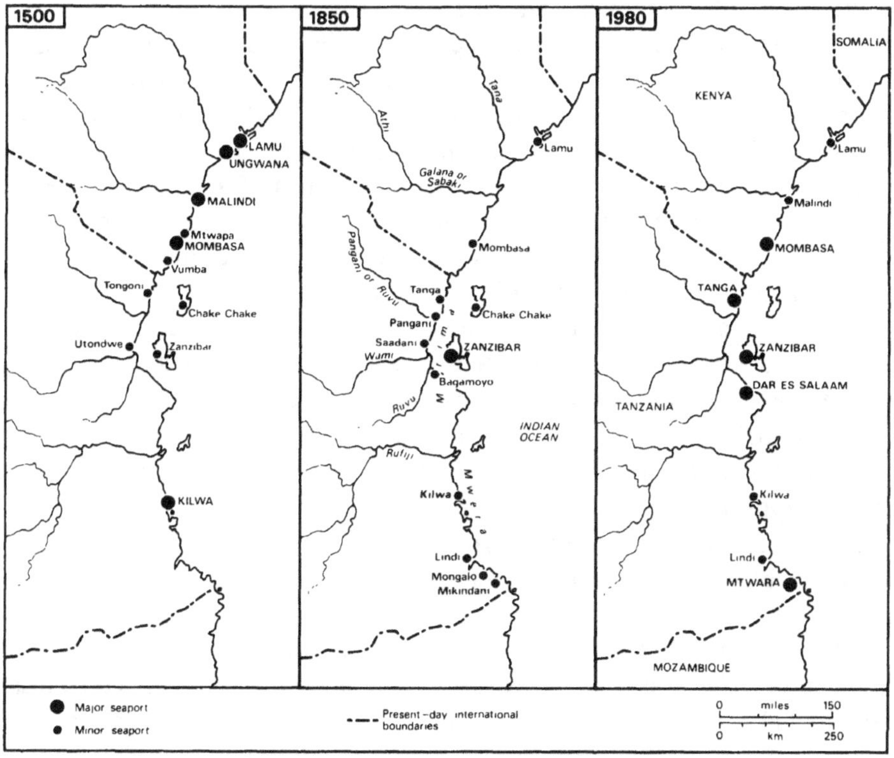

FIGURE 3.2. The seaports of East Africa in 1500, 1850 and 1980.

Kilwa Kisiwani were now of little significance; only Mombasa and Lamu remained fairly active. But as Omani commercial activity became increasingly concentrated upon Zanzibar, a range of new or revived settlements arose as mainland outports on the *Mrima* and *Mwera* coasts: these included Tanga, Pangani, Bagamoyo, Kilwa Kivinje, Lindi and Mikindani (Fig. 3.2b). "Each coastal settlement had its governor, customs officials, a few Baluchi soldiers, its Indian merchants counting their riches by the debts owed to them, and the Arabs, organising expeditions, setting off, or returning. Usually these people could build stone houses, often with plantations and provision grounds attached, whilst the African population lived in the traditional clusters of huts. Each settlement had its own hinterland and routes to the interior, and its own pattern of trade with Zanzibar and the rest of the world" (Gray, 1963, 224-5).

Seyyid Said concentrated his attention from the first on the regulation, simplification and extension of East African trade. The former extreme irregularities of port dues and customs tariffs were replaced by a five per cent import duty on all goods except bullion. The old range of products extracted from the interior of East Africa was not diversified in any degree, nor were new methods of commercial exploitation introduced. But the old methods were applied with new vigour, and the area tributary to Zanzibar was soon far greater than the hinterlands of all the seaports of East Africa had previously been. Trading caravans were larger, some new routes were opened, and new settlements founded; the new pattern of trade, which partly replaced and to some extent became integrated with African trading activities in the interior, "was extended and elaborated far beyond the more or less casual operations in which the Arabs of the coast had been engaged for ages past" (Coupland, 1938, 304-5).

The principal trade routes which Said's caravans used led from bagamoyo (Brown, 1970), the principal mainland outport of Zanzibar, to Tabora, approximately along the line of the present-day railway from Dar es Salaam to Lake Tanganyika; from Kilwa Kivinje south-westwards towards Lake Nyasa; and from the Tanga area via the Pangani valley towards Lake Victoria (Alpers, 1967 and 1969). Tabora, previously known as Kazeh (Burton, 1872, vol. 2, 325ff.), was the principal inland centre of Arab trade, the focus of a widely spread network leading westwards beyond Lake Tanganyika, and northwards via Karagwe to Buganda and Bunyoro (Gray, 1947b; Thomas, 1949). By this latter route Indian calico was received in Buganda in exchange for ivory, but neither Buganda nor

Bunyoro was ever an Arab hunting ground for slaves. The paths along which these trading caravans progressed often became impassable in the wet season, like many East African country roads today, and a start was therefore made from Zanzibar after the 'greater rains' of April and May; when a distant objective such as Tabora was reached, the slow moving caravan would rest there during the 'shorter rains' of October and November, and might be away from the coast for two or even three years. There is evidence that one caravan penetrated as far as Benguela on the west coast (Anon., 1854; Gray, 1961). Located at the seaward terminus of the principal trans-Tanzanian caravan route, Bagamoyo became important as a trading entrepôt; by mid-century a regional trade network concentrating upon dried fish, gum copal and salt was well established, and the trade in ivory and slaves which involved a more extensive hinterland probably developed as an extension and elaboration of this older, more local system (Brown, 1970, 74-5).

Attention was also directed to the economic development of the islands of Zanzibar and Pemba and to the expansion of markets for East African produce. Large areas of the best land in the islands was planted, on Said's orders, with clove seedlings obtained from French islands in the Indian Ocean. These plantations soon became the primary economic activity at Zanzibar, apart from the entrepôt trade, and initially required a large slave population to work them. By 1856, apart from slaves, the annual clove crop was second in value only to ivory amongst items of trade at Zanzibar; today, Pemba and Zanzibar still produce a very high proportion of the world's clove supply. The market for cloves was found to be lucrative; Said's own vessels sailed to Marseilles and London, laden with cloves, and the general market for East African goods was again extended to include India, south-east Asia and China.

Under the leadership of Seyyid Said mid-nineteenth century Zanzibar "witnessed the formation of an Arab-dominated colonial settler society . . . supported on the twin pillars to cloves and slave labour from the mainland, which endured with little essential modification right through the period of European colonial rule until the Revolution" (of 1964) (Alpers, 1969, 46). The overall effect of Said's commercial activities was to bring the entire East African coast from Mogadishu to the Rovuma river, together with the hinterland of the coast as far as it was then known and developed, within the range of a single political and economic system. Said's rule did not extend effectively beyond the coastal strip and islands, but his influence penetrated deep into the interior. Not surprisingly, the wide, deep contacts which Said developed in East Africa were quickly taken advantage of by other newcomers, and traders from other lands profited from the activities that Said stimulated. American traders set up business houses in Zanzibar in the 1820s as an offshoot of their whale fishing in the south Indian Ocean and their trade with China (Bennett, 1961); cotton cloth from Massachusetts was their main contribution to the commodity flow in East Africa, an item greater in quantity and superior in quality to Indian cottons, much desired for barter in the interior, and still known today by the Swahili term *amerikani.* German traders from Hamburg became established in Zanzibar in the 1840s, and the French engaged in the general trade of the coast, especially in oil-bearing grains, as an offshoot of their interests in Indian Ocean islands; British trade was very small until the later years of the century. Most of the trade passing through the port of Zanzibar in the nineteenth century was in Indian hands; Indian traders, especially Hindu Banyans from Kutch and Kathiawar, were strongly encouraged by Said both for their trading expertise and because they provided much of the capital necessary to finance caravan expeditions (Alpers, 1969, 46-48).

A useful illustration of the level and pattern of the trade of Zanzibar in the late 1850s is provided by General Rigby in his *Report on the Zanzibar Dominions* (Russell, 1935, 326-53). Comparing trade in the 1850s with that in the 1830s, Rigby commented that "the trade which has been created subsequent to the above period is certainly surprising, when it is considered that it has been developed under the primitive rule of an Arab chief; and it affords a proof of the great resources of Eastern Africa" (*ibid.*, 343). Table 3.1, based on information given by Rigby, shows the main items in the external trade of Zanzibar in 1859. At that time Zanzibar was the chief world source of ivory, cloves and gum copal, but no reliable figures are available to show the number or value of slaves sold at Zanzibar. Many of the imported goods, especially beads, wire and muskets, were used as barter for ivory in the interior. Gum copal was obtained from the mainland coast, cloves from Pemba and from Zanzibar itself, and sesamum chiefly from the Lamu district.

Several factors brought about a gradual decline in the trade of Zanzibar in the late 1850s; amongst these, a severe cholera epidemic in 1859 "carried off about twenty thousand persons in the Island of Zanzibar, and almost depopulated several towns on the opposite coast" (*ibid.*, 337); a

TABLE 3.1
EXTERNAL TRADE OF ZANZIBAR, 1859

Commodity	Volume	Value (£)
Exports		
Ivory	448,600 lb.	146,667
Cloves	4,860,100 lb.	55,666
Cowries	8,016,000 lb.	51,444
Gum copal	875,875 lb.	37,167
Sesamum	8,338,360 lb.	20,800
Total (incl. others)		755,666
Imports		
American cotton	6,950 bales	93,744
Indian cotton	204,500 pieces	53,778
English cotton	150,300 pieces	37,711
Rice	18,640,000 lb.	34,445
Venetian beads	868 barrels	21,880
Muskets	22,780	18,840
Muscat loongees and turbans	200 bales	11,889
Gunpowder	11,912 barrels	8,875
Ghee	175,000 lb.	7,778
Brass wire	2,000 barrels	7,556
Wheat and jowaree	3,831,000 lb.	7,022
Total (incl. others)		908,911
Total trade		1,664,577

(Source: Russell, 1935, pp. 343–344.)

concentration of French activity on the mainland to the south diverted local vessels that would otherwise have brought trade to Zanzibar; a rebellion against the Sultan and a threatened invasion from Muscat did nothing to increase traders' confidence. More significant than these, however, as a reason for the declining trade of Zanzibar, was the death of Seyyid Said in 1856; his successors did not take such a keen interest in the promotion of trading activity. Later, in 1872, a hurricane devastated Zanzibar island, destroying most of the clove and coconut plantations and wrecking the vessels in the harbour, thus depriving Zanzibar of the principal means of exerting authority over the mainland outports.

The growth of western commerce in East Africa, welcomed and encouraged by Said, was however parallelled by an increase in the activities of European explorers and missionaries. The gradual restriction and final abolition of the slave trade, due largely to British efforts on land and sea, effectively removed a traditional item of export from the East African coast. Britain declared the slave trade to be illegal for British subjects in 1807, and this prohibition was extended in 1811 to British Indian subjects. Slavery itself was not declared illegal in British colonies until 1833. The campaign against the Arab slave trade began in 1822 with the Moresby Treaty, and continued with a further treaty in 1845; both agreements attempted to limit the areas within which slaves might be transported without fear of interception by British warships. The slave trade was not, however, altogether stopped officially until 1873; in that year the old slave market at Zanzibar, the last to operate in East Africa or in any territory with which Britain was associated, was finally closed. Elton (1879, 42-44) provides a graphic description of the public slave market at Zanzibar a few weeks before its closure, and of the clearance of the market (pp. 57-58). On the site there now stands the Cathedral Church of Christ, built between 1873 and 1879 by the Universities Mission to Central Africa which was founded as a result of the work of the explorer Dr. David Livingstone. Slavery itself, however, continued to be legal in Zanzibar and the coastal ports even after the establishment of British rule, and many slaves were marched up the coast and slipped across the Gulf of Aden to Arabia even in the twentieth century.

The old Arab trade routes converging upon Zanzibar were used in the later nineteenth century by missionaries and explorers. The epic journeys of Krapf and Rebmann, the travels of Livingstone and Stanley, Burton and Speke, by which the dual aims of geographical discovery and Christian conversion were gradually effected, are well documented. Many of the travellers set out from Zanzibar, so that the port came to fulfill a new function as an important source of aid, advice and encouragement; their journals contain important, detailed accounts of the character and trade of the port (e.g. Burton, 1872). Bagomoyo became the seat of the first permanent European mission station on the East African mainland when the Holy Ghost Fathers from Zanzibar were granted land there in 1868 (Oliver, 1965, 20) and established an agricultural colony for liberated slaves. The town continued to prosper as a growing urban settlement and trading port: "the caravan trade was ever enriching Bagamoyo's economy by creating a demand for increased goods and services, which in turn resulted in an enlargement of the market, a proliferation of craftsmen, shopkeepers and labourers – and a population boom" (Brown, 1970, 75). The slave trade abolition treaties apparently did little, initially, to reduce the town's prosperity, but from the 1890s transport and trade were increasingly concentrated at Dar es Salaam.

To the pattern of interior trading posts were soon added many mission stations, and the main outlines of the geography of East Africa became known to the rest of the world within a relatively short space of time. But as European exploration succeeded, the Arab commercial domain foundered; the old relationship with Oman was broken, the authority of the Sultan of Zanzibar contracted to the offshore islands and the interior was partitioned between Britain and Germany. Arab domination of the East African coastlands, of its trade and ports, had lasted for at least a thousand years, interrupted only briefly by the Portuguese. Towards the end of the century, as European influence in the interior strengthened, and the beginnings of European colonial administration were established, Zanzibar began to find herself no longer in a competitive position. The focus of trade and port activity on the East African coast moved away from Zanzibar to the mainland, and the modern utilisation of the deep-water harbours began.

A study of the growth of port activity on the East African coast before the present century thus reveals a series of interacting processes on the mainland, on the offshore islands, and in the wider spaces of the Indian Ocean. A long succession of traders came to the shores of East Africa – Arabs, Shirazi, Portuguese, Omanis, Europeans, Americans; indigenous trading networks developed in interior East Africa, at first in relative isolation but later more expansively. The seaports of the East African coast, which initially were almost exclusively oriented towards the trade circulations of the Indian Ocean, gradually came to fulfill more effectively the classic seaport role – each an intermediary node linking land and sea transport networks. As the internal trading systems of interior East Africa were extended to include the coastlands, and as the variety and intensity of Indian Ocean trade increased, the coastal ports modified their commercial orientation and became, effectively for the first time, growth points in the maritime facade of a major continental area brought within the trading system of the world.

The East African interior and the Indian Ocean thus produced over time a series of contrasted hierarchies of ports along the coastal zone of conflict and interaction. In the absence of alternative evidence we can only assume an initial period of concentration upon the mysterious pre-Islamic port of Rhapta, and a diffusion of small-scale port activity along the coast in the early Islamic period. The fuller development of the Islamic coastal cultures in the fourteenth and fifteenth centuries included a concentration of port activity at a higher level at Lamu, Malindi, Mombasa and Kilwa, but the impact of the Portuguese engendered an era of relative decline and port diffusion in the succeeding centuries. The rise of Zanzibar as a major nineteenth century entrepôt under the Omani Arabs clearly represents renewed concentration, but as indicated earlier this was supported by the diffusion of a series of outports located at important mainland caravan terminals. The twentieth century has seen, first, a new beginning on several mainland port sites, representing a diffusion of port activity in a new technological era; and second, increasing concentration of activity at the principal modern East African seaport of Mombasa, which thus emerges after not less than eight centuries of continuous trading activity as a centre *par excellence* of *sustained port dominance.*

The processes and patterns of port development analysed in this chapter indicate in outline the experience over time of one selected area of the Third World. But these patterns and processes are also of interest in that they are, to a certain extent, representative of the experience of the Third World as a whole. Many parts of the former colonial world – West Africa, Malaysia, Brazil and tropical Australia are relevant cases – suggest a not dissimilar pattern in terms of historical experience and modern port systems. In most cases, the high cost of modern port infrastructures is a major factor encouraging *port concentration*; but we should not forget the importance of technology in more general terms, of changing forms of political organization and association, of new patterns of economic development and interaction, and perhaps above all the importance of the changing balance between the various scales – local, national, regional, global – at which port systems operate and on which modern world society is organised. It would be going too far to suggest that East Africa represents the Third World in microcosm – it has too many specific attributes for that to be true – but a study of the development of the area over time can provide a useful starting point for a comparative analysis of other areas and for a more detailed appreciation of the transport problems of the Third World as a whole.

REFERENCES

Alpers, E.A. (1967), *The East African slave trade* (Nairobi, East African Publishing House; Historical Association of Tanzania Paper No. 3).

Alpers, E.A. (1969), 'The coast and the development of the caravan trade', in I.N. Kimambo and A.J. Temu (eds.), *A history of Tanzania* (Nairobi, East African Publishing House, for the Historical Association of Tanzania), 35-56.

Anon. (1854), 'Notice of a caravan journey from the east to the west coast of Africa', *Journal of the Royal Geographical Society* 44, 266-271.

Ayany, S.G. (1970), *A history of Zanzibar: a study in constitutional development, 1934-64* (Nairobi, East African Literature Bureau).

Baxter, H.C. (1944), 'Pangani: the trade centre of ancient history', *Tanganyika Notes and Records* 17, 15-25.

Beachey, R.W. (1967), 'The East African ivory trade in the nineteenth century', *Journal of African History* 8, 269-290.

Bennett, N.R. (1961), 'Americans at Zanzibar, 1825-45, *Tanganyika Notes and Records* 56, 93-108; 57, 121-138.

Bird, J.H., (1971), *Seaports and seaport terminals* (London, Hutchinson).

Boxer, C.R. and C. de Azevedo (1960), *Fort Jesus and the Portuguese in Mombasa*, 1593-1729 (London, Hollis and Carter, for the Calouste Gulbenkian Foundation).

Brown, W.T. (1970), 'Bagamoyo: an historical introduction', *Tanzania Notes and Records* 71, 69-83.

Burton, Sir R.F. (1872), *Zanzibar: city, island and coast* (London, Tinsley Brothers, 2 vols.).

Chittick, N. (1963), 'Kilwa and the Arab settlements of the East African coast', *Journal of African History* 4, 179-190.

Chittick, N. (1965), 'The Shirazi colonization of East Africa', *Journal of African History* 6, 275-294.

Chittick, N. (1967), 'Discoveries in the Lamu Archipelago', *Azania* 2, 37-67.

Chittick, N. (1968), 'The coast before the arrival of the Portuguese', in B.A. Ogot and J.A. Kieran, *Zamani: a survey of East African history* (Nairobi, East African Publishing House).

Chittick, N. (1969) 'A new look at the history of Pate', *Journal of African History* 10, 375-391.

Coupland, R. (1938), *East Africa and its invaders* (London, Oxford University Press).

Dames, M.L. (ed.) (1918, 1921), *The book of Duarte Barbosa* (London, Hakluyt Society, 2 vols.).

Datoo, B.A. (1970a), 'Misconceptions about the use of monsoons by dhows in East African waters', *East African Geographical Review* 8, 1-10.

Datoo, B.A. (1970b), 'Rhapta: the location and importance of East Africa's first port', *Azania* 5, 65-75.

Datoo, B.A. (1971), 'East African ports', in S.H. Ominde (ed.), *Studies in East African geography and development* (London, Heinemann), 63-72.

Datoo, B.A. (1975), *Port development in East Africa: spatial patterns from the ninth to the sixteenth centuries* (Nairobi, East African Literature Bureau).

Datoo, B.A. and A.M.H. Sheriff (1971), 'Patterns of ports and trade routes in different periods', in L. Berry (ed.), *Tanzania in maps* (London, University of London Press), 102-105.

Duyvendak, J.J.L. (1949), *China's discovery of Africa* (London, Probsthain).

Elton, J.F. (1879), *Travels and researches among the lakes and mountains of eastern and central Africa* (London, John Murray; repr. Frank Cass, 1968).

Ferrand, G. (1913), *Relations de voyages et textes géographiques* (Paris, 2 vols.).

Flint, J.E. (1965), 'Zanzibar, 1890-1950', in V. Harlow and E.M. Chilver (eds.), *History of East Africa*, vol. 2 (Oxford, Clarendon Press), 641-671.

Freeman-Grenville, G.S.P. (1955), 'Ibn Battuta's visit to East Africa, A.D. 1332: a translation', *Uganda Journal* 19, 1-6.

Freeman-Grenville, G.S.P. (1962a), *The East African coast: select documents from the first to the earlier nineteenth century* (London, Oxford University Press).

Freeman-Grenville, G.S.P. (1962b), *The medieval history of the coast of Tanganyika* (London, Oxford University Press).

Freeman-Grenville, G.S.P. (1963), 'The coast, 1498-1840' in R. Oliver and G. Mathew (eds.), *History of East Africa*, vol. 1 (Oxford, Clarendon Press), 129-168.

Gray, Sir J.M. (1947a), 'Rezende's description of East Africa in 1634', *Tanganyika Notes and Records* 23, 2-28.

Gray, Sir J.M. (1947b), 'Ahmed bin Ibrahim, the first Arab to reach Buganda', *Uganda Journal* 11, 80-97.

Gray, Sir J.M. (1961), 'Commercial intercourse between Angola and Kilwa in the sixteenth century', *Tanganyika Notes and Records* 57, 173-174.

Gray, Sir J.M. (1963), 'Zanzibar and the coastal belt, 1840-1844', in R. Oliver and G. Mathew (eds.), *History of East Africa*, vol. 1 (Oxford, Clarendon Press), 212-251.

Hollingsworth, L.W. (1953), *Zanzibar under the Foreign Office, 1890-1913* (London, Macmillan).

Huntingford, G.W.B. (ed.) (1976), *The Periplus of the Erythraean Sea* (London, Hakluyt Society, 2nd series, vol. 151).

Ingham, K. (1962), *A history of East Africa* (London, Longmans).

Kirkman, J.S. (1954), *The Arab city of Gedi: excavations at the great mosque* (London, Oxford University Press).

Kirkman, J.S. (1956), 'The culture of the Kenya coast in the later Middle Ages', *South African Archaeological Bulletin* 11, 89-99.

Kirkman, J.S. (1960a), 'The tomb of the dated inscription at Gedi', Royal Anthropological Institute, *Occasional Paper No. 14*.

Kirkman, J.S. (1960b), *The Arab city of Gedi – the Palace* (The Hague).

Kirkman, J.S. (1964), *Men and monuments on the East African coast* (London, Lutterworth Press).

Kirkman, J.S. (1974), *Fort Jesus: a Portuguese fortress on the East African coast* (Oxford, Clarendon Press; British Institute in Eastern Africa, Memoir 4).

Lamphear, J. (1970), 'The Kamba and the northern Mrima coast', in R. Gray and D.

Birmingham (eds.), *Precolonial African trade: essays on trade in central and eastern Africa before 1900* (London, Oxford University Press), 75-101.

Lucas, Sir C. (1922), *The partition and colonization of Africa* (Oxford, Clarendon Press).

McMaster, D.N. (1962), 'Speculations on the coming of the banana to Uganda', *Journal of Tropical Geography* 16, 57-69.

McMaster, D.N. (1966), 'The ocean-going dhow trade to East Africa', *East African Geographical Review* 4, 13-24.

Martin, E.B. (1973), *The history of Malindi: a geographical analysis of an East African coastal town from the Portuguese period to the present* (Nairobi, East African Literature Bureau).

Martin, E.B. (1978), *Zanzibar: tradition and revolution* (London, Hamish Hamilton).

Martin, E.B. and C.P. (1978), *Cargoes of the East: the ports, trade and culture of the Arabian seas and western Indian Ocean* (London, Elm Tree Books/Hamish Hamilton).

Mathew, G. (1956), 'The culture of the East African coast in the seventeenth and eighteenth centuries', *Man* 56, 65-68.

Mathew, G. (1963), 'The East African coast until the coming of the Portuguese', in R. Oliver and G. Mathew (eds.), *History of East Africa*, vol. 1 (Oxford, Clarendon Press), 94-127.

Miller, J.I. (1969), *The spice trade of the Roman Empire* (Oxford, Clarendon Press).

Nicholls, C.S. (1971), *The Swahili coast: politics, diplomacy and trade on the East African littoral, 1798-1856* (London, Allen and Unwin).

Ogundana, B. (1970), 'Patterns and problems of seaport evolution in Nigeria', in B. S. Hoyle and D. Hilling (eds.), *Seaports and development in tropical Africa* (London, Macmillan), 167-182.

Oliver, R. (1965), *The missionary factor in East Africa* (London, Longmans, 2nd edn.).

Oliver, R. and J.D. Fage (1972), *A short history of Africa* (Harmondsworth, Penguin Books, 4th edn.).

Prins, A.H.J. (1967), *The Swahili-speaking peoples of the East African coast* (London, International African Institute, 2nd edn.).

Russell, Mrs. C.E.B. (ed.) (1935), *General Rigby, Zanzibar and the slave trade* (London, Allen and Unwin).

Sargent, A.J. (1938), *Seaports and hinterlands* (London, Black).

Sinclair, J.H. (1923), *Report on the Zanzibar Protectorate from 1911 to 1923* (Zanzibar, Government Printer).

Smith, A. (1963), 'The southern section of the interior, 1840-84,' in R. Oliver and G. Mathew (eds.), *History of East Africa,* vol. 1 (Oxford, Clarendon Press), 253-296.

Stevenson, E.L. (1932), *The Geography of Claudius Ptolemy* (New York).

Strandes, J. (1968), *The Portuguese period in East Africa,* trans. Jean F. Wallwork, ed. J.S. Kirkman, originally published as *Die Portugiesenzeit von Deutsch- und English- Ostafrika* (Berlin, 1899); Nairobi, East African Literature Bureau for the Kenya History Society, 2nd edn.).

Sutton, J.E.G. (1966), *The East African coast: an historical and archaeological review* (Nairobi, East African Publishing House; Historical Association of Tanzania Paper No. 1).

Thomas, H.B. (1949), 'Arabic correspondence captured in south-west Bunyoro in 1895; with a note on Arab traders in Bunyoro', *Uganda Journal* 13, 31-38.

Wheatley, P. (1964), 'The land of Zanj: exegetical notes on Chinese knowledge of East Africa prior to A.D. 1500', in R.W. Steel and R.M. Prothero (eds.), *Geographers and the Tropics* (London, Longmans), 139-187.

Zanzibar Protectorate (1920 *et seq.*), *Report on the Public Works Department for the year 1920 (et seq.)* (Zanzibar, Government Printer).

4 Modern Seaport Systems

An understanding of port operations and functions, and of their role in national and regional development, requires an appreciation of the patterns of physical port growth in modern times. The quayside represents a crucial interface between land and maritime transport systems, and as the technology of transport has evolved the degree of intermodal integration across this interface has been enhanced. The physical layout of a modern seaport reflects a process of technological change linking the most primitive with the most sophisticated methods of cargo handling, each technological stage being represented (in the past and/or today) by an appropriate range of physical facilities at the water's edge. The analysis of port growth, in this technology-dependent context, is a valuable aid to an understanding of the problems that confront port authorities and employees today; and whilst the analysis of a single seaport may be interesting in these terms, a more useful approach involves the study of a national or regional port complex on a comparative basis within the framework of a general model. Such a model is outlined in this chapter, and in order to demonstrate the relevance of the model to the process of port development in the Third World, the method of analysis is then applied to the East African seaport complex.

The 'Anyport' Model

The concept of a hypothetical *Anyport* was introduced by Bird in 1963, in the context of British seaports, as a pattern and standard against which to compare the actual development of individual members of the port complex (Bird, 1963, 23-34). Each historical stage in the development of *Anyport* involves a change in layout, and thus the way in which the present pattern of port facilities has evolved may clearly be seen. The application of the concept to a group of related ports provides a framework for an assessment of the comparative progress and patterns of development at the various individual components of the group. The development of *Anyport* begins "when the two-way exchange between land and water transport is regularly performed at a place, even if there are no port installations of any kind upon the shore" (*ibid.*, 26). Since land and water transport systems can never be precisely integrated, the provision of storage and handling facilities is necessary; their construction, and that of a jetty designed to steepen the gradient between land and water, marks the beginning of the first or *primitive* era in the development of *Anyport* (Table 4.1). Pressure on land space, and the increasing size and number of vessels, soon demand an expansion from the port nucleus which sometimes takes the form of a new beginning on a slightly different site.

TABLE 4.1
SUMMARY OF THE GENERAL THEME OF THE DEVELOPMENT OF A MAJOR BRITISH PORT

	Era	Terminated by
I	Primitive	Overflowing of the port function from the primitive nucleus of the port, or the change in location of the dominant port function
II	Marginal quay extension	Change from a simple continuous line of quays
III	Marginal quay elaboration	Opening of a dock or the expansion of the harbour
IV	Dock elaboration	Opening of a dock with simple lineal quayage
V	Simple lineal quayage	Provision of oil berths in deep water
VI	Specialised quayage	Occupation of all waterside sites between the port nucleus and the open sea

(*Source*: J.H. Bird, 1963, *The major seaports of the United Kingdom.* London: Hutchinson, p. 34.)

These events mark the beginning of the second era of development, that of *marginal quay extension*, which involves lineal extension of quays beyond the confines of the *primitive* nucleus. Distance from the nucleus, and physical obstacles, set a limit to this process and introduce the third era of *marginal quay elaboration*, which is characterized by the construction of jetties extended into the water and of quays developed with the help of land excavation, known respectively as water-encroaching and land-encroaching sites. Pressure on water space initiates the next era, that of *dock elaboration*, in which the first docks are built, equipped with locks, to enclose a number of ships and to minimize the effects of the tides on the activities of the port. Such docks, equipped with warehouses, often have quite elaborate outlines, since their designers wish to obtain the maximum length of quayage in relation to the available water area. The complex patterns of these docks, characteristic of nineteenth-century port development in Britain, have meant that in modern times, as the size of ships has rapidly increased, their usefulness has become limited, and the cost of making extensive alterations is prohibitive.

A new period of lineal development thus becomes necessary; this is termed the era of *simple lineal quayage*, and it has enabled *Anyport* to berth the largest ships efficiently and with flexibility. However, *specialised quayage* is required by many modern vessels such as oil tankers and bulk ore and grain carriers, and the development of facilities to meet these needs marks the beginning of the sixth era of *Anyport's* development. Oil tankers, in particular, require specialised treatment. Large tankers cannot easily negotiate many harbours; the unloading of oil is a simple and rapid process; and for security reasons it is preferable that oil installations should be sited away from other port facilities, often, in fact, in deep water. In the modern era *specialised quayage* is often carried a stage further: a series of berths serves public utilities, gas works and generating stations; and certain berths may specialize in handling certain types of cargo, a certain class of vessel, or ships of a particular company. In this process of specialisation elements of former eras are adapted to modern needs. As trade increases and ship design changes, and as one era of development moves into another, the facilities of earlier eras become adapted to serve later ones, often in a secondary capacity. This process of adaptation poses many problems, especially at large ports, but facilities representative of various eras of development may often be seen in present-day port layouts. The usefulness of the *Anyport* concept is thus not only that it draws attention to different eras of port development but also that, bearing the concept in mind, attention is more readily drawn to any unusual or unique features in the growth of an individual port.

An Application of the 'Anyport' Model to East African Seaports

A useful test of the validity of any model, particularly one derived from the experience of a limited range of case study evidence, is of course the degree to which it can be applied to alternative evidence from contrasted areas. In the context of port development on a global scale, it is perhaps especially interesting to test the applicability in the setting of less-developed countries of a model originally designed to analyse advanced-country conditions and experience. The transfer of economic or geographical theory, like the transfer of technology, from advanced to less-developed countries does not always prove to be very satisfactory, and it is unlikely that the *Anyport* model would be found useful in all parts of the Third World. In the case of East Africa, however, it is possible to outline the growth of a group of seaports within the framework of a modified version of the model, and this method provides some useful insights into the comparative patterns and levels of port development that have been achieved. In order to link this analysis with the discussion of changing port hierarchies in Chapter 3, it is important first of all to emphasise that the new orientation of the East African coastlands in the later nineteenth century was a result of several interrelated factors: the movement of African traders to the coast; the increased inland trading activities of the Arabs (from about 1825); the process of European exploration of the interior (from 1856); and the establishment of European administration (from 1885). Together these factors helped to create a situation in which it became impossible for Zanzibar to continue as East Africa's principal seaport and overseas trading centre. Modern port development in East Africa has therefore taken place primarily on mainland sites, the selection and initial establishment of which coincided in most cases with the period of political partition by colonial powers, which was also a period of rapid technological change in navigational terms. The growth patterns of the modern seaports of East Africa represent, in chronological summary, the economic development of East Africa as a whole; and their present-day patterns of activity indicate the extent to which modern economic development in the area has been successful.

There are several reasons why the Bird method of analysing the development of *Any (British) port* is not applicable in every detail to the seaports of East Africa. Many British seaports have been active since medieval times, but the major seaports of present-day East Africa are largely twentieth-century developments as far as material port facilities are concerned. The pattern of development of *Any (British) port* is closely related to the characteristic siting of major British seaports on tidal estuaries; physical influences upon port development in East Africa have been somewhat different – since all the major mainland seaports are sited on drowned estuaries, most have deep-water sites and the tidal range is relatively small. The creation of enclosed docks has not been necessary; the era of *dock elaboration*, a result of estuarine sites and of the peculiar tidal regime around the British coasts, is thus not represented in East Africa. Further, Britain is a small area of highly concentrated, advanced economic activity, whereas East Africa is a much larger area still in a relatively early stage of economic development. Britain is thus served by a large number of complex ports with overlapping hinterlands; the sixth era of *specialised quayage* has reached an advanced stage and traffic flow has reached a high level. In East Africa, on the other hand, a small number of ports with a relatively small traffic flow and with hinterlands that are to a large extent mutually exclusive, exhibits a much simpler pattern of development and activity.

TABLE 4.2
SUMMARY OF THE GENERAL THEME OF THE DEVELOPMENT OF A MAJOR EAST AFRICAN SEAPORT

	Era	Terminated by
I	Dhow traffic	Construction of the first port facilities on the modern harbour site
II	Primitive	Construction of the first lighterage quays
III	Marginal quay extension	Opening of the first deep-water berths
IV	Simple lineal quayage	Provision of oil berths in deep water
V	Specialised quayage	Development of a container terminal
VI	Containerisation	Occupation of all deep-water sites within the confines of the harbour

The six eras of port development that may be recognised at the major seaports of East Africa are summarised in Table 4.2 and represented cartographically in Figure 4.1. The *dhow traffic* era, extending from the earliest times to the end of the nineteenth century, involved the development of flexible hierarchies of ports at different periods; the construction

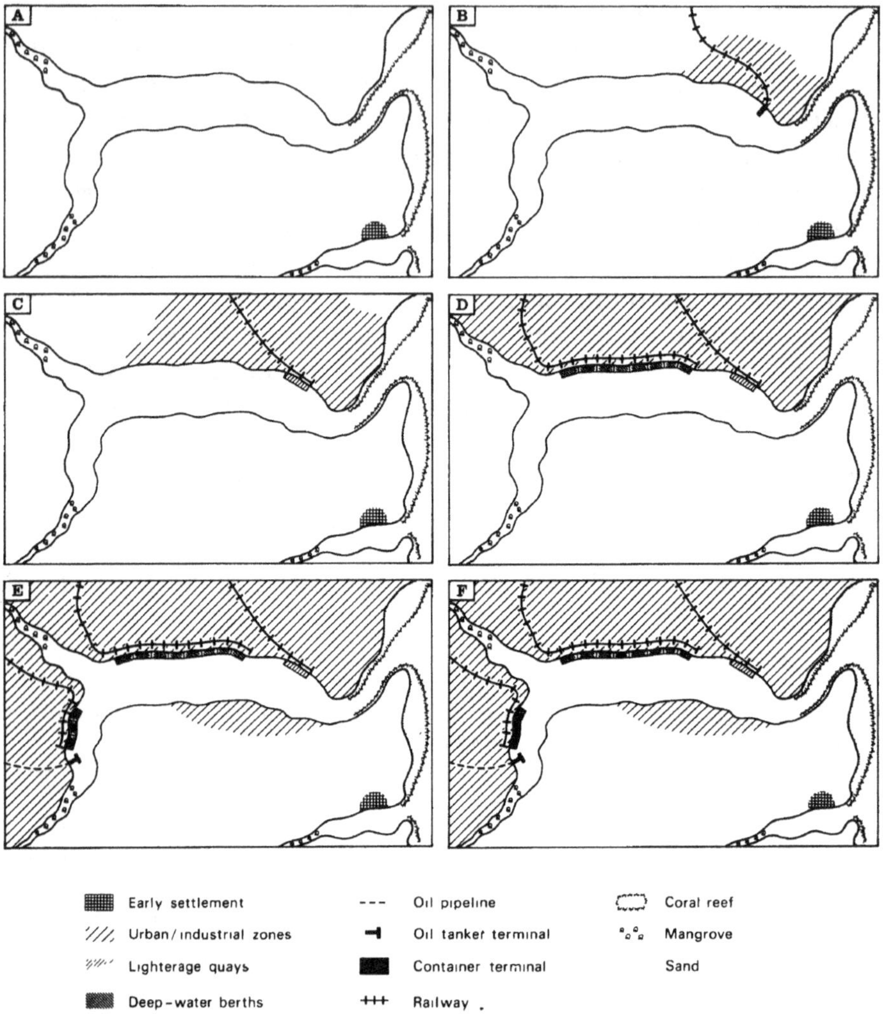

FIGURE 4.1. 'Anyport': the hypothetical development of a major East African seaport.

of substantial port facilities was not necessary and thus flexibility of port sites was an important keynote (McMaster, 1966). Towards the end of the nineteenth century, however, historical factors stimulated a crystallisation of the pattern of port development into a more permanent system which became the basis of the present-day hierarchy. Around the turn of the century, there was a geographical shift from a series of harbours or open roadsteads used by the dhows to the series of harbours constituting the present major East African seaports; this movement was made necessary chiefly by the increasing size and increasing manoeuvrability of ships and affords an illustration of the way in which the design of ships rather than the natural conditions of harbours is the pacemaker in sea transport developments. The *dhow traffic* era is concluded, and the *primitive* era introduced, by the construction of the first port facilities on the site of the nucleus of the modern port. In most cases this development is associated with the change from sail to steam propulsion and with the building of railways inland. The concentration of traffic at particular points by the simultaneous development of land transport and port facilities rapidly induced an increase in port traffic in the early colonial period. The *primitive* era is thus shortlived, superseded by the era of *marginal quay extension* the beginning of which is marked by the opening of the first properly constructed lighterage wharves, as opposed to the somewhat makeshift jetties of the *primitive* era.

The two eras which succeed that of *marginal quay extension* in the development of *Any (British) port*, the eras of *marginal quay elaboration* and *dock elaboration*, are not represented in the growth of *Any (East African) seaport.* The small size of the ports and their rate of growth in relation to their sites meant that *marginal quay extension* could continue without difficulty, no part of the port being too far away from the original nucleus or from the township area with which it was associated. Similarly the necessity for *dock elaboration* did not arise, since the tidal range in the deep-water harbours of East Africa is never sufficiently great to affect shipping movements seriously. Enclosed docks are thus unnecessary, and slipways are generally adequate for small-scale ship repairs. Plentiful shipping space, and deep water at all stages of the tide, enabled *Any (East African) seaport* to move on directly to the era of *simple lineal quayage*, introduced by the construction of the first deep-water berths in response to increasing ship size and increasing traffic.

Specialised quayage constitutes a fifth era of development at *Any (East African) seaport*, and has become increasingly important in recent years in response to global trends in maritime transport towards bulk handling of cargoes. Small-scale specialised equipment – for the export of soda ash from Magadi through Mombasa, for example – has been available for many years, but from the mid-1960s specialised export and import facilities have been introduced in connection with an increasing range of commodities. During this period the introduction of facilities for the reception of crude oil in association with the construction of oil refineries has been an important feature. Global trends towards cargo unitisation have not left the seaports of the less-developed countries unaffected, and in recent years *Any (East African) seaport* has progressed towards a sixth era of port development based on *containerisation*; this has involved the redevelopment of some quayside and storage areas and the substantial modification of port operation procedures.

TABLE 4.3
COMPARISON OF DATES OF TERMINATION OF PORT DEVELOPMENT ERAS AT MAJOR EAST AFRICAN SEAPORTS

Era	Mombasa	Dar es Salaam	Tanga	Mtwara
Dhow traffic	1896	1900	1892	1920
Primitive	1907	1907	1914	1954
Marginal quay extension	1926	1956	1972	–
Simple lineal quayage	1963	1966	–	–
Specialised quayage	1975	1975	–	–

In this way the technologically limited *dhow traffic* era has been succeeded by a variety of eras which, seen in an historical context, have followed one another with considerable rapidity (Table 4.3). The *primitive* era was essentially a brief transition, a mere beginning on the modern port site, leading to the two most significant periods in which lighterage quays and deep-water quays were respectively developed. For the sake of easy comparison with Bird's analysis of the eras of development of *Any (British) port*, the terms *marginal quay extension* and *simple lineal quayage* have been retained, but the distinction between the two forms of lineal development is simply that of the presence or absence of deep-water facilities, which in East Africa is a reflection of physical site conditions as well as of traffic levels. The most complete pattern of development of *Any (East African) seaport* is seen in the cases of the larger seaports of Mombasa and Dar es Salaam, at which all the (East African) eras are represented; elsewhere certain eras have either been omitted or have not yet been reached. The termination of an era by the inauguration of its successor does not mean that the earlier era came to a sudden end or that the constructions belonging to that era ceased to be of service. *Any (East*

African) seaport is still a dhow port, although vestiges of this period may soon vanish altogether; and although few elements representative of the brief *primitive* era now remain, the facilities constructed during the eras of *marginal quay extension* and *simple lineal quayage* constitute the basis of the present range of equipment. Further development of *simple lineal quayage* is in fact continuing during the most recent eras of *specialised quayage* and *containerisation.*

The Modern Development of Tanga

Tanga was the first of the modern seaports of the East African mainland to be developed, but its disadvantageous situation and site conditions have seriously hindered its progress. Situated between Mombasa and Dar es Salaam, both of which have better water sites, superior port facilities and more extensive direct rail connections inland, Tanga has been effectively prevented from developing as a major seaport serving a wide area of the East African hinterland. Tanga remains predominantly a port of small, almost local importance, deriving the bulk of its traffic from the sisal and coffee growing areas of north-east Tanzania.

Little information is available on the earliest stages of Tanga's development. The harbour was used by dhow traffic, but the once-flourishing port of Pangani, located a few miles south of Tanga Bay, perhaps has the strongest claim to represent the *dhow traffic* era in the Tanga area (Baxter, 1944); and Rhapta, East Africa's first seaport, was probably located on the northern stretch of the Tanzanian coast, possibly near the mouth of the Pangani river (Datoo, 1970). The modern development of Tanga (Table 4.4) dates from the early years of German colonial rule. In 1891 the German East Africa Company undertook to construct and operate ports and railways in German East Africa, through its subsidiary company *Eisenbahn Gesellschaft für Deutsch Ostafrika*, and the construction of port facilities at Tanga was to be its first undertaking. It was originally intended that three lines should be built: Tanga was selected as the seaward terminus of a line heading north-westward in the direction of Kilimanjaro and known as the Usambara line; a second line was planned to connect Dar es Salaam with Kigoma, on Lake Tanganyika; and a third was proposed, but never built, from Kilwa south-westward towards Lake Nyasa (Gillman, 1942). Preparatory work for the Usambara line was started in

TABLE 4.4
DEVELOPMENT OF THE PORT OF TANGA

	Era	Terminated by	Present-day symbols
I	Dhow traffic	Construction of a primitive jetty to unload railway materials, 1892	
II	Primitive: jetty for the unloading of railway materials	Construction of a lighterage quay, 1914	Lighterage quay
III	Marginal quay extension: lighterage quay, 1914; extended 1954	Construction of fertilizer (multipurpose) jetty, 1972	Lighterage quay
IV	Specialised quayage: fertilizer jetty 1972		Fertilizer jetty

1891, and actual construction in 1893. The building of a small jetty in 1892, designed to receive imported railway materials, marks the beginning of the *primitive* era of Tanga's port development (Hill, 1957). Unfortunately, owing to bad workmanship, part of the jetty collapsed in 1896. Attention was focused upon Tanga and the Usambara line at this early period, rather than upon Dar es Salaam and the central line, for two main reasons: it was thought that the Usambara line would be easier to build (although in fact it was very badly constructed and did not reach Moshi until 1911); and the German East Africa Company had already acquired vast tracts of land in the Usambara Mountains and several coffee and rubber plantations had been started. The railway proved, as was expected, an effective stimulus to the further development of plantation agriculture in this area. It was also in 1893 that sisal was introduced into the Tanga area from Florida, an event which laid the foundation stone of a major element in Tanzania's modern agricultural industry and contributed substantially for many years towards the export traffic channelled through the port of Tanga (Hitchcock, 1959).

Tanga did not move into the era of *marginal quay extension* until 1914, some years later than either Mombasa or Dar es Salaam. Funds for improvements were not available until 1909 when the German Government voted 1,500,000 DM for the construction of a lighterage quay, together with sheds and ancillary equipment. Completed in 1914, the project was "an ignominious failure . . . In 1913 the shore at Tanga was littered with thousands of tons of reinforced concrete piles cast at Mannheim on the Rhine. They had been carried by river barges to Rotterdam and thence shipped to Tanga. The available records provide no answer to the question why these concrete works were not cast at Tanga. Soon after completion, part of the quay wall collapsed, another example of bad design, bad work and lack of common sense" (Hill, 1957, 75).

No further major extensions took place at Tanga for 40 years. Any further German developments were prevented by the First World War, after which, in the context of an East Africa unified under British administration, it seemed more reasonable to concentrate development on the larger ports of Mombasa and Dar es Salaam. From time to time, considerable sums were spent in major repairs to the single lighterage wharf, but no strong pressures for an extension of the available facilities came until 1944 when the then Chief Engineer, Tanganyika Railways, recommended the postwar construction of two deep-water berths at Dar es Salaam and one at Tanga (Farquharson, 1945). This recommendation in respect of Tanga has never been implemented, since traffic levels do not yet appear to warrant the heavy expenditure that would be involved. Certain major improvements were completed in 1954, however, at a total cost of £1 million, and at a time when congestion at Mombasa was particularly severe. The original 1914 lighterage quay was extended 235 m towards the north-east, and large new warehouses were built, together with a modern passenger terminal, port offices, a small dockyard and a marshalling yard. Certain improvements were effected at the same time at the old wharf, and modern cargo handling equipment was installed.

Increased pressure on port facilities at Dar es Salaam and Mombasa, particularly in the context of growing Zambian traffic through East African ports, has raised again in recent years the question of possible port expansion at Tanga. The development of a line of deep-water berths at the port would seem to present no serious physical obstacles, but the costs involved would require careful justification in the context of traffic forecasts. Tanga has thus not yet moved on into the era of *simple lineal quayage*, but a multipurpose jetty (opened in 1972) designed primarily to serve a large fertilizer plant may be regarded as *specialised quayage*; and although the number of containers handled at Tanga is increasing, the port cannot yet be described as having entered the *containerisation* era.

PLATE 4.1. Mombasa: An aerial view from the northeast, showing in the foreground the old harbour during the dhow season. Kilindini Harbour lies in the distance, beyond the island on which the town is sited. (*Source:* Kenya Railways Corporation, Nairobi.)

The Modern Growth of Mombasa

Mombasa is distinguished amongst the seaports of East Africa by its possession of two harbours, one suited to medieval conditions of navigation and trade and the other to more modern circumstances. Old Mombasa harbour has been used for centuries as a dhow port, but the deep-water facilities of Kilindini harbour have not been extensively utilized until the present century. The point of departure for the modern development of the seaport was the purchase in 1895 by Mr. (later Sir) George Whitehouse of 372 acres of land near Kilindini harbour as a base from which to direct the building of the Uganda railway from Mombasa to Victoria Nyanza, in connection with which one of the most immediate problems was the provision of some kind of port facilities for the unloading of the steamers bringing railway materials from overseas. Cargoes from the earliest steamers to use Kilindini Harbour were landed on the beach; "the lighters

PLATE 4.2. Kilindini beach in 1895: unloading materials for the Uganda railway. (*Source:* Kenya Railways Corporation, Nairobi.)

PLATE 4.3. Kilindini pier and beach office, 1900. (*Source*: Kenya Railways Corporation, Nairobi.)

were brought as near high water mark as they would float, then they were allowed to ground and they were off-loaded between half-flood and half-ebb tides" (Hill, 1949, 148). In 1896 a jetty was built on the Mbaraki side of Ras Kilindini, an event which marks the transition of the port of Mombasa from the era of *dhow traffic* to the *primitive* era (*ibid.*, 145-146). Contemporary evidence indicates the simultaneous beginnings of quayage, lighterage, mechanization and rail services: the jetty, partly embanked and partly of timber piling, "was built so that fully loaded lighters could lie alongside at any tide and be off-loaded by steam cranes direct into wagons" (*ibid.*, 148). In 1898-99 an experienced engineer, Sir Guildford Molesworth, visited East Africa and reported on the progress of the railway and harbour developments. With regard to Kilindini, the development of which he strongly recommended in preference to the Old Harbour of Mombasa, he commented that "the port possesses great facilities for development as well as sites for warehouses and wharves of almost indefinite extension" (Molesworth, 1899). Molesworth's views were strongly endorsed by another inspector, Colonel T. Gracey, who wrote in 1901 that "the most urgent necessity at Kilindini is a deep-water berth, along which large vessels can lie connected by rail with railway warehouses . . . The first thing necessary is the preparation of a comprehensive plan showing what will be the ultimate aim and object to be attained when traffic largely develops . . ." (Gracey, 1901).

The *primitive* era came to an end with the construction of a lighterage wharf in 1907 (Table 4.5). The earlier wooden structures rotted away and traffic continued to increase. The new wharf, 168 m long and built in concrete, represents the inauguration of the era of *marginal quay extension* at Mombasa. It was hoped that additional quays would be built to relieve the increasing congestion, but in fact almost all traffic was handled at this wharf until the first of the deep-water berths was opened almost 20 years later; apart from some temporary wartime constructions, the only exception to this was a concrete pile wharf built in 1913 on the present site of berths 9 and 10 to handle exports of soda ash from Magadi – a minor early example of *specialised quayage*. Immediately prior to the First World War, considerable pressure upon port facilities developed at Mombasa, and efficient working was further handicapped by the very irregular arrival of steamers. Complaints arising from delay and damage were frequent, and in 1914 the British Government made available £700,000 for the building of much needed deep-water berths. The project was,

TABLE 4.5
DEVELOPMENT OF THE PORT OF MOMBASA

	Era	Terminated by	Present-day symbols
I	Dhow traffic: largely confined to Mombasa harbour	Construction of first port facilities at Kilindini: Mbaraki jetty, 1896	Continuing (though slight) dhow traffic in Mombasa harbour; landing place
II	Primitive: Mbaraki jetty	Construction of first lighterage quay, 1907	Slipways south of Ras Kilindini
III	Marginal quay extension: lighterage quays	Opening of first deep-water berths, 1926	Lighterage quays south of Ras Kilindini
IV	Simple lineal quayage: deep-water berths	Opening of Kipevu oil terminal, 1963	Deep-water berths Nos. 1–5, 7–14, 16–18
V	Specialised quayage: oil terminal and other facilities for handling bulk cargoes	Opening of Kipevu container terminal, 1975	Kipevu oil terminal (jetty and facilities); other bulk cargo handling facilities
VI	Containerisation		Kipevu container terminal

however, abandoned on the outbreak of war in August of that year. During the war, Kilindini harbour was taken over by the navy and closed to public traffic; most of the imports and exports to and from Uganda and the East Africa Protectorate (Kenya) had therefore to pass through the old harbour at Mombasa which was entirely inadequate for the purpose, even though lack of shipping space severely curtailed trade.

Mombasa's entry into the era of *simple lineal quayage* was thus postponed by the war and its aftermath until 1926. The need for deep-water berths had increased as the railway system was extended and as European settlement and export crop production increased. Investigations at a site immediately north of Ras Kilindini, first begun in 1912, were resumed in 1920. Deeper water offshore, and a less strong tidal current, made this part of the coast of Mombasa Island more suitable for port development than the Mbaraki area. In 1926, berths 1 and 2 were completed, and at the same time a comprehensive plan was drawn up for the extension of deep-water quayage north-westward along the shore of the island; a contract was placed immediately for the building of berths 3 and 4, which were completed in 1929. A fifth deep-water berth was opened in 1931, at about the same time as a new lighterage wharf and the bulk oil jetty at Shimanzi.

No further major developments took place before the Second World War. A significant test of the capacity of the harbour came in the early months of 1940, when as a result of the closure of the Red Sea all north-bound British shipping in the Indian Ocean was sent to Kilindini to await orders. The pilot service at Kilindini had to be expanded quickly, and a rapid survey was made of Port Reitz as a useful extra space for anchorage. Later, Mombasa became important as a naval base, and to improve the turnround facilities two new deep-water berths (numbered 7 and 8, with a total length of 371 m) were built in 1942-44. At one time during the war a total of 217 ships of all kinds were berthed or anchored in Kilindini

PLATE 4.4. Port installations at Mombasa: deep-water berths 1-5 and 7-10 (extreme left) are backed by transit sheds and storage areas. Lighterage quays are visible (bottom right). (*Source:* Kenya Railways Corporation, Nairobi.)

PLATE 4.5. Port installations at Mombasa: deep-water berths 1–5, with transit sheds and storage areas. In this photograph all berths are occupied and several vessels lie at anchor in the harbour, awaiting a vacant berth. (*Source:* Kenya Railways Corporation, Nairobi.)

Harbour. The site of berth 6 was not developed, for reasons connected with the instability of the site which includes a natural drainage channel.

During the immediate postwar period, increases in traffic handled made necessary further development of port facilities, but unfortunately adequate finance was not available and congestion in the port was the inevitable result. However, work on two further deep-water berths (9 and 10) was begun in 1953; two years later berth 9 was completed, and in 1954 a new lighterage wharf with eight stub jetties was opened south of Ras Kilindini. Berth 10 was not completed, however, until 1958, owing to an unfortunate setback in 1954 when the greater part of the construction work collapsed into the harbour as a result of subsidence, apparently related to submarine geological conditions.

The opening of berth 10 in 1958 completed the possible programme of port works on Mombasa Island since no suitable sites for the further development of deep-water quays remained unutilized. Attention was therefore directed to the nearby mainland at Kipevu, where further development of *simple lineal quayage* has continued. Here, on a site running in an east-west direction, connected to Mombasa Island by a road/rail causeway built in 1957, the Kipevu Project initially involved the construction of four additional deep-water berths. Two of the berths (11 and 12) were fully equipped and brought into service in 1961; the second pair (13 and 14) were not immediately utilized but were brought into service in 1967 in response to increasing traffic pressure. The line of deep-water berths at Kipevu has subsequently been extended westwards along the northern shore of Port Reitz: there is no berth 15 owing to unsuitable site conditions, but three additional berths (16-18) were constructed in the mid-1970s with the aid of substantial World Bank loans.

A further development of great importance has been the building of an oil jetty at Kipevu to receive large tankers bringing crude oil supplies to a refinery established at Changamwe. This event marks Mombasa's entry into the fifth era of *specialised quayage*. An earlier site for a refinery at Likoni was abandoned in favour of the Changamwe site because the latter is near the main Mombasa-Nairobi road and railway routes, in a developing industrial zone, and within 3.5 km of the tanker jetty site at Kipevu, to the west of the new deep-water berths. The £15 million project involved, in addition to the building of the refinery itself, the construction of a tank farm on the foreshore at Port Reitz, adjacent to the oil jetty, and the dredging and deepening of the approach channel to Mombasa harbour to allow the entrance of large oil tankers. These operations were completed in 1961-63. Subsequently, the entrance channel to the harbour has been modified to facilitate the entry of larger vessels.

An interesting trend at Mombasa in recent years has been the increasing provision for the bulk handling of a variety of commodities other than oil. Facilities are now available for the bulk export of bagged cement and Magadi soda, and for the bulk import of maize. These developments represent an important aspect of the increasing range of *specialised quayage* now available in the port. Mombasa has also responded very positively to another important trend in global maritime transport and has entered the *containerisation* era with the establishment of a well-equipped container terminal at berths 17 and 18.

The Origin and Growth of Dar es Salaam

In contrast to Mombasa, the harbour of Dar es Salaam has no history of commercial activity before the third quarter of the nineteenth century. Arab and Portuguese navigators and writers largely ignored the coast between Kilwa and Bagamoyo. The hostility of local inhabitants may have deterred an early Arab settlement, and the harbour is well hidden from the open sea and may have remained for long unknown; among others, Captain Owen failed to realize the existence of the harbour at Dar es Salaam during his hydrographic survey of the coast in 1824-26 (Owen, 1833), and in 1850 the explorer Krapf put in at Msasani but ignored the

TABLE 4.6
DEVELOPMENT OF THE PORT OF DAR ES SALAAM

	Era	Terminated by	Present-day symbols
I	Dhow traffic: the open roadstead port of Bagamoyo; Seyyid Majid's attempts to develop Dar es Salaam	Construction of first port facilities at Dar es Salaam, 1900	Beach at Bagamoyo; no present port activity
II	Primitive: masonry stairways and shoots, 1900; railway contractors' jetty, 1905	Opening of first lighterage quay, 1907	Town Quay; masonry shoots
III	Marginal quay extension; lighterage quay, 1907; extended 1929, 1933	Opening of deep-water berths, 1956	Town quay
IV	Simple lineal quayage: Main Quay (deep-water berths)	The provision of modern facilities for the reception of crude oil, 1966	Main quay; additional deep-water berths
V	Specialised quayage: Kigamboni jetty and Mjimwema SBM for the reception of crude oil	The provision of container handling facilities, 1975	Kigamboni jetty, Mjimwema SBM and associated oil refinery
VI	Containerisation		Container terminal

large harbour nearby (Krapf, 1860). The scene of the *dhow traffic* era in the growth of port activity in the Dar es Salaam area (Table 4.6) lies a few miles to the north at Bagamoyo; and the development of a new port at Dar es Salaam and the simultaneous decline of Bagamoyo provide an interesting example of the interaction of geographical circumstances and historical events. Standing at the seaward terminus of the long overland caravan route to Lake Tanganyika, a route traversed by countless slaves and unknown quantities of ivory and other goods, the port of Bagamoyo flourished in the mid-nineteenth century because of its proximity to the principal emporium at Zanzibar, which it served as a kind of mainland outport. Moreover, in the days of sailing ships and small, easily handled cargoes, the relatively flat sandy shore was quite adequate and no port facilities were necessary; whereas Dar es Salaam with its almost enclosed harbour, awkward entrance and strong winds, tides and currents was far less suitable. As ships and cargoes increased in size, and as more accurately controllable steamships were introduced, the advantages of shelter and deep water at Dar es Salaam became increasingly clear, and Bagamoyo declined into insignificance (Brown, 1970).

The foundation of a new port and town within the harbour of Dar es Salaam, near the site of a small village called Mzizima, was the work of Seyyid Majid, who succeeded his father Seyyid Said as Sultan of Zanzibar in 1856. Majid realized the advantages of a large and sheltered harbour, and decided to create there a new seaport, a new centre of trade, and an alternative, somewhat cooler residence to Zanzibar. His precise motive, like the motive of his father in moving to Zanzibar, is obscure, but seems to have been not so much the extension of Seyyid Said's trading network as a desire to escape from the political insecurity and intrigues of Zanzibar. Controversy surrounds the origin of the name 'Dar es Salaam'; derivation from the Arabic phrase *Bandar-ul-Salaam* (harbour of peace) is commonly accepted (Hartnoll, 1937) although this may be challenged on both linguistic and historical grounds (Allen, 1945; Sutton, 1970). There is evidence that Seyyid Majid formally opened Dar es Salaam as a seaport in 1867 (Gray, 1962a); the acting British consul at Zanzibar, Dr. Seward, did not rate the chances of success of the new venture very highly, writing that "the conception is good but the want of labour promises to be fatal to its realization; no considerable body of slaves could be kept together there . . . The settlements of Lamoo and Mombassa are flanked by tribes more dangerous to the fugitive slave than the Arab, but the country behind Dhar Salaam has no such flight-restraining terror" (Seward, 1866). Sutton (1970) suggests that Majid's scheme may have been partly a move to counteract British influence (and the antislavery campaign) that received encouragement from French diplomats and missionaries.

In 1870, however, Seyyid Majid died and was succeeded by Seyyid Barghash, who did not share his brother's enthusiasm for the development of Dar es Salaam. A hurricane in April 1872 caused much damage, and the buildings of the new town, many incomplete, were left to decay. Joseph Thomson, first of the early explorers to begin his expedition from Dar es Salaam, visited the town in 1879 and described its desolation: "the tenantless houses give shelter only to bats, owls, lizards and snakes, and the whole place wears the aspect of an old, battered and deserted city, instead of a new one just springing to life . . . But certainly, from the advantages which Dar es Salaam possesses over most places on the coast, there can be no doubt that it will, sooner or later, become all that its founder wished it to be" (Thomson, 1881, vol. 1, 73-75).

A new phase in the development of the port was marked by the establishment of a small trading station and of a mission settlement in 1887 at the beginning of the period of German activity. Dar es Salaam became the main military depot of German East Africa, while Bagamoyo was retained for a time as the seat of government. In 1891, however, the government was transferred to Dar es Salaam, several commercial enterprises moved over from Zanzibar, and a customs department was created. Yet in 1898-99 the export customs revenue at Dar es Salaam was only one third of that at Bagamoyo (Gillman, 1945, 7). A few port facilities were established at this time: the buoying of the intricate harbour entrance was begun in 1891, and a lighthouse was built on an outer coral reef in 1892-94; Bornhardt records that in 1900 "a series of masonry stairways and shoots, up and down which all cargo was manhandled into lighters, led from the natural narrow beach up the steep slope of the lowest coastal terrace to sheds and warehouses perched along the latter's upper edge" (Bornhardt, 1900, 198). Some of these masonry shoots are still visible today. A floating dock came into service in 1902, and a small dockyard was built near the entrance to Southern Creek; the small fleet of coastal vessels continued to grow, and repair facilities were provided for naval vessels.

Thus the period of Seyyid Majid's unsuccessful attempts to develop Dar es Salaam and the earliest years of the German period lead gradually into

PLATE 4.6. Dar es Salaam about 1906. Ascribed to Dr Bruckner, this photograph predates the lighterage quay, but shows the masonry stairways and shoots, the railway jetty and various German administrative buildings along the waterfront. (*Source:* National Museum of Tanzania.)

the *primitive* era in the evolution of the port. The year 1900, when evidence first becomes available of some simple aids to the unloading and loading of cargo, may be taken to mark the beginning of this era. A major stimulus to the development of the port came, as at Mombasa and Tanga, with the construction of a railway to the interior, a project essential for the consolidation and extension of German political control and for the continued growth of Dar es Salaam at the expense of Bagamoyo, served only by slow-moving caravans. Surveys for a railway to Lake Tanganyika began in 1894 and construction commenced in 1905; closely following the route of the old slave caravans, except at its seaward end, the railway reached Tabora in 1912 and Kigoma in 1914. To facilitate the unloading of railway materials, a small jetty was built at Dar es Salaam in 1905, and in the same year work was begun on a large customs shed and upon a more substantial quay equipped with cranes and joined to the town by road and rail. These developments form the basis of the present-day Town Quay. As early as 1906 the desirability of deep-water berths was pointed out (Paasche, 1906, 190-194), but it was not until 50 years later that this objective was achieved.

The entry of Dar es Salaam into the era of *marginal quay extension* was marked by the opening of the first lighterage wharf in 1907. No further significant changes occurred until the end of the First World War when, after the defeat of Germany, Tanganyika emerged as a League of Nations mandated territory under British administration. In 1921, under the terms of the Milner-Ortz Convention, sites at Dar es Salaam and Kigoma were leased to the Belgian Government, in return for an annual rent of 1 franc, to facilitate the handling of traffic to and from the eastern Belgian Congo; the Dar es Salaam site was originally the northernmost of the two lighterage berths on the Town Quay. These berths were lengthened in 1929 and again in 1933, marking a continuation of the era of *marginal quay extension*. The interwar period was also marked by a considerable improvement in the entrance to the harbour, achieved by dredging after a careful survey. Traffic growth in the 1920s included increased mineral exports from the then Belgian Congo and warranted the addition of a large new transit shed and marshalling yard to the terminal facilities. The depression of the 1930s meant, however, that for a time little use was made of these facilities and, as Gillman emphasized, "reminded optimistic enthusiasts that the reviving port's vast hinterland was not a land of unlimited dormant wealth . . . but at best a somewhat precarious borderland . . . a realm where prudent

PLATE 4.7. Dar es Salaam: the lighterage wharf in 1949, before the development of deep-water quays. (*Source:* National Museum of Tanzania.)

stocktaking of resources rather than adventurous boasting . . . was the only correct way of approach" (Gillman, 1945, 16).

The post-1946 period has shown very considerable advances in tonnages handled at Dar es Salaam, and in terms of port facilities the principal reflection of this growth has been the provision of deep-water berths. The decision to proceed with the construction of two deep-water berths was taken in 1949, and the Belgian Government, conscious of the need to develop its own share of the facilities of the port, decided to finance the construction of a third deep-water berth. Work on the three berths, now known collectively as the Main Quay, was completed in 1956, and marked

PLATE 4.8. Dar es Salaam in the later 1960s: beyond the city centre, the passenger pier and lighterage quays are separated by Kurasini Creek from the three deep-water berths opened in 1956. The site of deep-water berths completed more recently is shown (top left) (compare Figure 5.2). (*Source:* Kenya Railways Corporation, Nairobi.)

the port's entry into the era of *simple lineal quayage*. At berth 1, a degree of priority is now given to ships discharging or loading more than 50 per cent of cargo destined for or originating from Zaire, Rwanda or Burundi, and the berth is administered by a quadripartite commission established by the four governments now involved, known as the Agence Maritime Internationale. The era of *simple lineal quayage* is still in progress at Dar es Salaam, as at Mombasa; additional deep-water berths have been added south of the Main Quay on the western side of Southern Creek. The demand for these facilities was considerably accelerated during the later 1960s by rapid increases in Zambian traffic through Dar es Salaam, and the construction of new deep-water berths has been supported by loans and grants provided by the Zambian government as well as by the World Bank (Hoyle, 1978). At the same time the port has moved on into the era of *specialised quayage*: modern facilities for the reception and refining of crude oil became available in 1966. An existing small jetty in Southern Creek was rehabilitated as a crude oil tanker terminal, linked by a submarine pipeline to an oil refinery located on the opposite side of the creek at Kigamboni. The increasing size of oil tankers and the physical limitations of the harbour in respect of depth of water and alignment of channels has necessitated the introduction of alternative facilities for the reception of crude oil, and in 1973 a single buoy mooring was established outside the main harbour at Mjimwema Bay, linked by a submarine pipeline and a land pipeline across the Kigamboni peninsula to the refinery. During the later 1970s the considerable growth in the number of containers handled at Dar es Salaam has signalled the effective entry of the port into the era of *containerisation*.

The Foundation and Development of Mtwara

The growth pattern of the port of Mtwara departs further from the standard of *Any (East African) seaport* than does that of any other East African ocean terminal. The *dhow traffic* era is comparable, but the transition into the *primitive* era did not take place, as at the other mainland seaports, as a result of railway building projects. The era of *marginal quay extension*, moreover, is completely unrepresented at Mtwara, for the port progressed directly from the *primitive* era into the era of *simple lineal quayage*. Known to navigators from the late eighteenth century at least,

Mtwara harbour remained virtually unutilized until changed economic circumstances in the hinterland made its development desirable in the mid-twentieth century; the port thus illustrates the general principle that the development of port facilities is not a direct reflection of good natural harbours, but is more closely related to changing navigational and economic circumstances and to changing patterns of land and sea traffic.

Two separate harbours are located in the inner reaches of Mikindani Bay: the shallow Mikindani harbour, and the deep-water Mtwara harbour. Mikindani harbour provided the setting for the *dhow traffic* era of port development in this area, and this small harbour stands as the southern counterpart of Mombasa's old harbour and of Bagamoyo and, like them, retains the form and function of earlier centuries since modern developments have utilized a different site. French traders, taking slaves from the mainland to their new plantations on the Ile de France (Mauritius) and Bourbon (Réunion) in the eighteenth century were probably among the first to become aware of the existence of Mikindani Bay. Sir John Gray has drawn attention to a reference to 'Miquimdany' by the Chevalier Saulnier de Mondévit, who made a hydrographical survey of part of the East African coast in 1787 (Gray, 1962b). The French were also responsible for a chart delineating Mtwara Bay, reproduced by Alexander Dalrymple, hydrographer to the East India Company, in 1796 (Gray, 1950). Dr. David Livingstone stayed at Mikindani in 1866 at the outset of his last journey, and described the bay as "a beautiful landlocked harbour . . . a first-rate harbour for Arab dhows . . . completely screened by the masses of trees growing all around it from seaward observation" (Gray, 1950, 31; Waller, 1874, vol. 1, 14-15). The reference is clearly to Mikindani harbour and not to Mtwara Bay. The first detailed survey of Mtwara harbour was undertaken by Captain J.W. Dixon of HMS *Nassau* in 1874 (Dixon, 1874). Dixon's chart remained unaltered until 1947, and it was on the basis of the promising figures marked on his chart that Mtwara was selected as the site of a new port 75 years later. The explorer Joseph Thomson passed through Mikindani and recorded in 1882 that it had "prospered immensely since Livingstone visited it in 1866 . . . The trade has increased exceedingly, almost the entire produce of the Rovuma region finding its way there – gum copal, rubber, millet, rice and other grains being the chief articles, though the trade in ivory and slaves . . . is by no means unimportant. South of Bagamoyo, Mikindany will now rank in importance next after Kilwa and Lindy" (Thomson, 1882, 76).

Again the reference is clearly to Mikindani rather than to Mtwara, but the account provides the first firm indication of significant commercial activity other than slave trading in the Mikindany Bay area.

Evidence of the transition from the *dhow traffic* era to the *primitive* era, and of a change in the balance of activity between Mikindani and Mtwara harbours, is provided in 1920 by the building of a small jetty on the western side of the entrance to Mtwara harbour. This jetty, the first port construction of any kind within Mtwara harbour, was developed to facilitate the export of sisal from an estate, originally a German undertaking, which then occupied much of the land around the harbour. The fact that the sisal transported over this jetty was subsequently transhipped at Mikindani reveals the dominant role still played at this time by Mikindani harbour. The sisal jetty, still in existence today but no longer used for its original purpose, is the only evidence of the utilization of Mtwara harbour for trade purposes before relatively recent years (Table 4.7).

TABLE 4.7
DEVELOPMENT OF THE PORT OF MTWARA

	Era	Terminated by	Present-day symbols
I	Dhow traffic: Mikindani harbour	Construction of a sisal wharf in Mtwara harbour, c. 1920	Mikindani harbour
II	Primitive: sisal wharf	Opening of deep-water berths, 1954	Sisal wharf
IV	Simple lineal quayage: deep-water berths		Deep-water berths

It was not until 1954, when deep-water berths were opened, that Mtwara moved on from the *primitive*.era to a more advanced stage of port development. The era of *marginal quay extension* was completely bypassed, since no lighterage quays were built, and the era of *simple lineal quayage* was introduced in rather artificial circumstances. In spite of its excellent site conditions, Mtwara has never been able to overcome its disadvantageous land situation, with a small and relatively unproductive hinterland. The necessary stimulus for post-*primitive* development at Mtwara was provided by the groundnut schemes of the immediate post-

1945 period, when there was a serious world shortage of edible oils and fats. Despite local advice to the contrary, it was envisaged that several centres in Tanganyika could quickly become the foci of major groundnut-producing areas. In 1946 the Overseas Food Corporation, in association with the British Government, drew up a plan for the establishment of 107 mechanized units of 30,000 acres each, designed to produce a minimum of 600,000 tons of groundnuts a year by 1950-51; of these units, the principal group of 55 was to be in the Southern Province of Tanganyika in the hinterland of Mtwara, with 25 elsewhere in Tanganyika, 17 in Northern Rhodesia and 10 in Kenya. Capital expenditure was estimated at £24 millions, and a profit of £10 millions a year was envisaged on the basis of the estimated minimum production of 600,000 tons (HMSO, 1947). Localized production for export on such a scale demanded the provision of port facilities which at that time were not in existence anywhere in Tanganyika, and considerable development was therefore necessary at whatever terminal might be selected. A Harbour Commission appointed by the British Ministry of Food visited Lindi and Kilwa in February 1947; these ports were initially thought to be able to provide adequate outlet facilities; but, finding their disadvantages of site too great for the construction of deep-water berths, the Commission recommended the development of an entirely new port within the harbour of Mtwara, designed to meet the needs of the groundnut project and of future developments in the area.

As first proposed, the groundnut schemes gave rise to considerable optimism which proved in the event to be unfounded. The scheme in southern Tanganyika was thought likely "to cause a revolutionary upheaval at Mtwara, one that will advance the area and its people and provide opportunities for such progress in so short a time that none could have dreamed possible . . . The villagers of Mtwara already speak of their village as a future Mombasa" (Johnston, 1947, 63-4). Construction work on the new port facilities began in 1948, and in the following year a railway was opened from Mkwaya, at the head of Lindi Creek, to Nachingwea, about 100 miles inland. The port of Lindi, meanwhile, was improved so as to serve the scheme until the Mtwara developments were completed. By 1951, however, local conditions and the world market made it apparent that large-scale groundnut production was not a practical proposition and the scope of the scheme was considerably reduced. The railway administration nevertheless hoped that general agricultural development might eventually provide sufficient traffic to cover operating costs on the new line within the space of a few years; the railway was completed and opened at the same time as the new deep-water facilities at Mtwara in 1954. The date marks the transition of the port from the *primitive* era of development directly into the era of *simple lineal quayage*. In 1958 a 23-mile rail extension to Masasi was added as a last bid to attract more traffic. There proved, unfortunately, to be no tendency for earnings to increase and the total freight traffic handled on the railway – amounting only to 32,616 tons in 1958, the peak year – never reached 25 per cent of the level originally envisaged. In addition to the failure to produce cash crops on the scale forecast, the eventual closing of the line in 1962 was partly caused by increasing road competition; road transport was the traditional method, focused on Lindi before Mtwara was developed, and the planned reorientation to the new rail-served port never took place to the expected extent. Furthermore, road hauliers avoided transhipment costs at the rail-heads and, by using the railway to absorb peak loads, could operate generally at full capacity.

The failure of the complex plans involved in the groundnut project had important repercussions at Mtwara. The town was never built as planned, but a few shops, a bank, a hotel and various government offices now stand in isolation, separated from each other by bumpy lanes and stretches of open grassland. The town was described in 1962 by an *Observer* correspondent as having been "built in small patches, like a crossword just begun." The closed railway to Nachingwea and Masasi was lifted in 1963, and the lines used elsewhere; the government of independent Tanganyika was not prepared to meet the annual losses of about £200,000 that were entailed. In a sense the port facilities now available at Mtwara are under-utilised; traffic at the port has traditionally followed a seasonal pattern, dominated by cashew nut and cassava exports in the November-January period, and although at this season the port sometimes works under pressure, for the remainder of the year activity reaches only a low level. The utilisation of spare capacity by Zambian traffic in the future has been considered.

Although they have been widely discussed, the reasons for the failure of the development schemes so closely associated with transportation in this corner of East Africa are not easy to assess. The basic reason was, probably, an urgent desire for rapid and spectacular results, of a type which Africa rarely yields, a desire that inevitably involved inadequate preparation and inadequate investigation of the complex ecological factors that to a large extent control development in such an area. The eventual total cost of the scheme – some £35 million – was not, however, entirely wasted. Southern Tanzania is now equipped with a deep-water port which, although not proving a marked stimulus to development within its hinterland, probably provides adequate port facilities for some time to come. Groundnut production in the Nachingwea area is quite considerable, and the agricultural pattern of this and other development areas associated with the groundnut project has to some extent been diversified. Skilled labour and professional services have also proved, in part, to be of permanent benefit. Although the political problems of the Tanzania/Mozambique frontier zone in the early 1970s may have retarded the further development of the area for a time, perhaps the most worthwhile result of the relatively unsuccessful attempts to establish a major seaport at Mtwara in the 1950s was a new and rather expensive demonstration of the fact that in Africa development schemes must make haste slowly and in full cognizance of the ecology of the areas involved.

The Development of Port Facilities at Zanzibar

When Seyyid Said finally moved his court and capital from Muscat to Zanzibar in 1840, the site he selected for the development of a new port and town was extremely well adapted to his purposes both in terms of local land and water site conditions and in relation to the East African mainland. Moreover, the site was virtually uninhabited except for a small fishing village; earlier settlements on the island had been located elsewhere – the most important town on the island when the Portuguese arrived was at Unguja Ukuu, whilst among the many ruins is a mosque at Kizimkazi bearing the oldest inscribed date along the coast: 500 A.H. or A.D. 1107. Until the end of the nineteenth century there were no port facilities in the modern sense and, as at the mainland seaports in operation at that time, the open beach served quite adequately for the loading and unloading of cargoes during the *dhow traffic* era (Table 4.8). In the mid-nineteenth century port activity chiefly took place near the tip of the Shangani peninsula, concentrating to the north or south of the point according to season. The name Shangani – 'the place of beads' – perhaps indicates early trading activity, and it was in this quarter, in the vicinity of

TABLE 4.8
DEVELOPMENT OF THE PORT OF ZANZIBAR

	Era	Terminated by	Present-day symbols
I	Dhow traffic	Various early landing steps and piers	Beaches around Shangani Point
II	Primitive	Opening of Customs Quay, 1892	Landing steps
III	Marginal quay extension		
	Customs Quay, 1892–1929	Opening of new wharf, 1929	People's Gardens
	The Wharf, 1929		Present port area

PLATE 4.9. Zanzibar: the beach at Ras Shangani, the site of much trading activity in the mid-nineteenth century (see Figure 4.2). The central building on the left was the British Consulate from 1841 to 1874; here at different times lived Speke, Burton, Grant and Kirk; David Livingstone stayed here and his body was brought here in 1874 on its long journey from Zambia via Southampton to London. (*Source:* Author.)

the present Kilele Square, that the slave market was originally sited. Movement of cargo over the beach was permitted at many points; the various consulates with water frontages, for example, imported goods over their own beaches since their land titles included foreshore freehold.

From the tip of the Shangani peninsula the focus of port activity at Zanzibar gradually migrated northwards (Fig. 4.2), although there were

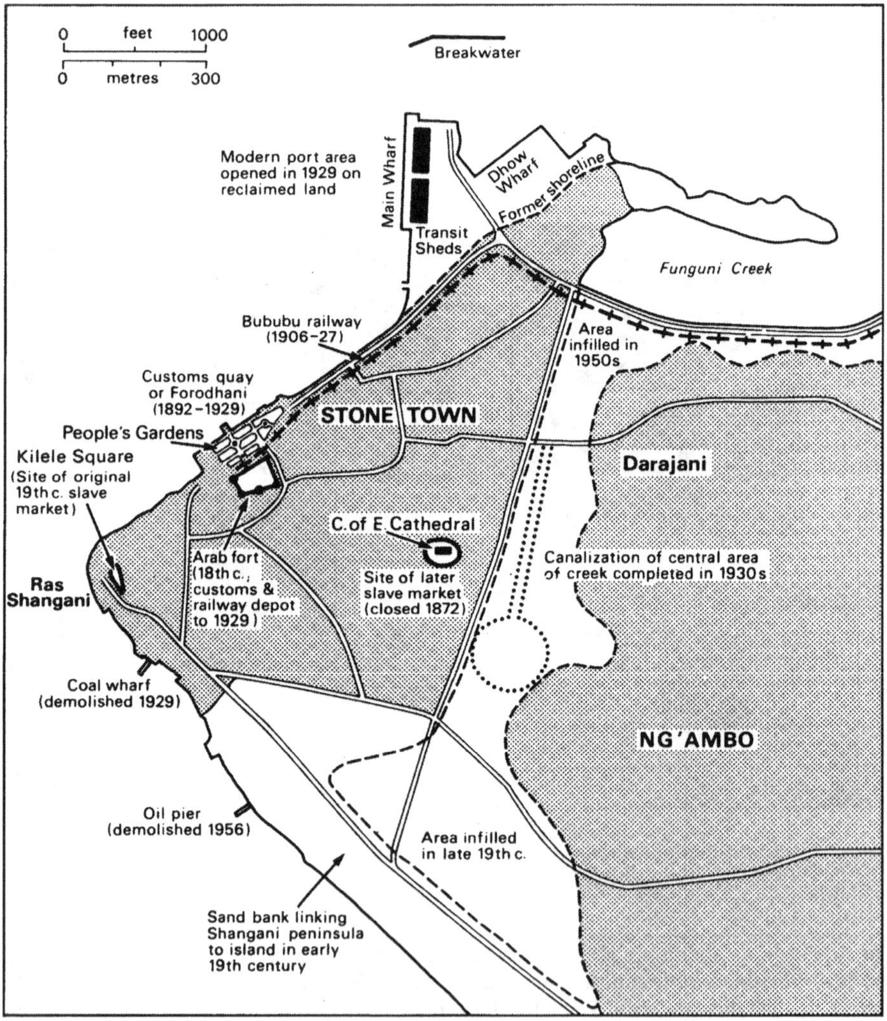

FIGURE 4.2. The development of port facilities at Zanzibar.

temporary structures on the southern side of the point including a wooden coal jetty used until 1929 and an iron oil pier which was not dismantled until 1956. In 1873 Elton described "slaves . . . busily loading coal at the wharf, watched by a group of idlers . . ." (Elton, 1879, 46). Towards the end of the nineteenth century it became increasingly obvious that modern port facilities were essential if Zanzibar was not to lose her trade supremacy on the East African coast. In 1892, before any of the mainland ports had moved on from the *dhow traffic* era to the *primitive* era, a small stone-built lighterage quay was completed at Zanzibar a short distance to the north of Ras Shangani (Hollingsworth, 1953, 67), thus representing the beginning of the era of *marginal quay extension* within which the port still remains today. The quay wall, about 260 m long, was continued north-eastwards as a sea wall for a further distance of some 300 m. The new lighterage quay, equipped with a lighthouse and several steam cranes, and backed by covered transit sheds, was generally known as the Customs Quay; the name 'Forodhani' (Swahili for 'customs') is still used for the main road along the seafront at this point. Immediately behind the port area, an eighteenth-century Arab fort was used partly for customs purposes, and partly as the main depot and workshops for a railway built in 1906 by an American company from this point to Bububu, a village near the coast seven miles north of Zanzibar town. The railway was closed in 1927 as a result of increasing competition from motor traffic.

The Customs Quay proved inadequate, however, due to its restricted land site and its exposure to the north-east monsoon. It was replaced in 1929 by the opening of a completely new port area, which marks the continuation of the era of *marginal quay extension* at Zanzibar on a slightly different site. The need for the development of more modern facilities, on a site less restricted than that afforded by the old Customs Quay, had been apparent for some years, but development had been retarded by the First World War. In 1919 a scheme was put forward for the construction of what was originally envisaged as a deep-water pier consisting of a three-berth reinforced concrete pile wharf backed by a reclaimed area of some twenty acres of land (Sinclair, 1923). On the eastern side of the reclaimed area provision was made for dhow traffic in the form of a sheltered basin with ancillary facilities; transit between the ocean wharf and the dhow wharf needed to be rapid and direct, since many imported goods were redistributed by coastal vessels, and a high proportion of export items (especially cloves from Pemba) were brought to

Zanzibar by sea also.

The project was approved by the British Secretary of State and in 1920 negotiations were completed between the Government of Zanzibar and the South African Government for the loan of a resident engineer and a foreman to supervise the construction of the new port works. A hydrographic survey of the harbour was undertaken and the exact bearing on which the new wharf was to be laid down was decided. The significance of the alignment, which is approximately south to north, is that the west-facing 250-m ocean wharf is sheltered by Shangani Point from the south-west monsoon and from the north-east monsoon by the reclaimed port area itself. The new port area thus reproduced, in part, the advantageous natural conditions associated with the similarly triangular Shangani peninsula in the *dhow traffic* era. After numerous practical and financial difficulties (the cost was originally estimated at £253,000, but eventually rose to over £400,000), the new port developments were opened in 1929 and the old Customs Quay fell into disuse (Zanzibar Protectorate, 1920 *et seq*.).

The 1964 revolution undoubtedly provided a turning point in the economic as well as the political and social history of Zanzibar (Flint, 1965; Ayani, 1970), but the effects upon port development have been limited. In that year, shortly after political independence from the British Protectorate had been achieved, armed rebellion caused the overthrow of the Sultan's government. In the early years of the post-revolutionary period, political factors undoubtedly had an adverse effect upon an already stagnant economy. In the 1970s, however, rising world clove prices encouraged economic diversification, industrial and infrastructural improvements, and further expansion of port installations has been considered. The modernisation and extension of the present port area in a north-easterly direction has been discussed: this would involve the infilling of the remaining tidal section of Funguni Creek. A new hotel, however, was built on the spit in an attempt to encourage a limited degree of tourism. Plans for a new port at Chake Chake, on Pemba Island, have also been considered.

'Anyport' in a Wider Perspective

These details demonstrate that there is a fundamental similarity in the pattern of development that each East African seaport has followed in modern times. As Bird has indicated, "there is one main reason why major ports should show similar features of layout, arranged in many different ways, even if they grew up independently on widely differing sites. All major ports serve the same world fleet of shipping, or similar cross-sections of it, with the result that they have the same incentives to provide terminals of similar dimensions and capacities" (Bird, 1963, 417). A major feature of the differential pattern of port development in East Africa is, however, that the growth of the individual terminals within the *Anyport* framework has reached widely varying levels (Fig. 4.3). Of the five members of the modern port group, only Mombasa and Dar es Salaam represent in their layout all eras of growth from that of *dhow traffic* to that of *containerisation*; Tanga has developed *specialised quayage* but has no deep-water berths; Mtwara, although equipped with deep-water facilities belonging to the era of *simple lineal quayage*, shows only vestiges of an earlier era; and Zanzibar has not progressed beyond the era of *marginal quay extension.* This differential pattern has arisen as a result of the complex interaction of a variety of physical, economic and political factors; and the modern hierarchy of East African seaports which has succeeded earlier hierarchies may have a greater degree of permanence because of heavy capital investment in port and railway facilities. The present-day ranking of members of the port group in terms of facilities and equipment does not accord closely with a ranking in terms of site potential; this is a measure of the importance of wider conditions of situation, particularly in terms of the economic development and political division of the hinterlands from the beginning of the colonial era. While all five seaports are of major significance in a local context, only Mombasa and Dar es Salaam could claim to be major terminals in an international sense. It is at these larger seaports that the fullest extent of development has been experienced, and towards them that an increasing proportion of the total traffic handled by the group has turned in recent years. Part of the usefulness of the Anyport model is that it brings to the analysis of port growth a frame of reference within which the chronological and the spatial elements are combined; its application to East African seaports helps to elucidate relationships between members of the port group as well as with their geographical setting.

The search for similarities in the development process within a port group can thus prove a useful exercise. *Anyport* was originally designed,

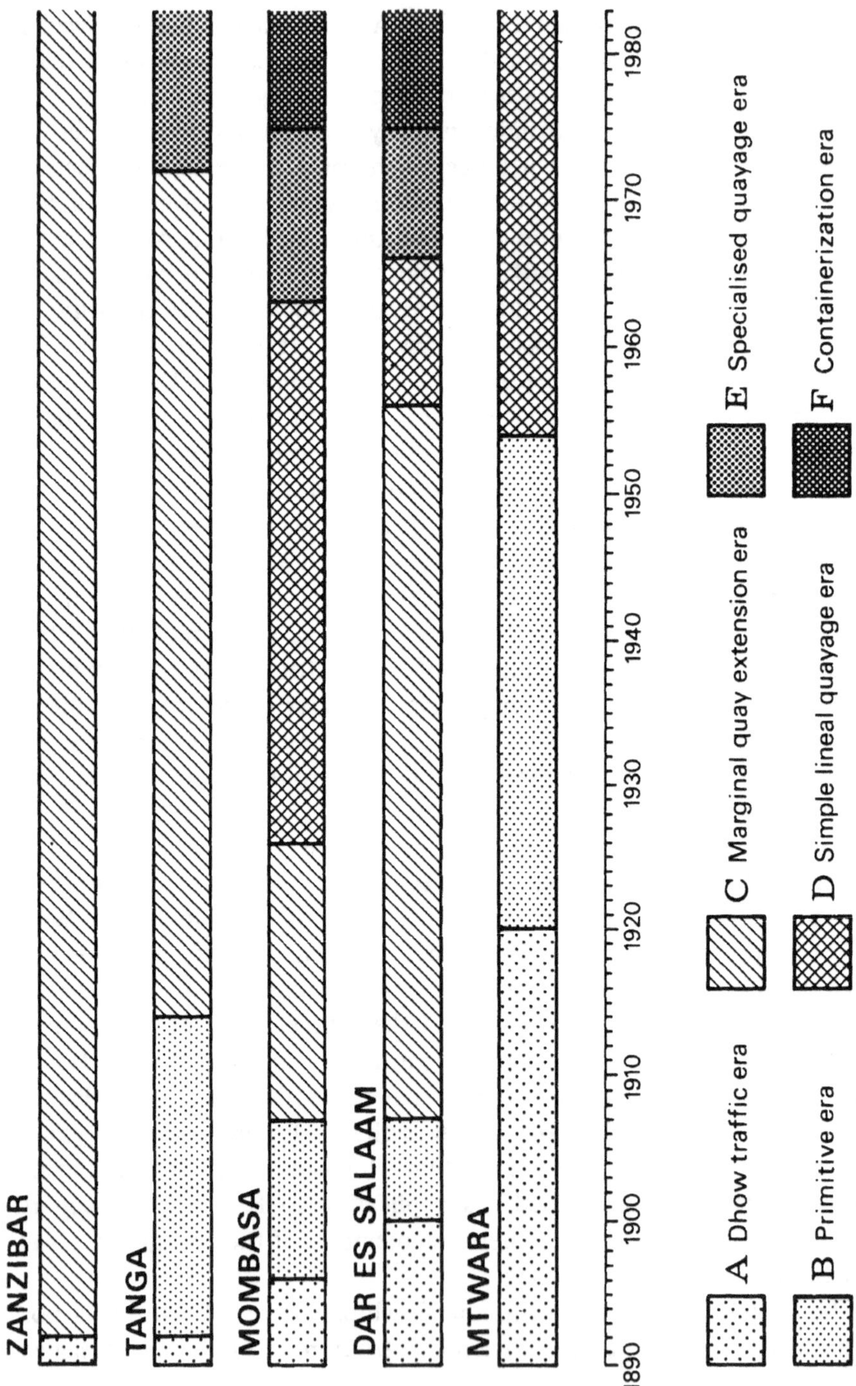

FIGURE 4.3. Comparative duration of development eras at major East African seaports.

however, as an aid to the understanding of the growth of large multifunctional ports in economically advanced countries. Small ports, and port groups, in less-developed countries are often too diverse or too specialised in function to lend themselves to this kind of approach. Political circumstances may explain, in part, why the model appears relevant to East Africa. Several of the mainland ports originated in their modern forms as vital elements within the process of colonization. Different European powers were involved, but the 'proclaimed impulse' (Bird, 1971, 24-26) of territorial acquisition was essentially the same. Elsewhere in tropical Africa it has been suggested that the model does not usefully illustrate the process of port development, although distinctive periods have been recognised in West Africa as a whole (Hilling, 1969) and also in Ghana (Dickson, 1965) and Nigeria (Ogundana, 1971). The originator of the model successfully applied a revised version to the seaports of Australia (Bird, 1968). Wiese (1981) has also used the model to illustrate his analysis of the South African seaport system.

Port layouts are designed to serve the basic port function – cargo transfer – and all large ports comprise installations built at different times. Tangible facilities, however, are not the essence of a port; defined as a place where the mode of transportation changes between land and water systems, a seaport exists to facilitate cargo transfer, and port facilities fulfill and express this function. As one era of development succeeds another, the introduction of new methods of cargo transfer may outwardly change the appearance of a port substantially, but these changes merely reflect new ways of fulfilling the same function. The search for similarities in the development of port layouts is justified by the fact that seaports do not grow in isolation but in response to changing opportunities and demands at different times, over different areas, on different scales and with different intensities. Whilst some factors involved are purely local, others are regional or global in their application. In a given technological era, for example, ports are likely to attempt to use similar methods of performing their functions. Today, major ports in both advanced and less-developed countries are becoming increasingly alike as they respond to current trends in the technology of cargo handling and maritime transport. Whilst Anyport may not rank, in detail, as a universal canon, the nomothetic principles underlying the design of the model are themselves of universal application.

REFERENCES

Allen, J.W.T. (1945), 'The name Dar es Salaam,' *Tanganyika Notes and Records* 19, 67-68.

Baxter, H.C. (1944), 'Pangani: the trade centre of ancient history,' *Tanganyika Notes and Records* 17, 15-25.

Bird, J.H. (1963), *The major seaports of the United Kingdom* (London, Hutchinson).

Bird, J.H. (1968), *Seaport gateways of Australia* (London, Oxford University Press).

Bird, J.H. (1971), *Seaports and seaport terminals* (London, Hutchinson).

Bornhardt, W. (1900), *Zur Oberflächengestaltung und Geologie Deutsch Ostafrikas* (Berlin, Dietrich Reimer).

Brown, W.T. (1970), 'Bagamoyo: an historical introduction,' *Tanzania Notes and Records* 71, 69-83.

Datoo, B.A. (1970), 'Rhapta: the location and importance of East Africa's first port', *Azania* 5, 65-75.

Dickson, K.B. (1965), 'Evolution of seaports in Ghana, 1800-1928,' *Annals of the Association of American Geographers* 55, 98-111.

Dixon, J.W. (1874), 'Mikindani Bay, east coast of Africa,' *Nautical Magazine*, 840-841.

Farquharson, J.R. (1945), *Tanganyika transport: a review* (Dar es Salaam, Government Printer).

Elton, J.F. (1879), *Travels and researches among the lakes and mountains of eastern and central Africa* (London, John Murray; repr. Frank Cass, 1968).

Gillman, C. (1942), 'A short history of the Tanganyika railways,' *Tanganyika Notes and Records* 13, 1-43.

Gillman, C. (1945), 'Dar es Salaam, 1860-1940: a story of growth and change,' *Tanganyika Notes and Records* 20, 1-23.

Gracey, T. (1901), 'Correspondence respecting the Uganda railway,' *Africa* 6 (cited in Hill, 1949, 204-210).

Gray, Sir J.M. (1950), 'Mikindani Bay before 1887,' *Tanganyika Notes and Records* 28, 29-37.

Gray, Sir J.M. (1962a), 'The opening of Dar es Salaam as a seaport,' *Tanganyika Notes and Records* 59, 224.

Gray, Sir J.M. (1962b), 'Mikindani Bay,' *Tanganyika Notes and Records* 59, 287.

Hartnoll, M. (1937), 'A story of the origin of the name Bandar es Salaam, which in the old days was called Mzizima,' *Tanganyika Notes and Records* 3, 117-119.

Hill, M.F. (1949), *Permanent way: the story of the Kenya and Uganda railway* (Nairobi, East African Railways and Harbours).

Hill, M.F. (1957), *Permanent way: the story of the Tanganyika railways* (Nairobi, East African Railways and Harbours).

Hilling, D. (1969), 'The evolution of the major seaports of West Africa,' *Geographical Journal* 135, 365-378.

Hitchcock, Sir E. (1959), 'The sisal industry of East Africa,' *Tanganyika Notes and Records* 52, 4-17.

HMSO, (1947), *A plan for the mechanized production of groundnuts in East and*

Central Africa (London, Cmd. 7030).

Hollingsworth, L.W. (1953), *Zanzibar under the Foreign Office, 1890-1913* (London, Macmillan).

Hoyle, B.S. (1978), 'African politics and port expansion at Dar es Salaam,' *Geographical Review* 68, 31-80.

Johnston, P.H. (1947), 'Mtwara Bay,' *Tanganyika Notes and Records* 24, 61-65.

Krapf, J.L. (1860), *Travels, missionary researches and labours in eastern Africa (London, Trubner).*

McMaster, D.N. (1966), 'The ocean-going dhow trade to East Africa,' *East African Geographical Review* 4, 13-24.

Molesworth, Sir G. (1899), 'Report on the Uganda railway,' *Africa* 5 (cited in Hill, 1949, 179-185).

Ogundana, B. (1971), 'The location factor in changing seaport significance in Nigeria,' *Nigerian Geographical Journal* 14, 71-88.

Owen, W.F. W. (1833), *Narrative of voyages to explore the shores of Africa, Arabia and Madagascar* (London, 2 vols., Bentley; repr. 1968, Gregg International Publishers, Farnborough).

Paasche, H. (1906), *Deutsche Ostafrika* (Berlin).

Seward, G.E. (1866), 'Report on Dhar Salaam in 1866, to the Political Department, Bombay,' *Tanzania Notes and Records* 71, 1970, 201-202.

Sinclair, J.H. (1923), *Report on the Zanzibar Protectorate from 1911 to 1923* (Zanzibar, Government Printer).

Sutton, J.E.G. (1970), 'Dar es Salaam: a sketch of a hundred years,' *Tanzania Notes and Records* 71, 1-19.

Thomson, J. (1881), *To the central African lakes and back* (London, 2 vols.; Sampson, Low).

Thomson, J. (1882), 'Notes on the basin of the River Rovuma, East Africa,' *Proceedings of the Royal Geographical Society* 4, 76.

Waller, H. (ed.) (1874), *The last journals of David Livingstone in Central Africa (London, 2 vols., John Murray).*

Wiese, B. (1981), *Seaports and port cities of southern Africa* (Weisbaden, Franz Steiner Verlag GMBH: Kölner Geographische Arbeiten 11).

Zanzibar Protectorate (1920 *et seq.*), *Report on the Public Works Department for the year 1920, et seq.* (Zanzibar, Government Printer).

5 Seaport Installations and Operation

The installations of a port, together with the system and mode of operation (including labour organisation), constitute the means whereby the basic port function of cargo transfer is performed. Installations and operation are subject to continuous review, and modifications are frequent, especially at larger seaports. The development of new facilities or methods may change considerably the outward appearance of a port or its efficiency of operation, but such changes merely introduce new ways of performing the basic function (Bird, 1971, 74). Port installations comprise, on the one hand, *infrastructures* designed to sharpen and stabilise the junction between land and water areas; and, on the other hand, *superstructures* for the purpose of assisting cargo movements to and from ships across the land/water junction. Most ports provide installations of both kinds, although the level of provision varies between wide extremes. The objectives, however, are everywhere the same: to accelerate ships' turnaround times by increasing cargo throughput. Faster flows may often be achieved by increasing the range of specialised port installations and by reducing the relative importance of common user facilities, but such developments may place a considerable strain upon hinterland transport services.

Port capacity depends essentially upon the range and level of installations, upon the system and mode of operation, and upon the relationship between these two sets of factors. Defined as the ability of a port to achieve a given level of throughput, port capacity may be assessed in a variety of ways. The quantification of a concept dependent upon such a wide range of variables is not, however, a particularly fruitful exercise. Different assessments of capacity may be given for any combination of an unlimited number of separate sets of circumstances, and will vary substantially according to the length and nature of the time period on which

PLATE 5.1. Infrastructures, superstructures and cargo transfer across the land/water junction: a quay-side scene at an East African seaport. (*Source*: Kenya Cargo Handling Services, Mombasa.)

the assessment is based. In whatever way it is assessed, port capacity is a crucial factor affecting the ability of a country to engage in overseas trade, and may operate as a permissive or as a restrictive influence upon economic development. The new states of the developing world are frequently highly dependent economically upon overseas trade, and the capacity of the seaports through which this trade passes (whether located within their own national boundaries or within those of a neighbouring state) may readily become an indicator of national development levels.

In this chapter an attempt is made to illustrate these principles by comparing the modern seaports of the East African mainland in terms of their present-day installations and in terms of some of their current problems of operation. An approximate indication of relative capacity is given in Table 5.1, which emphasises the wide variety that exists within

TABLE 5.1
INSTALLATIONS AND EQUIPMENT AT EAST AFRICAN SEAPORTS, 1982

	Mombasa	Dar es Salaam	Tanga	Mtwara	Total
Deep-water berths					
Number	16	11	–	2	29
Length (m)	3,044	2,018	–	380	5,442
Dredged depth (m)	10	10	–	10	
Bulk oil berths	2	1	–	–	3
Single buoy mooring	–	1	–	–	1
Bulk dry cargo jetty	–	–	1	–	1
Bulk dry cargo berths					
Number	2	–	–	–	2
Length (m)	315	–	–	–	315
Lighterage and dhow wharves					
Number	2	4	2	–	8
Length	412	588	381	–	1,381
Handling points	9	5	9	–	23
Transit sheds					
Number	30	20	6	4	60
Floor area (m^2)	185,050	106,863	15,028	16,723	323,664
Cargo lighters					
Number	43	71	58	–	172
Capacity	9,200	11,030	17,030	–	37,260

(*Sources*: Kenya Ports Authority [for Mombasa] and Tanzania Harbours Authority [for Tanzanian ports].)

the modern East African seaport hierarchy. The value of comparative data of this kind is to some extent reduced, however, by the fact that berths and cargo-handling appliances are not necessarily in continuous use, since the flow of traffic through the ports varies considerably over time. The level and variety of port installations, and the varied demands made upon the ports by their customers, are subjects of continuous debate and frequent contention, especially when problems of congestion arise. It may be said at the outset, however, that the abolition of port congestion is virtually an impossibility, given on the one hand the dangers of overcapitalisation and on the other hand the widely varying demands made upon ports in terms of the composition of their cargo mix and in terms of the pattern of their cargo flow. Without irresponsible overcapitalisation it is not possible to satisfy all of a port's customers all the time. Given the very wide range of factors affecting port operation – economic and political, social and historical, physical and technical – a port may be deemed to be doing a reasonably good job if most of the customers are satisfied for most of the time.

Port Installations at Mombasa

There is no doubt that Mombasa is at present the best equipped of the seaports of East Africa in terms of the extent and variety of installations available (Fig. 5.1). In spite of this Mombasa has frequently suffered from congestion which at times has been serious. The modern port of Mombasa, or Kilindini, is divisible into three main functional zones. The south-western shore of Mombasa Island between the Likoni ferry and Ras Kilindini is occupied by a series of lighterage wharves, the Liwatoni fish quay, ship repair facilities and the bulk cargo handling quay at Mbaraki. Along the north-western shore of the island, between Ras Kilindini and Makupa Creek, there is a series of nine deep-water berths (1-5 and 7-10), and the Shimanzi oil terminal. On the mainland at Kipevu, connected to the island by a road/rail causeway, a series of seven deep-water berths (11-14 and 16-18) has been developed, together with the Kipevu oil terminal. All the deep-water berths are dredged to approximately –10 m. The extent and predominance of deep-water facilities is an important feature of Mombasa which contrasts with the position at the other major East African ports, although the extent of the disparity between Mombasa

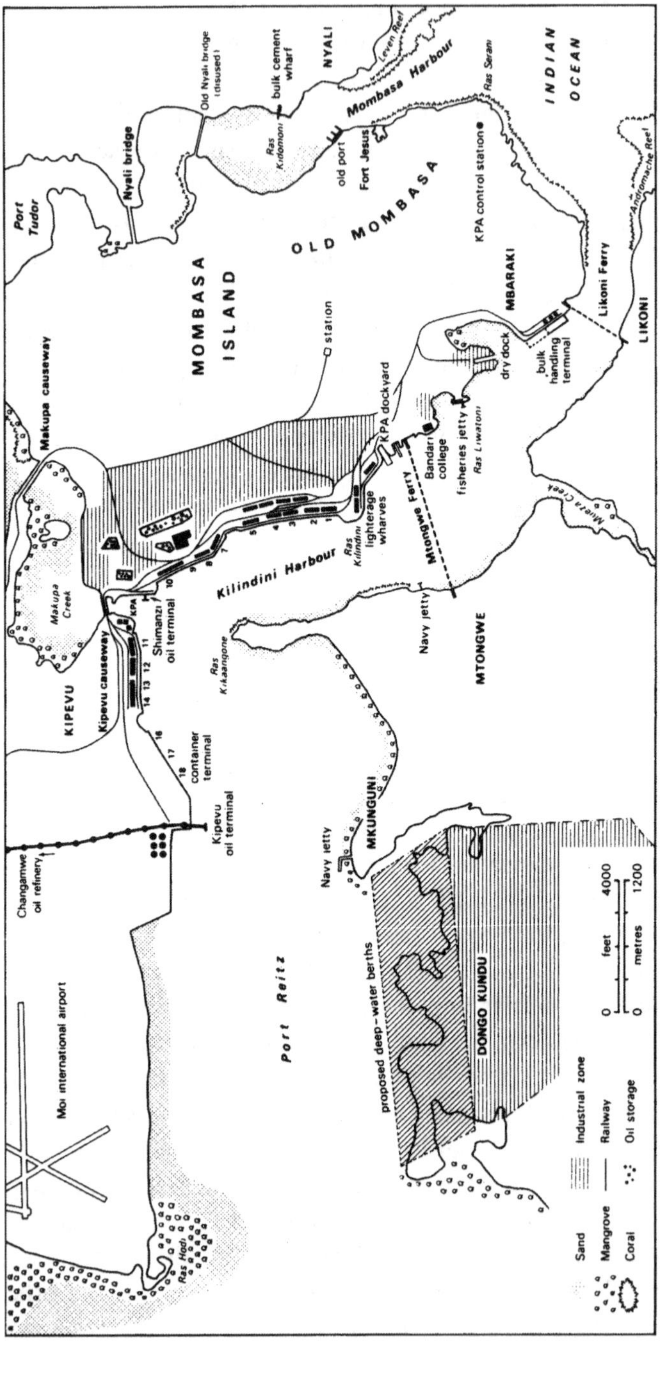

FIGURE 5.1. The port of Mombasa. (*Sources*: Based on Admiralty Charts 616 and 666; Survey of Kenya 1/14,000 special sheet, Mombasa Island and environs; and data provided by the Kenya Ports Authority.)

PLATE 5.2. Bulk export of soda ash at Mombasa: the overhead conveyors transfer soda ash from storage areas to the quayside at berth 9. (*Source:* Author.)

and Dar es Salaam has been considerably reduced in recent years.

In common with major seaports in many other parts of the world, Mombasa demonstrates today an increasing tendency towards specialisation of activity at the waterfront; the current era of *Anyport* development, that of *containerisation* (and its immediate precursor, that of *specialised quayage*) are essentially expressions of important global trends in the technology of maritime transport. Specialisation is most commonly based on the type of cargo handled, but it can also arise from the size or technical character of vessels, or from politico-economic conditions in the hinterland. In a limited sense, specialised quayage has existed at Mombasa for many years: bulk loading facilities for the export of soda ash from Magadi were introduced at Kilindini in 1913; the modern equivalent comprises two overhead gantries carrying conveyor belts for the transfer of bulk soda ash from rail-served storage facilities on the hill behind the port to the quayside at berth 9. In the same area a privately owned tank for the storage of molasses is linked to the quayside by a pipeline slung below one of the soda ash gantries. Coal is handled at the bulk cargo-

PLATE 5.3. Bulk export of molasses at Mombasa: a pipeline slung below one of the soda ash conveyors (Plate 5.2) connects storage tanks with the quayside at berth 9. Flexible pipes link the fixed pipeline with ships' manifolds – sometimes, as in this photograph, across the decks of another vessel discharging cargo at the quayside. (*Source:* Kenya Railways Corporation, Nairobi.)

handling quay at Mbaraki; some other bulk cargoes such as grains are handled at general cargo berths, where only limited specialised handling facilities are available. In one sense it may be argued that the development of a container terminal is merely a particular form of *specialised quayage*, but it is probably more realistic to regard the rapid growth in the number of containers handled since the mid-1970s as the beginning of a major new era and as a turning point in the development of the port not only as a transport node but also as an industrial complex.

In Mombasa Harbour the dhow jetties, which serve dhows mainly between November and April and receive other small coastal vessels throughout the year, represent a type of specialisation with deep historic roots. The principal modern specialised facility within the old harbour is

PLATE 5.4. The bulk cement wharf at Mbaraki, Mombasa. (*Source*: Kenya Ports Authority.)

the bulk cement loading berth at Ras Kidomoni, suitable for vessels not exceeding 130 m in length and 8.5 m draught, built in 1970 for the Bamburi Portland Cement Company. In Kilindini Harbour, a 300-m bulk-cargo berth was opened at Mbaraki in 1971 through which the BPCC exports bagged cement and clinker; this berth is also used for fluorspar exports. Pneumatic grain pumps are available at general-cargo berths for handling imported wheat and maize and also for loading maize exports. North of Mombasa Island, on the margins of Port Tudor, the Kenya Meat Commission has developed a jetty for cattle imports.

Bulk oil cargoes are handled at two specialised Mombasa terminals. The Kipevu oil terminal, located on the mainland to the west of the deep-water berths, normally accepts tankers of up to approximately 50,000 dwt or 13.4 m draught; the jetty was developed in 1962 to import crude oil in bulk and is connected by pipelines with the Changamwe refinery, some 3 km to the north. The Shimanzi oil terminal is located on the north-western shore of Mombasa Island, was built in 1931 and receives smaller tankers of up to about 30,000 dwt, not exceeding 194 m in length or 9.75 m in draught; it is used for the export of refined oil products and also for the import of other bulk liquids such as vegetable oils and chemicals.

The various quays and jetties at Mombasa are backed by some 30 transit sheds; additional facilities include a cold store, a passenger baggage hall and extensive open stacking areas used to store cargoes for which protection from sun and rain is not essential. Many of the older deep-water berths are deficient in terms of the character and extent of stacking areas available, and the transit sheds are generally inadequate in view of slow cargo clearance rates. Mombasa has developed essentially as a rail-served deep-water port, and all the transit sheds and stacking areas at Kilindini and Kipevu, and the Mbaraki bulk-cargo handling quay, are rail-served. The rail and road communication system within the port area is extensive and connects with the mainland system via the Makupa and Kipevu causeways; marshalling yards are located at Changamwe, and also at Kipevu and on Mombasa Island.

Port Installations at Dar es Salaam

The range of port facilities at Dar es Salaam is considerably smaller than at Mombasa, in spite of major recent developments. Whereas Mombasa is able to accept ships of up to about 65,000 dwt and can accommodate over 50 ships at one time, the more restricted harbour of Dar es Salaam with its more limited facilities is only able to accept ships of up to about 20,000 dwt and cannot provide simultaneous anchorage within the harbour for more than 19 deep-water vessels.

Port installations es Dar as Salaam may be divided on a functional basis into three zones (Fig. 5.2). To the north of Kurasini Creek lies the older part of the port where there are four lighterage wharves which in 1981 were badly in need of modernisation and were scheduled for complete rehabilitation. To the south of Kurasini Creek, a series of deep-water berths has been built along the western shore of Southern Creek; three were completed in 1956, five more during the period 1970-72, and three more berths in the mid-1970s. The port is now therefore equipped with a total of 11 deep-water berths and most of the more obvious sites for development within the harbour are now occupied. These recent extensions reflect a transformation in the scale of port activity at Dar es Salaam from the early 1970s, due primarily to the extension of the hinterland of the port to include Zambia (Hoyle, 1978). Extranational trade has long been important at Dar es Salaam, however, as at Mombasa; berth 1 was constructed in 1956 at the expense of the Belgian Government to facilitate traffic destined for or originating from the then Belgian Congo and Ruanda-Urundi. Today priority is given at this berth to vessels discharging or loading more than 50 per cent of cargo to or from Zaire, Rwanda or Burundi (ZRB), and traffic across this quay is administered by the Agence Maritime Internationale (AMI) on behalf of the four governments involved.

At present all deep-water and lighterage berths at Dar es Salaam are rail-served; berths 1-6 are served by the Tanzania Railway Corporation and berths 6-11 by the Tanzania-Zambia Railway. The berths are served by 20 transit sheds. There are two small passenger and baggage sheds, and extensive open stacking areas. A depot at Ubungo (10 km west of Dar es Salaam on the Morogoro road) was established in 1975 to provide transhipment facilities for Zambian exports and imports through the port. A substantial increase in the number of containers handled at Dar es Salaam during the later 1970s propelled the port firmly into the *containerisation* era; berth 9 was rehabilitated and equipped as the temporary focus of the port's container terminal during the present phase of development. Bulk cement-loading facilities are available at the Malindi Wharf (the southern-

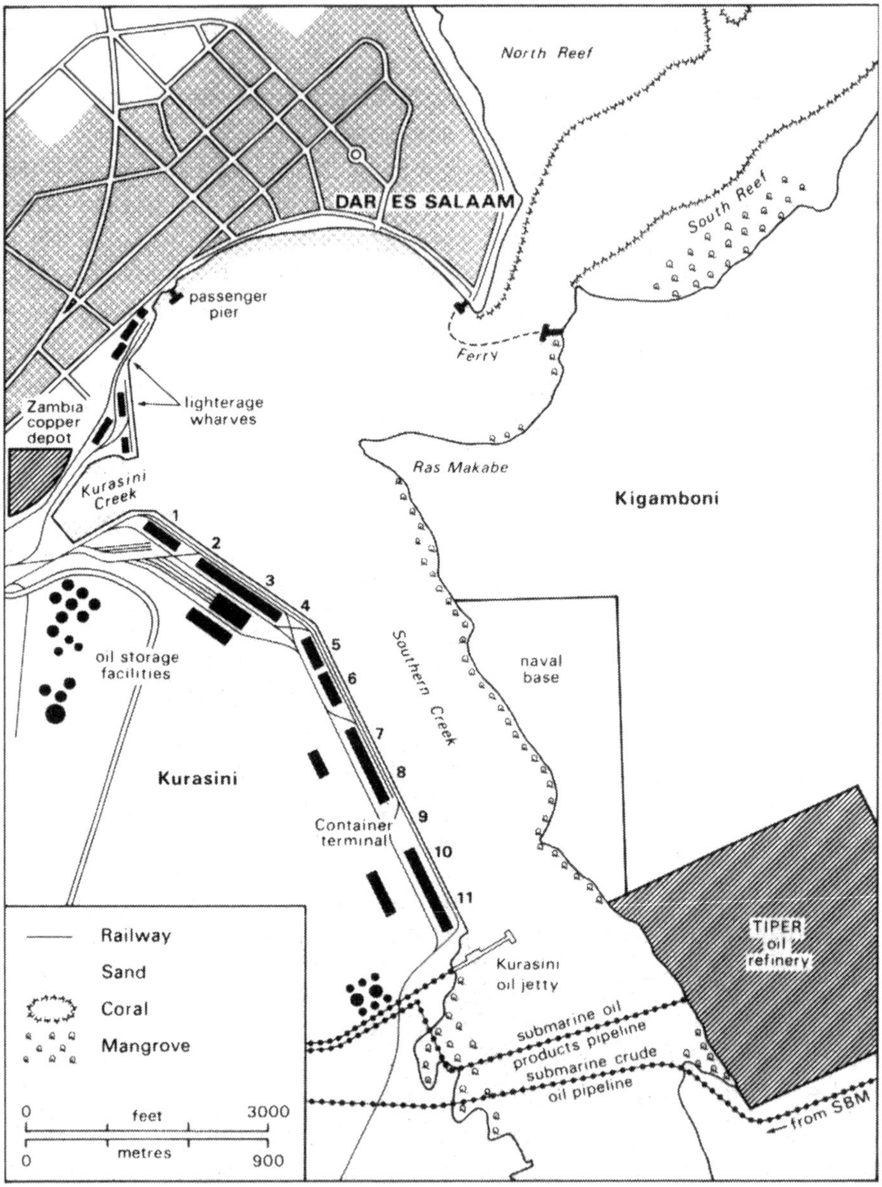

FIGURE 5.2. The port of Dar es Salaam. (*Sources:* Based on Admiralty Charts 674 and 693; Survey and Mapping Division, Tanzania, 1/50,000 series, sheet 186/4; and data provided by the Tanzania Harbours Authority.)

PLATE 5.5. Oil-handling facilities at Dar es Salaam: the single buoy mooring (SBM) facility at Mjimwema Bay. Taken in April 1973, this photograph shows the tanker *Long Phoenix* (the first tanker to use the SBM) offloading 50,000 tonnes of crude oil. (*Source*: Tanzania Harbours Authority, Dar es Salaam.)

most of the lighterage wharves), and miscellaneous bulk liquids are handled by pipelines at berth 11.

Facilities for the bulk handling of petroleum are available both within Dar es Salaam harbour and outside the harbour at Mjimwema Bay. The Kurasini oil jetty, located at the southern end of the deep-water berths in Southern Creek, has a minimum depth alongside of 10 m and can accommodate tankers not exceeding 20,000 dwt. Originally designed to receive refined products, the jetty has also served as a crude-oil terminal since the opening in 1966 of the TIPER oil refinery (Tanzanian and Italian Petroleum Company Ltd) on the Kigamboni peninsula between Southern Creek and the Indian Ocean; the jetty is linked to the refinery by a submarine pipeline. Increasing demands for oil in Tanzania and Zambia in the later 1960s emphasised the need for improved oil reception facilities. As a direct result of the Rhodesian unilateral declaration of independence in 1965 the traditional northward flow of oil supplies into Zambia was stopped, and since at that time road links between Tanzania and Zambia were unsatisfactory and rail links nonexistent, a pipeline from Dar es Salaam was introduced (Griffiths, 1969). Opened in 1968, the TAZAMA oil pipeline links the port with the Zambian copperbelt; originally used to transport oil products from the TIPER refinery, the pipeline now carries crude oil to the INDECO (Industrial Development Corporation) refinery at Ndola, Zambia, which was opened in 1973. At Dar es Salaam, the extension of deep-water berths and the physical limitations of the harbour underlined the practical and economic advantages to be gained by providing alternative crude oil reception facilities outside the harbour so that larger tankers could be used. A single buoy mooring (SBM) installation at Mjimwema Bay was introduced in 1973 and has provided a satisfactory solution to this problem (East African Harbours Corporation, 1971). The SBM installation is basically an offshore tanker berth which can be used in all but the most severe weather conditions; it is linked to the refinery by a submarine pipeline and by land pipelines, and is capable of accepting tankers of up to 100,000 dwt.

Port Installations at Tanga

Facilities at the port of Tanga are much more limited than at the two larger East African seaports. Basically, Tanga is equipped as a lighterage

PLATE 5.6. The port of Tanga: lighters and dhows may be seen near the lighterage quay; cargo vessels are being worked at anchor in the harbour. (*Source:* Author.)

port, as a result of restricted draught at all points near the shoreline. There are two lighterage quays (total length 381 m) with 9 lighter handling points; additional facilities include a passenger landing pier and a dhow wharf (Fig. 5.3). The inner harbour provides safe anchorages for six ocean-going vessels not exceeding 213 m in length and 9.4 m draught. Six further anchorages are available in the outer harbour for ships exceeding 9.4 m draught, the minimum depth at these anchorages being 13.7 m.

The port facilities are situated on the south side of Tanga Bay, immediately below the town. Six transit sheds and additional stacking areas are served by rail and road. Bulk oil products are received in coastal tankers from Dar es Salaam at a shallow mooring berth at the western end of the port and are discharged into storage tanks via a submarine pipeline. Lighterage is, of course, an awkward and time-consuming process, but since Tanga's main function remains the export of sisal fibre and coffee the delays and damage often associated with the lighterage process are less important than they might otherwise be. In 1982 the port had a fleet of 58 lighters.

In 1972 an important new installation came into service at Tanga in the form of a 700-m multipurpose jetty aligned north-eastwards off Ras Kazone and designed to receive bulk carriers up to 50,000 dwt. Developed under the auspices of the Tanzania National Development Corporation (NDC), the jetty is designed primarily to import raw materials in bulk

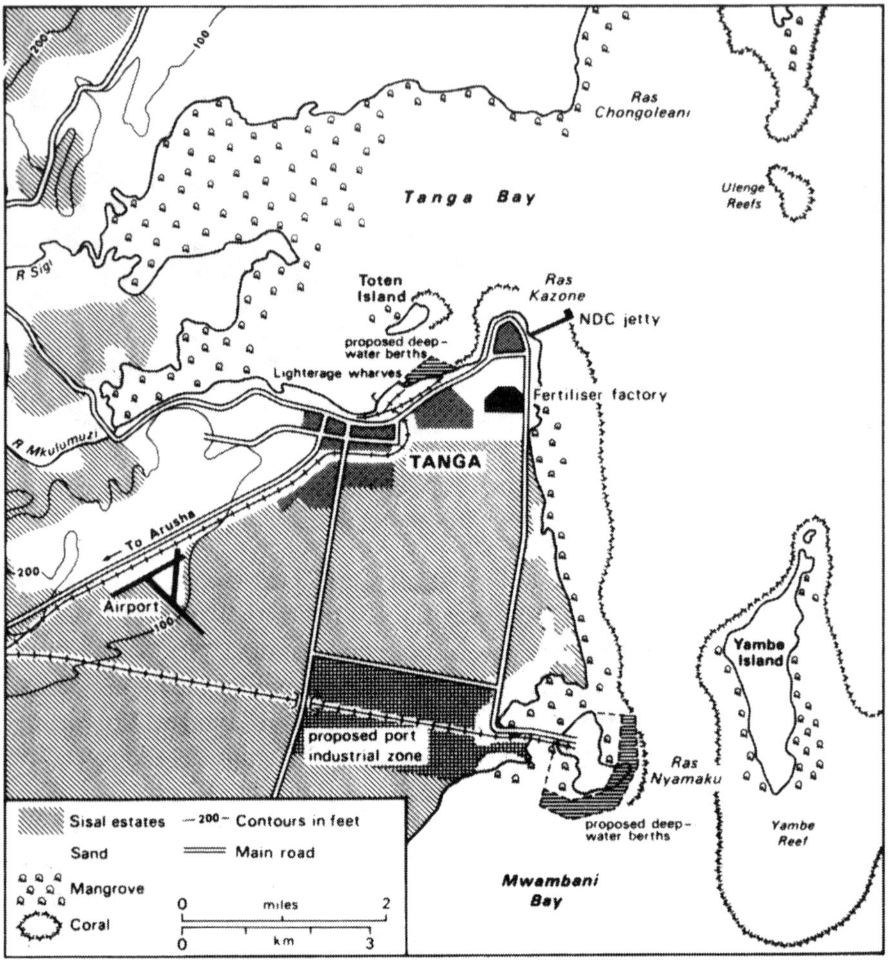

FIGURE 5.3. The port of Tanga. (*Sources:* Based on Admiralty Chart 663; DOS 1/50,000 series, sheet 130E/1; and data provided by the Tanzania Harbours Authority.)

(rock phosphate, sulphur, liquid ammonia) for the Tanzania Fertilizer Company's plant located about 1 km away. With a minimum depth alongside of 13.5 m, the jetty is Tanga's first specialised deep-water installation, and is capable of receiving vessels very much larger than the 20,000 dwt ships which normally call at the port. The fertilizer factory, which is also an NDC undertaking, produces mainly triple superphosphate.

Port Installations at Mtwara

At East Africa's most southerly ocean port of Mtwara, port facilities bear little relation to the extensive deep-water harbour that is available (Fig. 5.4). In spite of the sharp turn near the narrowest part of the entrance channel, Mtwara is able to accept ships of up to 175 m in length. The 380-m deep-water quay is located on the south side of the harbour, and provides two berths for deep-sea ships (minimum depth alongside -9.75 m) and a small berth reserved for coastal vessels. There are four transit sheds and additional stacking areas. Pipelines connecting the deep-water quay to an oil products depot and to bulk cement silos outside the port area allow these commodities to be discharged at the general cargo berths. There is also a small dhow and schooner jetty near the harbour entrance. The port is served by road transport facilities but rail services were withdrawn in 1963.

Port Installations at Zanzibar

Although the 1929 wharf at Zanzibar was originally conceived as a deep-water pier, the port remains essentially a lighterage port since neither the wharf itself nor the dredging alongside were ever completed to the original specifications. The main quay is 250 m long, and the depth alongside increases seawards to a maximum of about 5.5 m. Small coastal vessels may thus be brought alongside, but otherwise the wharf is used for the loading and unloading of lighters. Larger vessels anchor a short distance offshore, where there is adequate space in deeper water. The dhow wharf is 168 m long and the depth of water alongside rarely exceeds 3.3 m. The area of reclaimed land behind the two wharves is occupied by a number of transit sheds. Although the port of Zanzibar is not very well equipped, either in terms of the level and range of facilities or of the general standard of efficiency of port working, the port is nevertheless able to deal with the type and level of traffic that passes through it with a minimum of delay, so that there has been little incentive to improve facilities from this standpoint. The general level of mechanization is extremely low, and some mechanical appliances are badly in need of renewal; transport between quayside, transit shed and warehouse is partly by means of human effort, aided by the traditional 'hamali' carts, which are elongated four-wheeled

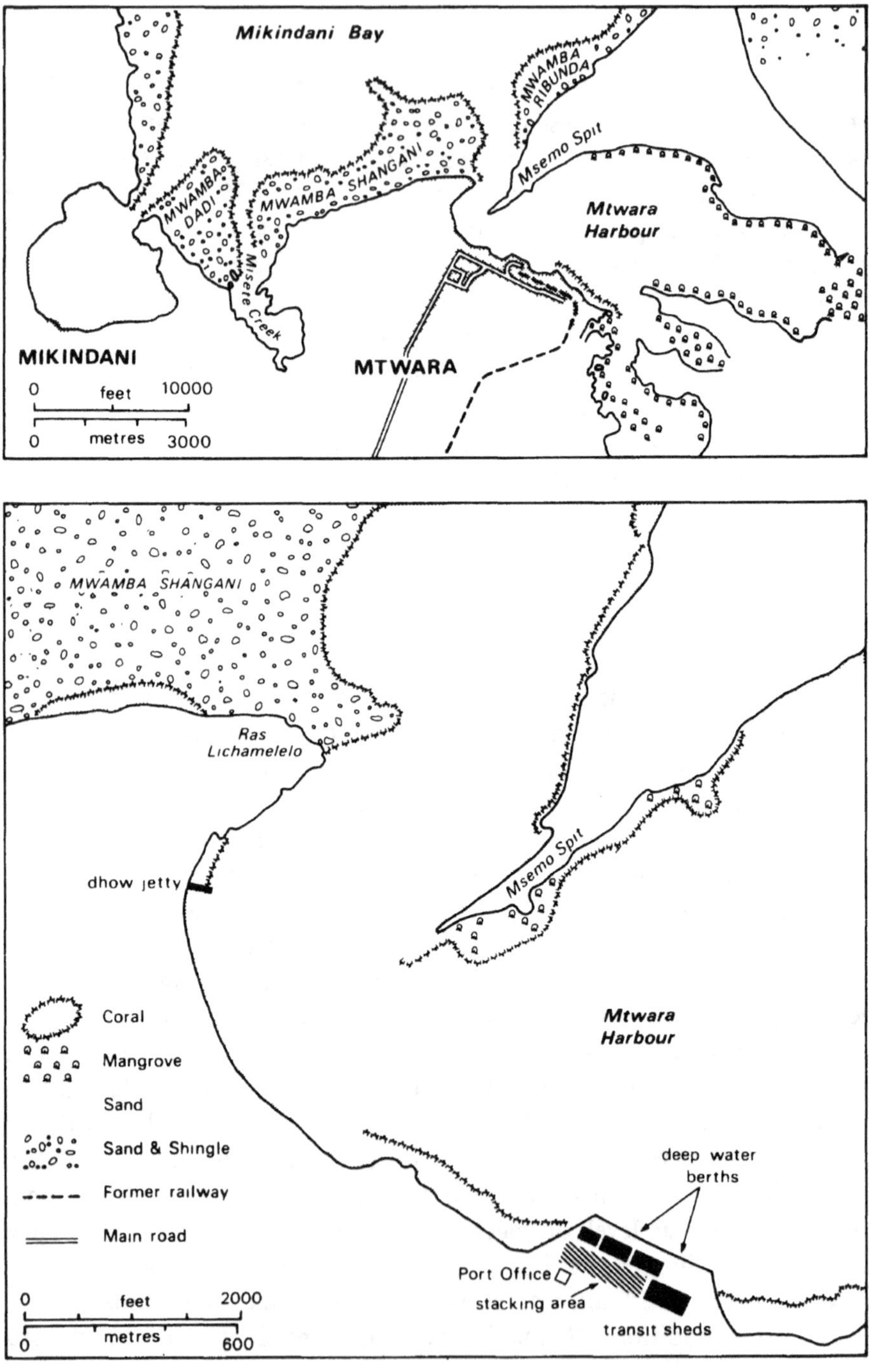

FIGURE 5.4. The port of Mtwara. (*Sources:* Based on Admiralty Charts 684 and 691, and data provided by the Tanzania Harbours Authority.)

trolleys capable of transporting up to a tonne load when propelled by four or five men. This traditional method of transport provides employment for a considerable number of people, and it is difficult to see how it could be completely replaced by a more efficient motorized system because of the location of many of the traders' warehouses within the 'stone town' where the streets are extremely narrow. Since the revolution of 1964, however, road haulage systems have been improved and the concentration of trading activity in the older part of the urban area of Zanzibar has been much reduced. In one sense, the port of Zanzibar is unsatisfactorily equipped in terms of the mechanization of equipment, but in another sense the port is overequipped for the handling of the amount of traffic that passes through it. The volume of traffic handled has not yet caught up with the facilities provided in 1929, and it is essentially the qualitative rather than the quantitative aspect of port facilities that is lacking. It is rare for a vessel to be kept waiting in the harbour before being worked; most vessels (other than dhows) calling at Zanzibar are worked in less than a day, partly because in many cases only a small proportion of their cargo is landed or shipped at the port.

Cargo Handling Appliances

A comparison of the level and range of equipment at the mainland seaports of East Africa in terms of cargo-handling appliances indicates again the very wide variation between the four centres. The variation in cranage capacity between the largest and the smallest ports is considerable, but the level and range of equipment at Dar es Salaam is now similar in this respect to that at Mombasa. The numbers of forklift trucks and other mechanical appliances, used for internal transfer work between quayside, transit shed and land transport systems, similarly varies within very wide limits. In general terms a high degree of mechanical working is in evidence, especially at Mombasa and Dar es Salaam; at Tanga all general cargo work is carried out by lighterage of vessels at anchor, and at Mtwara all ocean-going vessels are worked by ships' derricks, the port's mobile cranes being normally used only for coastal vessels.

The Problem of Port Congestion

The adequacy of the facilities provided by the seaports of East Africa in relation to the varied demands made upon them is a subject of continuous debate and frequent contention in the ports themselves and in the hinterlands. Smooth and efficient port operation always requires the co-ordination of numerous factors, including port administration, labour organisation, navigation and ship operation, and land transport integration. Whenever problems arise or inefficiency is allowed to develop in any one of these areas of activity, some degree of congestion at the quayside is a likely result; too frequently, however, the causes of congestion are attributed to the port administration, or to cargo-handling systems or labour problems, whereas in reality the causes of the difficulties may lie elsewhere.

In East Africa pressure upon port facilities has varied considerably over time, and varies also from port to port. Table 5.2 summarises the position in respect of average monthly occupancy rates at general-cargo berths at mainland seaports for the years 1971-75 and 1976-80, and illustrates the striking contrasts between the very high rates characteristic of the ports of Dar es Salaam and Mombasa and the much lower rates achieved at Tanga and Mtwara. It is rare for vessels to be kept waiting for a berth at Mtwara (Table 5.3) or for more than a few hours at Tanga. More serious delays have occured from time to time at the two larger ports, for a variety of reasons, but it should be remembered that part of the waiting time spent by a vessel outside the harbour is often at the ship's convenience rather than because a berth is not immediately available.

At Mombasa serious port congestion has arisen on several occasions as pressures on the port have increased in recent years. In the mid-1950s, for example, the average waiting and working days in port per ship were unacceptably high, and the opening of the Kipevu extensions in 1961 did little more than keep pace with traffic increases. In 1965-66, and again in 1973-74, there were periods of acute congestion when ships were kept waiting for several days, double berthing was quite frequent, and the transit sheds and storage areas were inadequate for the demands being made upon them. Fortunately, such periods of extreme pressure are normally relatively shortlived. They arise from a variety of causes, including the simultaneous arrival of an unusually large number of ships with heavy cargoes, the shortage of railway wagons and road vehicles for off-loading imported goods from the port, and the difficulties experienced by the port labour organisation in responding promptly and efficiently to a situation involving rapidly rising demands. Additional port labour is

TABLE 5.2
AVERAGE MONTHLY BERTH OCCUPANCY RATES AT EAST AFRICAN SEAPORTS, 1971–80

	Mombasa		Dar es Salaam		Tanga		Mtwara	
	1971–75	1976–80	1971–75	1976–80	1971–75	1976–80	1971–75	1976–80
January	92.0	85.6	100.0	99.3	42.7	75.6	31.3	29.2
February	87.7	81.0	99.4	100.0	42.1	80.9	38.6	28.4
March	86.8	87.1	98.6	100.0	78.2	70.8	32.7	39.7
April	89.5	87.3	99.3	100.0	52.0	84.3	35.4	23.0
May	90.9	90.7	99.5	99.7	50.7	80.0	36.5	16.1
June	93.1	84.7	97.3	100.0	48.2	68.3	41.0	30.6
July	92.3	75.2	88.7	99.9	57.3	56.8	27.9	38.8
August	89.1	78.6	96.1	99.9	40.3	49.3	30.2	33.4
September	91.1	76.6	97.3	100.0	48.2	49.6	31.0	19.0
October	88.8	76.1	99.4	99.9	47.8	64.6	39.5	30.5
November	86.8	83.7	96.8	99.9	51.2	64.5	32.0	29.4
December	88.2	83.9	96.6	100.0	46.1	72.3	32.3	41.7
Annual average:	89.7	82.5	97.4	99.9	50.4	68.1	34.0	30.0

(*Sources*: East African Harbours Corporation, Kenya Ports Authority and Tanzania Harbours Authority. Data for Mombasa refer to general cargo berths; those for specialised bulk cargo berths are normally rather lower.)

TABLE 5.3
AVERAGE DAYS IN PORT PER SHIP AT EAST AFRICAN SEAPORTS, 1960–81

	Mombasa		Dar es Salaam		Tanga		Mtwara	
	Waiting	Working	Waiting	Working	Waiting	Working	Waiting	Working
1961–65 Average	0.89	3.12	0.43	1.63	0.39	1.47	0.37	1.06
1966–70 Average	1.06	3.65	0.85	2.74	0.12	1.42	0.22	1.64
1971	1.76	4.18	1.88	5.18	0.13	1.92	0.00	2.28
1972	1.02	3.56	1.47	4.64	0.05	1.64	0.00	1.95
1973	2.27	4.45	1.03	4.99	0.09	2.00	0.10	3.10
1974	2.49	5.37	3.77	6.85	0.22	3.23	0.05	1.31
1975	0.10	3.29	1.09	5.59	0.27	3.41	0.00	2.81
1976	0.49	3.36	1.05	6.42	0.11	2.84	0.40	1.33
1977	1.31	3.73	2.18	7.64	1.60	2.40	0.73	1.59
1978	1.49	3.91	5.69	7.86	0.00	4.64	0.00	3.85
1979	0.59	3.89	1.61	6.89	0.00	5.00	0.00	2.14
1980	0.81	4.02	1.41	9.61	0.00	4.51	0.00	2.22
1981	0.82	3.54	1.14	7.12	0.00	3.95	0.00	1.92

(*Sources*: East African Railways and Harbours, *Annual reports* [for 1961–68]; East African Harbours Corporation, *Annual reports* [for 1969–74]; Kenya Ports Authority [for Mombasa, 1975–81]; and Tanzania Harbours Authority [for Tanzanian ports data, 1975–81].)

normally recruited as quickly as possible in such circumstances, but it has often been demonstrated that at Mombasa (as at all major ports) the margin of spare capacity over and above 'normal' working conditions is relatively small. A fundamental reason involved is, of course, the shortage of capital for port expansion schemes, together with the obvious dangers of overcapitalisation and high interest charges on external loan finance. The provision of adequate installations is, however, only one factor in the complex web of circumstances affecting cargo flows through a port, and the effects of congestion at the quayside spread far beyond the port itself. Whenever congestion occurs at a port for any length of time, conference lines are inclined to impose surcharges on freight rates, and the hidden costs of delays may be felt in innumerable ways throughout the hinterlands.

At Dar es Salaam there was a marked improvement in shipping turnround immediately following the opening of deep-water quays there in 1956, an event which relieved a considerable degree of congestion that had built up, and changed the character of the principal port operations at Dar es Salaam from lighterage to normal wharfage. At the time this development gave rise to the widespread opinion that the port was equipped with adequate facilities for handling the likely volume of traffic for a good many years to come. Ten years later, this optimistic opinion was no longer justified, and plans were announced for the extension of deep-water quayage. The rapidity of port extensions at Dar es Salaam during the 1965-75 decade, in part a direct reflection of the extension of the hinterland of the port to include Zambia, and in part a response to increasing demands upon the port from more traditional sources, has not solved the problem of congestion in the port as the data set out in Tables 5.2 and 5.3 amply demonstrate. Throughout the 1970s, berths in the port of Dar es Salaam were rarely unoccupied, the average waiting time never fell below 24 hours during this period (and reached unacceptably high levels in 1977-78), and the average working days per ship have continued to rise to very high levels, primarily as a result of low labour productivity in the port.

Pressures on facilities at the two smaller ports is not so marked. At Tanga, where sisal remained throughout the 1970s the principal export commodity handled, signs of congestion are relatively rare. This reflects the comparatively low level of total throughput, and the predominance of a few major export commodities, but may also result from the general situation of Tanga between the two larger East African terminals. In normal circumstances, that is when the Kenya/Tanzania boundary is open to normal commercial traffic, goods destined for the port of Tanga could without great difficulty be diverted through Dar es Salaam or Mombasa in the event of congestion developing at the northern Tanzanian port. Port growth and throughput at Tanga have clearly been affected in a variety of ways by the intermediate location of the port; the expansion of lighterage facilities at Tanga in 1954 took place at a time when port congestion at Mombasa was particularly severe, and one of the main factors stimulating the physical growth of Tanga was the function of the port as an overflow for Mombasa, a role which Tanga could perhaps fulfil more effectively today if political circumstances allowed. In the 1970s the possible expansion of Tanga has been discussed in the context of relieving pressures upon the port of Dar es Salaam. Attempts were made to divert traffic – particularly imports destined for Tanzania – from Dar es Salaam to Tanga, so that goods destined for Zambia, Zaire, Rwanda and Burundi could be more easily handled at the larger port. Much publicity surrounded the diversion to Tanga in 1973 of a Japanese vessel with a cargo of cement. Opposition from shipping concerns, and the inadequacy of road/rail networks in Tanga's hinterland, meant that the diversion scheme met with little success. It is possible, however, that in future Tanga will handle an increasing proportion of Tanzanian domestic imports and exports.

Mtwara, situated in the far south of Tanzania, is too far away from the main East African centres of export crop and mineral production to serve a similar function in relation to Dar es Salaam. Congestion has only very rarely made itself felt at Mtwara – the average berth occupancy rates (Table 5.2) are very low, and the average waiting days (Table 5.3) are negligible – and the port has fallen far short of fulfilling its originally planned function as a major groundnut exporting port. Delays have occasionally occurred at Mtwara, however, as a result of the traditionally highly seasonal character of the export traffic of the port. At the larger East African seaports, exports of certain major agricultural commodities are concentrated in certain seasons of the year, but export peaks tend to occur at different times so that seasonal congestion is to some extent avoided. At Mtwara, however, facilities are very limited and throughout the 1960s and early 1970s there was only one major export item – cashew nuts; exports took place mainly during the November-March period, and sometimes coincided with shipments of cassava and sisal. In the later 1970s exports of cashew nuts declined, and those of cassava increased, and any serious congestion is very unusual. During the greater part of the year, port facilities at Mtwara are definitely underutilised, and comparatively little traffic passes across the quays. The possibility of utilising the spare port capacity available at Mtwara to absorb some of the congestion experienced at Dar es Salaam – for example, by rerouting some Zambian traffic through the port – has been discussed on numerous occasions, but political circumstances and hinterland transport difficulties, together with the attitudes of ship operators, have to date prevented the implementation of any such schemes.

Port Development Plans

Port installations must be kept continuously under review, given that the *raison d'être* of a port is to provide an appropriate and efficient method of integrating land and maritime transport systems serving the economies of the hinterlands and forelands. As these systems and economies change, the installations and operational procedures of a port must respond in order to maintain and enhance the efficiency with which goods are transferred across the crucial land/maritime interface at the quayside. These considerations have become all the more important in the developing countries in recent years in the context of major changes in world trading patterns and in the technology of maritime transport. Seaports in all less-developed countries have been confronted, in particular, with the need to consider to what extent it is in their interest to participate in an innovation of global importance – the revolution in transport technology commonly symbolised by the term 'containerisation' (Hunter and Wilson, 1969; United Nations, 1970). World trends towards the increasing unitisation of cargo (Mayer, 1973), stimulated by the need to increase efficiency and keep down transport costs, have not left the less-developed countries unaffected, since all ports serve the same world fleet of shipping (or similar cross sections of it) and must attempt to provide at least a minimum range of similar facilities in order to attract traffic.

The continued expansion of the seaports of East Africa – especially the two larger ports – is essential to the growth of the national economies of Kenya, Tanzania and Uganda, and to the economic well-being of the neighbouring landlocked countries of Zambia, Rwanda and Burundi. Substantial growth of traffic during the 1960s – especially at Dar es Salaam and

Mombasa – led to the first Development Programme (1969-72) of the East African Harbours Corporation, and to physical expansion on the basis of World Bank loans. Traffic forecasts made for the period 1970-80 by the Economist Intelligence Unit (1970) formed the basis for the estimate of resources required during the period of the Corporation's second Development Programme (1972-76). The Programmes were designed essentially as outline structure plans, indicating the main areas for improvement and expansion and the probable cost, but retaining the necessary flexibility to respond to changing circumstances during the plan period. Part of the cost of implementing the second Development Programme (£24.5m) was covered by internal East African sources (£6m) but the Programme relied substantially upon long-term IBRD and other external loans amounting to £18.4m. Numerous studies have been made in order to arrive at a realistic appraisal of likely trends during the period from the mid-1970s to the end of the century; these have included investigations undertaken by the Economist Intelligence Unit and by private consultants; some of these reports are listed in the references at the end of this chapter (Bertlin and Partners, 1975, 1977 and 1979; Economist Intelligence Unit, 1981). In all cases the analyses included a wide variety of factors affecting port installations and throughput; traffic forecasting and the estimation of berth requirements is not, however, a particularly exact science. Data from these studies are not reproduced here in detail, but their main conclusion is reiterated: that pressure on facilities at Mombasa and Dar es Salaam will continue, and may increase substantially; further investment in facilities and in rehabilitation programmes is therefore necessary if the ports are to continue efficiently to meet an increasing variety of demands from their customers and if serious congestion is to be avoided in the future. Substantial increases in throughput are also forecast for the port of Tanga, raising again the question of whether deep-water general-cargo berths should be provided; but at Mtwara it appears that the existing deep-water berths will prove adequate for anticipated traffic levels for some considerable time to come.

The completion of deep-water berth extension programmes at Mombasa (to berth 18) and at Dar es Salaam (to berth 11) in the 1970s suggested that in both cases most of the obvious sites for port expansion had been taken up. At Mombasa consulting engineers have recommended that during the 1980s port development policies should focus upon the consolidation, redevelopment and rehabilitation of existing facilities rather than upon the extension of the port to new areas which would involve heavy capital investment in infrastructural provision. Traffic growth in the short term is likely to be matched by improved cargo-handling rates resulting from the adoption of more modern methods involving especially the development of bulk-cargo and containerisation facilities, so that major berth extensions are not likely to be needed before the 1990s. During the 1980s, however, it is planned to extend the bulk cargo-handling facilities at Mbaraki to provide for soda ash exports and coal imports, and to reserve adequate land areas for storage; to redevelop the north lighterage quay for small coastal and short-sea trading vessels, leaving only the south quay for lighterage operations; to undertake further dredging operations in the main harbour entrance and deep-water channel; and to improve the general layout of the port operational area behind the Kilindini deep-water berths. It is also recommended that berths 6 and 15 should be constructed; these were omitted in earlier expansion schemes because of difficult site conditions, resulting from the fact that both occur where small tributary valleys enter the main ria and offer very considerable thicknesses of clay and alluvia. The further development of the container terminal at berths 16-18 may involve a limited RO/RO facility immediately to the west of berth 18. In 1978 the estimated cost of these and related developments at Mombasa (including investigations for longer-term projects) was 715 million Kenya shillings (approximately £43 million), of which the estimated foreign element was 402 million shillings or £24 million.

Three main areas have been identified for port development at Mombasa in the period beyond the later 1980s: the northern shore of Port Reitz, west of the Kipevu oil terminal; the southern shore of Port Reitz, between Dongo Kundu and Mkunguni; and the southern side of the entrance to Kilindini Harbour, between the Likoni ferry and Mueza Creek. To the west of the Kipevu oil terminal, shallow water and the considerable thicknesses of silt and clay below the floor of the harbour largely preclude any further development of marginal deep-water quays, but a series of specialised T-head jetties more or less in line with the Kipevu oil terminal would be a practical possibility. On the south side of Port Reitz the deep-water channel runs close to the shoreline at Dongo Kundu, and between this point and the Kenya Navy jetty at Mkunguni there is an excellent site for a further series of deep-water berths; the plateau area behind the shore zone provides a possible zone for the development of a major maritime industrial complex in the longer term, and a site for a coal-fired power station has already been identified. The shoreline between Mkunguni and Mueza Creek is physically unsuited to berth construction, and much of the Mtongwe area is occupied by the naval base. Between Mueza Creek and the Likoni ferry, however, the waterfront offers a good site for future deep-water berth construction, although there are no plans to develop this area in the foreseeable future.

The future pattern of rail, road and pipeline communication in the port area itself and within the expanding cityport industrial complex as a whole requires further detailed consideration. Road links between Mombasa Island and the north mainland were greatly improved by the opening of a new bridge in 1980, and the possibility of building a high-level road bridge across Kilindini Harbour is under consideration. A road/rail crossing of Port Reitz from Ras Hodi to Dongo Kundu has also been proposed, but alternatives are being considered in case hydrological studies suggests that siltation problems may arise. Although the Kipevu and Shimanzi oil terminals are expected to serve adequately all anticipated requirements for many years to come, a potential site for an SBM has been identified at Tiwi (20 km south of Mombasa) suitable for handling tankers of 200,000 dwt and above. The further development of port facilities at Mombasa may also be influenced to some degree by the eventual outcome of proposals to construct a second deep-water port on the Kenya coast (Republic of Kenya, 1974 and 1979). This question is discussed in some detail in Chapter 8.

At Dar es Salaam the EAHC 1972-76 Development Programme provided for the completion of the deep-water quayage extensions up to and including berth 11; but the opening in 1975 of the TAZARA railway linking the port with the Zambian copperbelt, and increases in Tanzanian traffic, meant that the port operated under severe pressure throughout the decade. On the assumption that the construction of additional deep-water facilities will be economically justified in the future, several studies have analysed possible strategies and sites for development (Bertlin and Partners, 1975 and 1979). In 1975 it was recommended that the general cargo facilities in the port should be extended by the construction of two further deep-water berths (12-13); that a new oil jetty for smaller tankers should be built on the Kigamboni side of Southern Creek; that the entrance channel should be straightened and dredged to a depth of −10 m to allow the entry of larger and more modern vessels; and that cargo-handling operations within the port should be improved by the removal of most of the rail transport facilities and the construction of new rail depots outside the port area. It was suggested that container traffic, which was not expected to increase very rapidly, should be handled at berths 7-9 as demand required. The rehabilitation of the lighterage wharves and improvements in layout at berths 1-4 were also recommended, together with the reservation of extensive areas outside the harbour for longer-term developments. The main objective of this mid-1970s strategy was to restrict investment in the later 1970s and 1980s to the further development of traditional port facilities – additional general-cargo berths designed for break-bulk cargo handling, with only limited development of specialised bulk terminals – in order to maintain planning flexibility during the closing years of the century and beyond. In view of the very poor and rapidly deteriorating cargo-handling performance at Dar es Salaam in the 1970s, it was emphasised that unless every effort was made to implement these recommendations and to improve port efficiency by all possible means the inevitable results would include not only increased delays to shipping and severe congestion in the port but also the very high probability of substantial adverse effects on the economy of Tanzania and of other hinterland areas. The estimated costs of the developments recommended in 1975 were 342 million Tanzanian shillings (£23 m) of which the estimated external element was 222 million shillings (£15 m).

By 1979 the combined effects of several factors had made it clear that some revision of these development proposals was necessary, and modified recommendations were therefore drawn up (Bertlin and Partners, 1979). The political independence of Angola and Mozambique in 1975, and subsequent transport problems arising from border closures, tended to increase the flow of Zambian traffic through Dar es Salaam which for a time was the only seaport generally available to Zambia. Other factors, however, such as the disintegration of the East African Community in 1976, higher world oil prices from 1973 and the depressed world copper market from the mid-1970s, together with the failure of the TAZARA railway from 1975 to carry the expected traffic load due to operational difficulties, all tended to reduce the expected increases in cargo throughput at Dar es Salaam. Within this general context the most immediate factor affecting port development plans was, however, the unexpectedly rapid rise in the number of specialised container ships introduced in the UK/Europe-East Africa services. The consultant engineers therefore recommended that berths 12-13 should be built as a matter of urgency as specialised container berths, and not as break-bulk general-cargo berths as previously suggested. An additional berth 14 was also proposed, together with accommodation for deep-sea RO/RO services if required. Improvements to the entrance channel, and the development of special rail facilities by the TRC and by TAZARA, were considered essential in order to allow these extensions to yield maximum benefits. Development plans for the 1980s also include a bulk grain wharf at berth 11, and the construction of new warehouses and storage areas outside the port for extranational transit traffic which has for some years been a major cause of congestion in the port. The revised estimated costs of the implementation of these developments during the 1980s were calculated in 1979 as 904 million Tanzanian shillings (£60 million) of which the external component was calculated as 537 million shillings (£36 million).

The occupation of all the available deep-water sites on the western side of Southern Creek, the construction of a naval base on the eastern side, and the limitations of the harbour entrance in terms of restrictions on the size of vessels that can be accommodated, suggest that as far as the longer-term development of the port of Dar es Salaam is concerned attention should be directed to areas outside the harbour towards the south. Marginal deep-water quays along the eastern side of Southern Creek, and near the harbour entrance, have been considered; but these sites present serious disadvantages from several points of view. Outside the harbour entrance the most likely area for future development seems to be the water area lying south of the Makatumbe Islands and sheltered from the east by Kendwa Island (Hoyle, 1978). A reef linking Makatumbe and Kendwa could be exploited to provide protection from the east; an entrance channel would be established from the west. Very large volumes of dredging and reclamation would be involved. Further to the south-east, favourable sites for deep-water berths exist at Mbwamaji, adjoining Mjimwema Bay, where deep water is available with some natural protection from the Sinda Islands. It has been suggested that this area might be reserved for future use by large bulk carriers, such as might be required for coal exports or bauxite imports. Extensive reclamation works would, however, be required. Sites north of the present harbour entrance, for example at Msasani Bay and Kunduchi, are unlikely to be developed for port purposes in view of the cost and difficulty of providing land communications and the present and proposed extent of residential and tourist development.

The general trend of port development plans at Dar es Salaam is therefore not unlike that at Mombasa, and many factors affecting port expansion are common to these and other ports. Recent developments in maritime transport methods have provided a major turning point in the development strategies of the two ports, as on other occasions in the past. In both cases, too, the continued pattern and pace of port development is to some extent conditioned in the early 1980s by politico-economic conditions in areas beyond the national hinterlands: the rate of economic recovery in Uganda is an unknown element in the complex web of circumstances affecting the fortunes of Mombasa; similarly, the extent to which Zambia will continue to use the port of Dar es Salaam, in the context of an independent Zimbabwe, is in the longer run an unknown factor affecting the future of the port.

Proposals for the extension of facilities at the smaller ports of Tanga and Mtwara are more tentative. Issues affecting the future pattern and level of port throughout at Tanga include the economic prospects of the sisal industry, the relative success of local industrial development, and the degree to which the hinterland of the port is extended beyond north-eastern Tanzania. Proposals to extend the Tanga-Arusha railway to Musoma on Lake Victoria have been made, with a view to directing some Ugandan and Rwandan traffic through the port; but the economic arguments in favour of these proposals are not strong. Political considerations clearly favour an increased degree of diffusion of port activity along the East African coast; such policies would certainly benefit Tanga and Mtwara, as well as minor ports, but economic incentives clearly favour the established trend towards increasing concentration at the larger ports of Mombasa and Dar es Salaam. It seems likely that, given certain relatively inexpensive improvements, the lighterage facilities at Tanga will prove perfectly adequate to handle the port's forecast traffic through the 1980s and perhaps beyond, and no new berth construction is economically justified in the short term. The case for transforming Tanga into a deep-water port would become stronger if the throughput total were to exceed 500,000 tonnes. Should this traffic level materialise, it would be economically sensible to develop deep-water berths rather than to increase the lighterage capacity of the port. Two possible sites for deep-water berths have been identified at Tanga: inside the existing port area, three or four berths could be constructed on a line extending north-eastwards from the lighterage quays; outside the port area, some seven kilometres south of Ras Kazone, a site at Ras Nyamaku in Mwambani Bay would allow the eventual development of up to 12 deep-water berths. Arguments in favour of deep-water berths at Tanga would be strengthened if a policy of diverting traffic from Dar es Salaam were to be successfully implemented; such a policy would depend in turn upon improvements in the efficiency of railway services at Tanga. Other factors affecting the future pattern of port development at Tanga include the possibility of bulk mineral export traffic (such as soda ash from Lake Natron) which could conveniently be handled via a loading jetty at Mwambani Bay; and, more locally, the transfer of oil products imports to the NDC jetty.

There are no plans to expand or develop port facilities at Mtwara during the 1980s, since it is clear that the port has considerable reserve capacity. If throughput levels should increase during the present decade, more intensive use could be made of existing facilities by increasing labour inputs and by introducing lighterage operations. Factors likely to affect the level and pattern of port development at Mtwara in the future include the development of a modern road linking the port with Dar es Salaam; the efficiency of coastal shipping services; and the prosperity of agricultural development in the hinterland. All are somewhat uncertain, but in the 1990s and beyond some increase in berth capacity may be required. The construction of a separate oil jetty, and a separate wharf for coastal vessels, would relieve any pressure that might develop on the deep-water berths. Beyond this, there is plenty of scope within Mtwara harbour for the extension of the present deep-water quays in either direction, westwards or eastwards, should this ever become necessary.

Port Operations

The administration and operation of port services invariably reflect a wide variety of economic, political, social and technological factors; these in turn are related not only to the specific conditions within the port area itself but also to the wider framework provided by the national and international contexts within which port activities are set. The evolution of port services and the ways in which they are organised reflect the interaction of these various factors and frameworks over time and on a variety of scales. Changes in the administration of port services in East Africa, as the modern port hierarchy has developed, illustrate these points particularly well; for the twentieth-century growth of port activity along the coasts of

Kenya and Tanzania has not only reflected the emergence and character of the national economies of the hinterland, but has also provided a sensitive parameter of the rising and falling tides of closer geopolitical union within the area.

In 1948, under the East Africa High Commission (EAHC), the Kenya and Uganda railways and harbours were amalgamated with the Tanganyika railways and ports services to form the East African Railways and Harbours Administration (EARHA). The emergence of independent states in East Africa during the period 1961-64 witnessed a restructuring of the EAHC which became the East African Common Services Organisation (EACSO); the EARHA continued, however, to provide services throughout the mainland states. The formation of the East African Community (EAC) in 1967 involved a further rationalisation of the administration of transport services; the EARHA was divided into two separate organisations, the East African Railways Corporation (EARC) and the East African Harbours Corporation (EAHC). These two bodies, together with the East African Posts and Telecommunications Corporation (EAPTC) and the East African Airways Corporation (EAAC), were responsible to the EAC through its Communications Council.

The EAHC was the statutory port authority for all the mainland seaports of Kenya and Tanzania from 1969 to 1976; the headquarters of the Corporation, and the office of the Director General, were located in Dar es Salaam (whereas those of the EARC and the EAAC were in Nairobi, and those of the EAPTC in Kampala); the office of the Deputy Director General was in Mombasa, and each of the four mainland ports was under the immediate control of a port manager. This relatively shortlived administrative system did not survive the decline and eventual disintegration of the EAC, which effectively ceased to operate in 1976. In the following year, in line with the predominant devolutionary trend towards national successor organisations for all the central service functions of the former Community, the EAHC was effectively subdivided into two separate bodies: the Kenya Ports Authority (KPA) and the Tanzania Harbours Authority (THA), a development subsequently ratified by the Kenyan and Tanzanian governments in 1977/78. The headquarters of the KPA are in Mombasa, and those of the THA in Dar es Salaam; each Authority is responsible for port management, the construction and maintenance of port installations, the provision of shore equipment, and the operation of port services such as pilotage. The control of the KPA extends to minor Kenyan seaports such as Lamu and Malindi, and that of the THA includes Kilwa, Lindi and Mafia but not Zanzibar.

All cargo handling on shore and on ship at Mombasa is carried out on behalf of the KPA by its agents, Kenya Cargo Handling Services Ltd. (KCHS); in Tanzania, similar services are provided for the THA by its own Directorate of Operations. The two cargo-handling organisations are responsible, at Kenyan and Tanzanian seaports respectively, for stevedoring, shorehandling, lightering and miscellaneous services in connection with the loading and discharging of exports and imports. This system came into operation in 1976, as a consequence of the collapse of the EAC under which the East African Cargo Handling Services Ltd. (EACHS) operated as sole agents for the EAHC. The EACHS system came into operation in 1964 as a result of a major reorganisation of cargo-handling operations which is part of the essential background to the present situation. Before 1964, cargo handling at the four ocean ports had been divided between the two complementary services of stevedoring and shorehandling. These services were carried out by different organisations: stevedoring by four privately owned commercial firms, shorehandling by the Landing and Shipping Company of East Africa Ltd, in which the EARHA held a majority of shares.

In 1962, at a time when productivity was declining at all East African seaports, and when labour unrest was causing serious concern, it became increasingly obvious that this system was unsatisfactory and was not conducive to maximum efficiency in port operation. The government of Tanganyika thereupon engaged Dr. Amos Landman, manager of the port of Haifa, to examine the working of the existing system with special reference to Dar es Salaam, and to make recommendations for improvements. Dr. Landman's report (Landman, 1962), which in many respects was taken to refer to all the four mainland seaports, recommended that, in the interests of cargo handling and the rational use of costly equipment and labour, complete coordination of ship- and shore-working operations should henceforward be effected through the medium of a single operating company under the direct authority of the EARHA. The division of responsibility for stevedoring between four private firms had led to a marked loss in efficiency, adversely affecting the number of days spent in port per ship and the time taken to clear cargo through the ports. This move towards the rationalisation of port working was widely supported and was accepted by the three East African governments. The result was the formation on 1 January 1964 of a unified organisation, the East African Cargo Handling Services Ltd, in which all shares were held by the EARHA. All the employees of the Landing and Shipping Company of East Africa Ltd and of the four commercial companies were offered employment in the new company, which took over the shares and assets of the defunct companies at agreed valuation. When the EARHA was divided in 1969 and the EAHC took control of port operations, a new agreement was signed between the port administration and the cargo-handling company; this was superseded in 1972 by a further agreement designed to cover the period 1972-76. The EAHC held a majority of EACHS shares; approximately 17 per cent were held by the EARC. The subdivision of the EAHC into the KPA and the THA in 1976 resulted in similar arrangements: in Kenya, 95 per cent of KCHS shares are held by the KPA, 4 per cent by the Kenya Railways Corporation and 1 per cent by the Kenya Ministry of Transport and Communications; in Tanzania the cargo-handling services form an integral part of the THA.

Employment

The East African port industry depends essentially upon its manpower resources, and the structure and organisation of port labour is a matter of considerable social and political as well as economic importance. Table 5.4 presents a statement of the numbers of persons employed in the four major mainland seaports by the Kenyan and Tanzanian port authorities and their respective cargo-handling agents, at the end of 1981. Overall employment in the ports exceeds 30,000, of whom 40 per cent work in Mombasa and a further 50 per cent in Dar es Salaam; the two smaller ports of Tanga and Mtwara employ only 8 per cent and 2 per cent respectively of the employees listed. About 38 per cent of those employed comprise the manual labour force, but not all of these are classified as permanent full-time employees. In Tanzania some 40 per cent of the manual labour is registered to cover seasonal requirements.

There have traditionally been some important differences between the four ports, and between Kenya and Tanzania, in terms of the categories of manual labour employed. During the 1960s there was a tendency to favour weekly-paid rather than monthly-paid manual labour, but this is no longer the case. At Mombasa the monthly- and weekly-paid manual grades have

TABLE 5.4
EMPLOYMENT IN THE SEAPORTS OF EAST AFRICA, 1981

	Mombasa	Dar es Salaam	Tanga	Mtwara	Total Tanzania	Total
KPA/THA						
Management	269	242	34	29	305	574
Operations	1,137	6,474	925	233	7,632	8,769
Engineering	1,901	1,256	247	60	1,563	3,464
Finance	335	252	85	24	361	696
Planning	16	17	–	–	17	33
Personnel/misc.	328	725	171	40	936	1,264
	3,986	8,966	1,462	386	10,814	14,800
KCHS/THA (Directorate of Operations)						
Management	173	42	7	1	50	223
Supervisory	524	420	18	5	443	967
Clerical	2,671	621	95	33	749	3,420
Manual	5,391	5,391	805	194	6,390	11,781
	8,759	6,474	925	233	7,632	16,391
Total	12,745	15,440	2,387	619	18,446	31,191

(*Sources*: Kenya Ports Authority [KPA], Tanzania Harbours Authority [THA] and Kenya Cargo Handling Services Ltd [KCHS].

long formed the essential permanent labour force, and the number of casual weekly-paid workers employed was always relatively small. In the Tanzanian ports, in contrast, all manual labour was either monthly-paid on a permanent basis or daily-paid on a casual basis, and at Dar es Salaam the number of casual workers was generally much higher than at Mombasa. At Tanga it was the normal practice for many years to employ only permanent manual workers, whereas at Mtwara the number of casual workers employed during the year normally exceeded the number of permanent manual workers, reflecting the highly seasonal character of traffic through the port. In 1973 an attempt was made to reduce these irregularities, and a central negotiating council was established with the specific aim of standardising all wages and conditions of employment throughout all branches of the EACHS. The result is that today, under the bipartite system introduced in 1976, all casual employment in Tanzanian seaports has ceased, and at all four mainland ports all port workers are now either monthly-paid on a permanent basis or are held on a weekly register (with a minimum weekly guaranteed wage) to cover seasonal requirements.

Detailed aspects of labour organisation in East Africa lie outside the scope of this volume, but the importance of trade union activity as an integral part of the socioeconomic and political structure of the port industry requires emphasis. In Kenya, the Mombasa Dockworkers' Union is one of many trade unions which belong to the Central Organisation of Trade Unions (COTU) at the national level. The equivalent body in Tanzania is the Jumuia ya Wafanyakazi Tanzania (JUWATA) or Union of Tanzania Workers which absorbed the former Dockworkers and Stevedores Union in 1964. The two unions, COTU and JUWATA, are involved in industrial relations with the port and cargo-handling authorities, subject to the national laws of the two countries concerned. The present system is the outcome of protracted and complex labour movements in both countries during the post-1946 period – although the roots of self-concious unity amongst port workers have been traced to the 1930s in both Tanzania and Kenya (Iliffe, 1970). During the 1950s the group consciousness of the port workers was directed primarily against the colonial system; the Mombasa strike of March 1955 marked a significant move forward in the growth of trade unionism, and consolidation and interterritorial association between the Mombasa and Tanganyika dockworkers' unions led to joint wage demands. By 1959 it was recorded that "the upsurge of the trade union movement . . . has been maintained, and it is now vying for pride of place with the nationalist movement" (Landing and Shipping Company of East Africa, 1960, 4). The strength of the trade unions in the port industry, and in East Africa more generally, was a basic factor in the formation of the EACHS in 1964 and in the consequent exclusion of private enterprise from the seaports of East Africa. In recent years there has been a certain degree of interstate competition between the unions in questions involving wage settlements, but an interstate joint industrial council achieved some degree of standardisation of wages and conditions of employment in the mid-1970s. A basic problem in this context arises from the contrasting politico-economic philosophies and development patterns of Kenya and Tanzania; in the field of industrial relations a desirable objective in one country may be totally unacceptable – or even contrary to national law – in the other.

Productivity in the Port Industry

A good deal of attention is devoted in the port industry to ways of measuring and assessing productivity, as a means of demonstrating the degree of efficiency with which the capacity of the ports is being utilised. Questions of port capacity, efficiency and productivity are difficult to define precisely, since all three terms are essentially arbitrary. Capacity is assessed in terms of the tonnage of goods that a port may be realistically expected to handle in a year, given the known circumstances of installations, labour conditions and methods of working. Efficiency is a concept in which the volume and cost of port throughput are set against productive resources of labour, land, capital and technical equipment. Measures of productivity are designed to describe aspects of port efficiency, but by their nature they can only be partial and selective. No accurate, realistic and comprehensive measure of port productivity is practicable, in view of the very wide range of factors affecting port throughput, many of which lie quite outside the control of the port and cargo-handling authorities. Various measures are commonly employed, however, and all seek to relate port throughout to one or more of the factors involved. These factors include basic variables – technological conditions, management systems, capital resources, and labour relations – and a number of less predictable but nevertheless crucial influences, including the late arrival of ships, land transport problems and heavy rain.

Basic data describing the volume of cargo handled at a port, or the average number of days required to work a ship, are not in themselves measures of port productivity. Port installations may be underused, even if total throughput is high, resulting in low efficiency; and ships of varying size obviously load or discharge varying proportions of their cargo at a given port. A measure of productivity which, to a large extent, successfully ignores these defects is that which describes variations in tonnages handled per ship working day (Table 5.5). Rates achieved at Mombasa are substantially higher than at Dar es Salaam, and the continued reliance upon lighterage tends to depress the rates at Tanga. At the larger ports one of the most potent factors affecting throughput per ship working day is the weather. During the early part of the year, especially the period March-May and again at the end of the year (October-December), the coastlands of East Africa experience heavy rainfall which frequently interferes considerably with ship working. Conversely, the peak rates achieved in the

TABLE 5.5
CARGO THROUGHPUT PER SHIP WORKING DAY AT EAST AFRICAN SEAPORTS, 1971–81*

	Mombasa	Dar es Salaam	Tanga	Mtwara
1971	504	404	376	394
1972	540	424	389	502
1973	537	404	388	605
1974	483	404	336	685
1975	531	456	327	704
1976	543	454	308	678
1977	487	421	251	778
1978	500	452	254	605
1979	555	411	270	530
1980	669	425	320	623
1981	768	487	337	604

(*Sources*: Kenya Ports Authority [for Mombasa] and Tanzania Harbours Authority [for Tanzanian ports].)
*In deadweight tonnes.

third quarter of the year represent better working conditions during the cool dry season.

Port productivity may also be measured in terms of throughput per gang/shift, which relates tonnages handled to hours worked by a known number of workers, given the facilities and equipment of the port. Average annual data for 1975-81 are set out in Table 5.6. Given increased tonnages

TABLE 5.6
AVERAGE CARGO THROUGHPUT PER GANG/SHIFT AT EAST AFRICAN SEAPORTS, 1975–81*

	Mombasa	Dar es Salaam	Tanga	Mtwara
1975	46.5	65.0	57.9	115.4
1976	50.0	69.3	57.1	106.8
1977	50.5	53.7	56.3	108.7
1978	56.7	48.3	60.7	100.3
1979	69.0	48.5	54.0	79.8
1980	98.3	57.7	59.9	74.6
1981	102.2	62.3	58.7	74.0

(*Sources*: Kenya Ports Authority [for Mombasa] and Tanzania Harbours Authority [for Tanzanian ports].)
*In deadweight tonnes.

handled, static or rising throughput data per man/shift obviously imply an increased labour force. Considerable caution is required when attempting to interpret these data, however, since rates depend not only upon working conditions and the type of cargo handled but also upon a variety of social factors (health, temperament, attitudes to work) that affect the efficiency of an individual worker. These various measures of port productivity have their individual merits and imperfections, and it may be argued that an index attempting to relate throughput to total costs of operation might prove to be a more realistic economic assessment. The KCHS appear to favour throughput per gang/shift as the most useful measure generally available, since it is used as the basis for the monthly net productivity index (Table 5.7). This shows, for Mombasa only, the monthly tonnage handled per gang/shift as a percentage of the tonnage handled per gang/shift during the equivalent month of 1960. Equivalent data for Tanzanian ports are not available.

Whatever measures of productivity are employed, it is generally accepted that cargo-handling rates at East African seaports are low by world standards, especially in terms of exports. Data for other tropical African seaports frequently reveal handling rates two or three times higher for exports, and significantly higher for imports, than those for Mombasa and Dar es Salaam. One reason for this situation is that some other ports handle larger volumes of homogeneous export cargo, but this can only be a partial explanation of an unsatisfactory situation. Significant improvements in productivity have already become apparent at Mombasa and may be expected elsewhere as port installations are modernised and as technical innovations in cargo-handling methods are introduced; the importance of staff training and retraining schemes at all levels is, however, an extremely important aspect of port development strategy in this context (United Nations Development Programme, 1972). The establishment of a Port Management Association for Eastern Africa in 1973 (United Nations Economic Commission for Africa, 1974) was designed to facilitate multinational cooperation in this field by setting up permanent machinery for discussion and improvement of port management techniques. In a more local context, the inauguration at Mombasa in 1980 of Bandari College as a training centre for KPA and KCHS staff is clearly a development of considerable significance likely to yield far-reaching benefits in the future. A similar institution, also known as Bandari College, was opened at Dar es Salaam in 1982. The colleges function as regional training centres for

TABLE 5.7
MOMBASA: MONTHLY NET PRODUCTIVITY INDEX,* 1972–80

	1972	1973	1974	1975	1976	1977	1978	1979	1980
January	129	126	124	121	116	124	142	111	150
February	110	110	114	111	111	131	157	96	149
March	135	111	111	106	122	123	153	110	135
April	110	109	114	106	129	132	152	123	179
May	119	111	104	106	127	133	148	121	172
June	115	117	106	106	125	135	119	111	156
July	115	143	111	107	126	133	134	115	161
August	125	103	121	109	123	133	110	92	139
September	114	103	114	110	120	132	169	122	162
October	109	118	112	109	121	133	109	121	142
November	104	127	104	108	121	135	104	123	128
December	126	116	108	110	123	138	124	173	114
Annual average	118	124	112	110	122	132	135	118	149

(*Source*: Kenya Cargo Handling Services Ltd.)

*The productivity index is derived by dividing the monthly revenue tonnage by the total net gang/shifts worked; the year 1960 is used as a base of 100. Thus the productivity index $= \frac{100x}{y}$ where x equals the tonnage handled per gang/shift during the month in question, and y equals the tonnage handled per gang/shift during the equivalent month of 1960.

the countries of East and Central Africa, and conduct international courses with the help of UNCTAD and other UN agencies.

REFERENCES

Bertlin and Partners, in association with the Economist Intelligence Unit (1975), *Dar es Salaam port development study: final report* (London, 4 vols., prepared for the IBRD and the EAHC).

Bertlin and Partners, in association with the Economist Intelligence Unit (1977), *East African ports development study: final report* (London, 5 vols., prepared for the IBRD and the EAHC).

Bertlin and Partners, in association with the Economist Intelligence Unit (1979), *Review of Dar es Salaam port development study* (London, 3 vols., prepared for the THA).

Bird, J.H. (1971), *Seaports and seaport terminals* (London, Hutchinson).

East African Cargo Handling Services Ltd, *General Manager's report for 1969, eq seq.* (Mombasa, annually to 1973).

East African Harbours Corporation (1970), *Annual report and accounts for the period 1 June to 31 December 1969* (Dar es Salaam).

East African Harbours Corporation, *Annual report and accounts for the year ending 31 December 1970, et seq.* (Dar es Salaam, annually to 1974).

East African Harbours Corporation (1969), *Development programme, 1969-72* (Dar es Salaam).

East African Harbours Corporation (1971), *Report on single buoy mooring for oil tankers and ancillary services at Mjimwema Bay, Dar es Salaam* (London: Rendel, Palmer and Tritton).

East African Harbours Corporation (1972), *Development programme, 1972-76* (Dar es Salaam).

Economist Intelligence Unit (1970), *East Africa transport study* (London, 10 vols.).

Economist Intelligence Unit (1981), *Traffic survey and forecast 1980-2000, prepared for the Kenya Ports Authority, final report* (London).

Griffiths, I.L. (1969), 'The Tazama oil pipeline,' *Geography* 54, 214-217.

Hilling, D. (1973), 'Container potential of West African ports,' in B.S. Hoyle (ed.), *Transport and development* (London, Macmillan), 151-166.

Hoyle, B.S. (1978), 'African politics and port expansion at Dar es Salaam,' *Geographical Review* 68, 31-50.

Hunter, E. and T.B. Wilson (1969), 'The increasing size of tankers, bulk carriers and containerships with some implications for port facilities,' *Research and Technical Bulletin* 5, 186-224 (London, National Ports Council).

Iliffe, J. (1970), 'A history of the dockworkers of Dar es Salaam,' *Tanzania Notes and Records* 71, 119-148.

Kenya Ports Authority (1977), *Development plan, 1977-83* (Mombasa).

Kenya Ports Authority, *Annual bulletin of port statistics, 1978, et seq.* (Mombasa, annually).

Kenya Ports Authority, *Annual report and accounts for the period 1 January to 31 December 1978, et seq.* (Mombasa, annually).

Landman, A. (1962), *Report on the port of Dar es Salaam* (Haifa).

Mayer, H.M. (1973), 'Some geographic aspects of technological change in maritime transportation,' *Economic Geography* 49, 145-155.

Mkinga, J.O. (1981), *Prospects and problems of transit ports: a study of the port of Dar es Salaam* (Cardiff, University of Wales Institute of Science and Technology, Department of Maritime Studies, unpublished dissertation for the Diploma in Port and Shipping Administration).

Landing and Shipping Company of East Africa (1960), *General Manager's annual report, 1959* (Mombasa).

Republic of Kenya (1974), *Development plan, 1974-78* (Nairobi, Government Printer).

Republic of Kenya (1979), *Development plan, 1979-83* (Nairobi, Government Printer).

Tanzania Harbours Authority (1978), *Revised ports development programme, 1978-82* (Dar es Salaam).

United Nations Conference on Trade and Development (1969), *Development of ports: improvement of port operations and connected facilities* (New York, TD/B/C.4/42/Rev.1).

United Nations Department of Economic and Social Affairs (1970), *Containers, pallets and other unitized methods for the intermodal movement of freight: application to developing countries* (New York).

United Nations Development Programme (1972), *Management's role in promoting productivity in the East African Community and the East African Corporations* (East African Community Project: Report of the 3rd Senior Executive Seminar, Arusha).

United Nations Economic Commission for Africa (1974), *Final report of the port management conference, Eastern Africa, Mombasa 1973* (Addis Ababa).

6 Seaport Throughput

The essential function of a port is to facilitate two-way cargo flows between land and water-borne transport systems. Port throughput is thus a measure of the functions and relative importance of a port, and a reflection of the combined effect of the various factors influencing port operation. The analysis and explanation of port throughput data are therefore not merely exercises in statistical description, but involve widespread reference to many factors operating at various scales over time and area. Just as a port, by definition, stands as a node in a complex web of transport links, so also port throughput represents in summary form the overall trading conditions in the areas served. Many approaches to the analysis of port throughput are of course possible, depending upon the objectives involved and upon data availability; the interests of port management in the operational and financial implications of throughput characteristics and trends are not necessarily the same as those of port labour organisations or of port users. All who are involved in the provision, operation and use of port facilities nevertheless share a common interest in the attraction, retention and structure of port traffic and in the effects and interaction of factors affecting its development. The explanation of throughput patterns at individual ports in less-developed countries presents a complex variety of questions and problems; but in this context as in others it is more profitable to consider the interactive factors and interrelated patterns within a national or international port complex rather than to focus exclusively upon individual terminals. In this chapter, data from the four mainland ocean ports of Kenya and Tanzania are used to illustrate the patterns of cargo flow that characterise Third World seaports; emphasis is placed on ways in which port throughput is a sensitive parameter of the economic geography of the hinterland areas as a whole. More generally, however, East Africa is used as a case-study area through which the problems associated with traffic flows across the waterfronts of the less-developed countries may be considered in a wider perspective.

Ship Arrivals

The number and net registered tonnage of ships entering the four major mainland ports of East Africa from 1960 to 1981 are indicated in Table 6.1. In general, the data for Mombasa and Dar es Salaam show that the increases in the number and tonnage of ships handled in the 1960s were not maintained in the 1970s, and that there has been a tendency for the number of ships entering these ports to decline. At Tanga and Mtwara there has been a more substantial reduction during the 1970s in both the number and the NRT of ships entering these ports as compared with the levels experienced during the previous decade. There is obviously a wide variation in the level of shipping activity between the four ports, but these contrasts are less marked than those between the corresponding cargo throughput data; in 1981, for example, Mombasa recorded 53.4 per cent of the number and 58.4 per cent of the NRT of ship arrivals at the four East African ocean ports, but in the same year handled 69.0 per cent of the total cargo throughput. One factor in this situation is that the same ships frequently call at several individual ports in the complex but tend to land or ship a greater proportion of their cargo at the larger terminals. It is also important to note that a declining, steady or only slightly rising number of ship arrivals does not necessarily indicate a lack of progressive trading activity, but may primarily reflect increases in average ship size and economies in sea freight movements.

Shipping services to the seaports of Kenya and Tanzania are still largely based on the concept of the cargo liner carrying break-bulk cargo, a concept which is becoming increasingly outmoded on most of the important searoutes as the global container network becomes more extensive. In recent years the seaports of many less-developed countries, including those of East Africa, have been substantially affected by these trends, and sharp rises in container traffic handled at the larger ports have been experienced as a result.

Data relating to the nationality of registration of ships entering the ports of Kenya and Tanzania are not given here in detail, but it is worth noting that an important place is still occupied by shipping of British registration, although in both absolute and relative terms the British component appears to be declining. The continued importance of British shipping at East African seaports is partly a reflection of Britain's past and present economic and political interests in East Africa, but relates also in

TABLE 6.1
NUMBER AND NET REGISTERED TONNAGE* OF SHIPS ENTERING EAST AFRICAN SEAPORTS, 1960–81

Year	Mombasa		Dar es Salaam		Tanga		Mtwara	
	No.	NRT	No.	NRT	No.	NRT	No.	NRT
1960–69 average	1,632	5,776	1,046	3,606	564	1,989	194	557
1970	2,011	7,288	999	3,310	503	1,902	149	389
1971	1,844	7,295	997	3,330	376	1,584	143	335
1972	1,904	7,189	1,031	3,676	450	1,630	185	408
1973	1,801	7,070	991	3,687	379	1,492	185	311
1974	1,699	6,582	965	3,362	357	1,388	190	293
1975	1,563	6,191	1,017	3,835	379	1,505	198	255
1976	1,282	5,570	1,033	4,164	390	1,619	163	223
1977	1,447	5,770	1,077	4,244	407	1,698	124	222
1978	1,597	6,298	957	3,887	417	1,856	105	235
1979	1,493	5,933	850	3,651	327	1,517	121	234
1970–79 average	1,664	6,519	992	3,715	399	1,619	171	291
1980	1,449	6,511	880	3,719	298	1,399	118	226
1981	1,391	6,525	802	3,233	302	1,179	109	229

Sources: East African Harbours Corporation, Kenya Ports Authority, Tanzania Harbours Authority.

*NRT data are given in thousand tonnes.

general terms to the strength of the British merchant marine on the world seas. The importance of shipping of Liberian, Greek and Dutch registration is of course a direct outcome of the substantially increased oil traffic handled in recent years. Shipping of other European nationalities remains important, whilst that associated with India, Japan and other Asian countries is also significant. Ship arrivals of Kenyan and Tanzanian nationality are quite numerous, but constitute only a small proportion of the total net registered tonnage. The East Africa National Shipping Line, formerly owned by the governments of Kenya, Tanzania, Zambia and Uganda, was disbanded in 1980; national shipping lines in Tanzania and in Kenya are in course of development.

Total Cargo Throughput

General aspects of the total cargo throughput at the major seaports of Kenya and Tanzania are represented in Tables 6.2 and 6.3. The most important feature is the rapid overall traffic growth achieved in recent years: during the years 1960-69 the total cargo throughput at the four major

TABLE 6.2
TOTAL CARGO THROUGHPUT AT EAST AFRICAN SEAPORTS, 1976–81*

	1976	1977	1978	1979	1980	1981
Exports						
Dry general cargo	2,329	2,090	2,014	2,031	1,751	1,664
Dry bulk cargo	603	686	656	590	574	748
Bulk liquids	671	698	477	625	795	1,393
Total	3,603	3,474	3,148	3,247	3,120	3,805
Imports						
Dry general cargo	2,030	2,638	2,656	1,941	2,703	2,500
Dry bulk cargo	189	216	283	193	729	778
Bulk liquids	4,838	4,555	4,692	4,396	5,213	5,145
Total	7,056	7,410	7,631	6,530	8,646	8,423
Total throughput†	10,670	10,895	10,786	9,783	11,774	12,234

Sources: Calculated from data provided by the Kenya Ports Authority and the Tanzania Harbours Authority.
* '000 dwt.
† Including transhipment.

mainland ports increased by 107.9 per cent, and during the years 1970-79 by a further 12.6 per cent. A large part of this increase is accounted for by growth of bulk oil flows, especially crude oil imports; increases in bulk cargo exports have also been important at the two larger ports; but the growth of break-bulk exports and imports has not generally been so marked. The data re-emphasise the predominance of Mombasa within the East African port complex: Table 6.3 sets out the total cargo throughput at each of the four principal seaports for the years 1960-81 as a percentage of the throughput of the port group as a whole. The proportion handled at Mombasa has never fallen below 54 per cent of the total during the period under review, and has risen to over 78 per cent, whilst in contrast that at Dar es Salaam has varied between 16 per cent and 41 per cent. The consistent 70 per cent/20 per cent balance maintained by Mombasa and Dar es Salaam during the earlier part of the period included in the table (1960-62) was temporarily disrupted by the introduction of crude oil imports at Mombasa in 1963 to serve the EAOR refinery at Changamwe; but the subsequent growth of crude oil imports at Dar es Salaam (for the TIPER refinery at Kigamboni and for the Zambian INDECO refinery at Ndola), together with the introduction of Zambian copper exports, have increased significantly the proportion of the total throughput of the port group now handled at Dar es Salaam, whilst tending to reduce the proportion passing through Mombasa. Nevertheless, Mombasa and Dar es Salaam together handle about 95 per cent of the total throughput of the East African mainland port group, and the pressures resulting from these disparities have inevitably caused serious problems. The two larger seaports contrast even more strikingly with the smaller seaports at Tanga and Mtwara, which together have not handled more than 10 per cent of the total throughput of the port group in any year since 1956, and from 1965 onwards their combined share of the total has been less than 6 per cent. In spite of significant percentage increases in throughput at both the smaller ports, the level of operation there remains low and the contribution made by Tanga and Mtwara to East African overseas trade is essentially very modest.

In the case of Mombasa these facts and figures represent the relatively advanced level of development achieved within many areas of the hinterland of the port. The level of development within the hinterland of the port of Dar es Salaam is generally much lower, but recent changes (notably the extension of the hinterland of the port to include parts of Zambia)

TABLE 6.3
PERCENTAGE OF TOTAL CARGO THROUGHPUT AT EAST AFRICAN MAINLAND SEAPORTS HANDLED AT INDIVIDUAL PORTS, 1960–81

	x_1 Mombasa	x_2 Dar es Salaam	$x_1 + x_2$	x_3 Tanga	x_4 Mtwara	PC Index
1960	69.8	21.9	91.7	5.2	3.1	73.41
1961	71.8	19.3	91.1	5.9	3.0	74.64
1962	71.6	20.0	91.6	5.4	3.0	74.60
1963	73.9	18.6	92.5	4.8	2.7	76.40
1964	77.3	16.0	93.3	4.2	2.5	79.09
1965	78.1	16.0	94.1	3.7	2.3	79.75
1966	74.2	20.5	94.7	3.4	1.9	76.99
1967	68.8	25.7	94.5	3.4	2.1	73.62
1968	68.3	26.5	94.8	3.1	2.2	73.36
1969	67.5	27.6	95.1	3.0	1.9	73.01
1970	66.9	28.4	95.3	3.1	1.5	72.77
1971	66.2	29.0	95.2	3.0	1.7	72.36
1972	62.3	32.9	95.2	2.7	2.0	70.53
1973	64.7	30.9	95.6	2.7	1.6	71.77
1974	61.4	33.2	94.6	3.6	1.8	69.91
1975	57.7	37.0	94.7	3.6	1.7	68.64
1976	55.2	40.0	95.2	3.3	1.6	68.27
1977	54.4	41.1	95.5	3.0	1.5	68.26
1978	56.3	38.4	94.7	3.7	1.5	68.28
1979	60.7	34.5	95.2	3.7	1.1	69.92
1980	63.8	31.9	95.7	3.3	1.0	71.41
1981	69.0	27.5	96.4	2.6	0.9	74.29

(*Sources*: Calculated from EARHA, *Annual reports*, 1960–68; EARH, *Annual reports*, 1969–73; KPA, *Annual reports*, 1974–80; and from data provided by the KPA and the THA.)

have considerably reduced the disparity between the two larger seaports. At Tanga the low level of traffic handled is directly related to the location of the port midway between the two larger centres; this aspect of the situation of the port, which implies limited hinterland growth, has traditionally restricted the activities of the port considerably. The small amount of traffic handled at Mtwara is not, of course, a reflection of inadequate or unsatisfactory site conditions, but rather of the low level of economic development attained in a hinterland served only by a limited transport network.

Another point of general interest is that at Mombasa and Dar es Salaam the volume of import cargo throughput far exceeds the volume of export cargo throughput, chiefly because of the large quantities of crude oil imported at these ports. If bulk oils are disregarded, dry cargo imports normally exceed dry cargo exports at Dar es Salaam; at Mombasa dry cargo exports have generally exceeded dry cargo imports by a considerable margin, but in 1980 a sharp rise in dry cargo imports reversed this trend. At the two smaller ports the tonnages of oil products imported are far lower, and traditionally exports have outweighed imports by a wide margin; this reflected the fact that the principal function of Tanga and Mtwara is the export of a limited range of primary agricultural products from geographically limited hinterlands which do not constitute major market areas for imported goods. During the 1970s, however, these established patterns of port throughput at Tanga and Mtwara have been modified by a general decline in the tonnages of cash crops exported through both these ports, and by the introduction of bulk fertiliser imports at Tanga, so that in 1980 at both the smaller ports imports exceeded exports, and this relationship was not affected by the relatively small quantities of oil imports involved.

On the basis of this evidence the concept of port hierarchies (Chapter 3) may be given quantitative expression. The composite structure of a port complex may be measured by using an index of port concentration:

$$I = \sqrt{x_1^2 + x_2^2 + x_3^2 + \ldots x_n^2},$$

where x is the percentage share of the total throughput of a port complex handled at an individual port. The index is derived from a technique devised by Hirschmann (1945) – an index of trade concentration – and has been used by Britton (1965), Ogundana (1970 and 1971), and is discussed by Bird (1971, p. 144). The index tends to be relatively low when the degree of port diffusion is high; and conversely the index tends to be high when the degree of port concentration is high. Applied to East African seaports over the period 1960-81 (Table 6.3), the index reflects the high degree of concentration at Mombasa, which increased during the year 1963-66 when the only East African oil refinery was located at that port, but shows also the rising relative importance of Dar es Salaam in the 1970s as the degree of concentration upon Mombasa has been reduced.

Export Cargo Throughput at Mombasa

Table 6.4 shows the general pattern of cargo throughput at Mombasa, and Table 6.5 lists the principal commodities exported, during the years 1976-81. As noted earlier, the total volume of imports considerably exceeds that of exports, primarily as a result of the large quantities of crude oil imported; but until 1980 the volume of dry cargo exports exceeded that of dry cargo imports. Specific commodity flows through Mombasa have shown considerable variation over time, as is the normal situation at all ports, but the main dry-cargo exports fall clearly into two categories: agricultural primary products and semiprocessed raw materials. In the first group coffee, tea and cotton have traditionally been the most important items. Cotton was outstanding as Mombasa's principal export item in the 1950s and 1960s, and in 1970 stood at over 100,000 tonnes. Political disruption in Uganda, the primary source of cotton exports through Mombasa, caused production there to fall off dramatically during the 1970s, so that by the end of the decade cotton exports had reached a very low level. Cotton production in Kenya is increasing, but most is absorbed in domestic textile industries.

Coffee is by far the most important agricultural export item handled at Mombasa. Stimulated by rising world market prices, coffee cultivation expanded rapidly in East Africa in the 1950s, but in the early 1960s falling prices and world overproduction discouraged further increases in output. The later 1960s and the early 1970s, however, saw a considerable improvement in the international coffee market, and exports through Mombasa again rose sharply. Coffee exports through Mombasa are derived primarily from Uganda and Kenya, with smaller quantities being exported from Rwanda; some coffee from the Kivu Province of Zaire and from Burundi also passes through Mombasa, although most of the output from these

TABLE 6.4
CARGO THROUGHPUT AT MOMBASA, 1976–81*

	1976	1977	1978	1979	1980	1981
Exports						
Dry general cargo	956	821	830	1,014	864	784
Dry bulk cargo	603	686	656	590	574	748
Bulk liquids	411	461	314	474	599	1,274
Total	1,970	1,968	1,800	2,078	2,037	2,806
Imports						
Dry general cargo	814	1,170	1,242	977	1,347	1,342
Dry bulk cargo	124	167	238	160	657	718
Bulk liquids	2,970	2,617	2,787	2,822	3,467	3,567
Total	3,908	3,954	4,267	3,859	5,472	5,627
Total throughput†	5,888	5,931	6,071	5,942	7,512	8,436

(*Source*: Kenya Ports Authority, *Annual bulletin of port statistics.*)

* '000 dwt.
† Including transhipment.

TABLE 6.5
PRINCIPAL COMMODITIES EXPORTED THROUGH THE PORT OF MOMBASA, 1976–81*

	1976	1977	1978	1979	1980	1981
Bulk oils	375	417	276	409	520	1,167
Bulk cement	434	533	523	426	460	530
Coffee	324	302	275	259	234	256
Soda ash	92	98	148	196	196	127
Fluorspar	91	111	104	78	97	106
Tea	84	96	101	111	91	91
Molasses	36	41	38	65	79	107
Canned fruit, etc.	35	57	56	50	51	54
Sisal	25	25	27	26	36	40
Bagged cement	69	65	9	37	29	55
Lubricating oils	15	25	22	26	26	7
Cement clinker	77	42	29	81	14	42
Cotton	26	11	14	5	6	4
Maize	128	8	24	159	1	0

(*Source*: Kenya Ports Authority, *Annual bulletin of port statistics.*)

Note: This table includes all individual commodities exports of which reached 25,000 dwt in one or more of the years 1976–81.

* '000 dwt.

areas is despatched via Dar es Salaam. As in the case of cotton, there was a decline in Ugandan coffee output during the 1970s, and this has substantially affected the total coffee throughput at the port. Other factors influencing the level of coffee exports include the implementation of the export quota system agreed by the International Coffee Organization, the shortage of land available for the expansion of coffee cultivation, the tendency of Ugandan coffee farmers to revert from cash crop to subsistence cultivation in times of political disruption, and the considerable potential for higher yields from existing coffee-producing areas as a result of irrigation and the increased use of fertilizers.

Several of these factors also apply in the case of tea exports through Mombasa, although the balance of production from the Kenyan and Ugandan hinterlands is the reverse of that for coffee. In the later 1970s approximately 75 per cent of the tea exports through Mombasa were derived from Kenya, roughly 20 per cent from Uganda and smaller consignments from Rwanda, Zaire and Burundi. Total tea exports through the port rose sharply during the later 1960s and early 1970s and reached a plateau at about 10,000 tonnes per annum at the end of the decade. Although production in Uganda has declined, that in Kenya continues to increase both from estates and from smallholders, and new plantings have been encouraged by the Kenya Tea Development Authority. In external terms there has been for some years a healthy relationship between supply and demand on the world tea market, and prices have shown a greater degree of stability than in the case of some other primary commodities. The case for expanding tea production in East Africa, both in terms of estate production and smallholder cultivation, largely rests on the relative efficiency of the industry in East Africa in relation to the major exporting countries elsewhere. Much of the tea industry of East Africa has been established fairly recently, under the influence of the latest technological methods, and market results indicate that the quality of East African tea is high. Further substantial increases in tea exports through Mombasa are therefore likely.

Although coffee is the most valuable commodity exported through Mombasa, pride of place in terms of volume of exports has frequently been taken in recent years by cement. The domestic market in Kenya for cement is served by factories at Nairobi and Mombasa, and there are plans to develop additional factories in western Kenya and in the coastal zone. In 1980 Kenyan cement production exceeded 1.25 million tonnes, of

PLATE 6.1. Mombasa: cargo handling at Kipevu. The layout of the Kipevu berths permits a greater degree of mechanisation than at the older berths on Mombasa Island. The travelling quay cranes are provided by the KPA and operated, together with a large number of fork-lift trucks and other appliances, by the KCHS. (*Source:* Kenya Ports Authority, Mombasa.)

which about 0.5 million tonnes were available for export, primarily to destinations in the western Indian Ocean. Almost all the cement exported from Kenya passes through Mombasa and is derived from the Bamburi Portland Cement Company's factory located a few miles north of the port; cement-loading facilities are located at Ras Kidomoni in Mombasa Harbour and at Mbaraki in Kilindini Harbour. Considerable increases in bulk cement exports are anticipated in the future; bagged cement exports, and exports by overland routes, are relatively limited.

Soda ash is another heavy item of export at Mombasa, and of much longer standing than cement, having been exported in quantity as early as 1913. Used mainly in glass manufacture, soda ash is derived from Lake

Magadi, Kenya, and exports are strongly regulated by overseas demand which at times has varied substantially and has been affected by political factors. Prior to 1964 most soda ash exports through Mombasa were shipped to South Africa, but in more recent years alternative markets have been developed in Japan and elsewhere. There were considerable increases in both bulk and bagged soda ash exports in the later 1970s, and further growth is anticipated as the Magadi Soda Company implements expansion plans.

A variety of other export commodities rank high in the structure of port throughput at Mombasa. Exports of fluorspar (from the Kerio valley in western Kenya) reached an annual level of about 100,000 tonnes in the later 1970s; exports of Ugandan copper, however, which used to be very important, ceased in the mid-1970s as a result of political and technological difficulties, but there is no basic reason why they should not be resumed. No other mineral exports are of major significance at Mombasa at present; several additional agricultural products appear in Table 6.5,

PLATE 6.2. Mombasa: fork-lift trucks handling agricultural exports at berth 11, Kipevu. (*Source:* Kenya Ports Authority, Mombasa.)

however, although none is likely to show rapid growth in the future. Exports of sisal increased steadily in the 1950s but declined in the 1960s and 1970s to a level of about 25,000 tonnes per annum as international trading conditions in natural hard fibres became increasingly difficult. World market prices for sisal remain very sensitive, and long-term prospects for sisal production and export are bleak. Exports of molasses from the Kenya sugar factories increased during the 1970s, but are likely to cease in future when factories designed to produce industrial alcohol from molasses are opened in western Kenya. In contrast, exports of maize vary between wide limits from year to year, as a result of the Kenya Government's policy of encouraging the production of an export surplus of maize sufficient to provide a safety margin against seasonal fluctuations in home production. Substantial quantities become available for export therefore only in occasional years, and imports are in fact quite frequently necessary.

PLATE 6.3. Export throughput at Mombasa: fork-lift trucks handling agricultural exports in the transit shed at berth 11, Kipevu. (*Source:* Kenya Ports Authority.)

PLATE 6.4. Sisal exports at Mombasa: sisal consignments from Kenya to Greece being shipped on board S.S. *Zuigo Maro* at berth 11, Kipevu. (*Source:* Kenya Ports Authority.)

Export Cargo Throughput at Dar es Salaam

The general pattern of export cargo throughput at Dar es Salaam for the years 1976-81 is shown in Table 6.6, and Table 6.7 lists the principal commodities exported. To a greater extent than other East African seaports, Dar es Salaam operates as a gateway for traffic to and from the landlocked countries and areas of eastern Africa beyond the national frontiers of Tanzania: Table 6.8 gives details of non-Tanzanian cargo throughput at Dar es Salaam for the years 1965-81, listing Zambian traffic separately from that linking the port with Rwanda, Burundi and eastern Zaire. Trading links

TABLE 6.6
CARGO THROUGHPUT AT DAR ES SALAAM, 1976–81*

	1976	1977	1978	1979	1980	1981
Exports						
Dry general cargo	1,118	1,045	913	759	705	673
Bulk liquids	260	237	163	151	196	119
Total	1,378	1,282	1,077	911	901	792
Imports						
Dry general cargo	1,065	1,299	1,206	915	1,150	1,032
Bulk liquids	1,821	1,894	1,862	1,542	1,702	1,537
Total	2,886	3,194	3,068	2,458	2,853	2,569
Total throughput†	4,265	4,478	4,146	3,370	3,759	3,362

(*Source*: Tanzania Harbours Authority.)

* '000 dwt.
† Including transhipment.

TABLE 6.7
PRINCIPAL COMMODITIES* EXPORTED THROUGH DAR ES SALAAM, 1976–81†

	1976	1977	1978	1979	1980	1981
Copper (Zambia)	660	636	552	358	411	368
Cotton	140	87	89	113	123	89
Bulk oils	182	147	121	117	115	96
Tea	19	21	22	23	30	25
Coffee	22	19	27	30	29	45
Tobacco	35	39	42	28	25	30
Sisal	53	37	24	31	22	16
Copper (Zaire)	67	62	37	12	19	24
Molasses	10	20	28	27	29	25

(*Source*: Tanzania Harbours Authority.)

* This table includes all individual commodities exports of which reached 25,000 harbour tonnes in one or more of the years 1976–81.
† '000 harbour tonnes.

between Dar es Salaam and the extranational hinterlands of the port predate the present century and have been a significant factor throughout the development of the modern port; these links have traditionally concerned Burundi, eastern Zaire and to a limited extent Rwanda, but their import-

TABLE 6.8
NON-TANZANIAN CARGO THROUGHPUT AT DAR ES SALAAM, 1965–81*

	Rwanda/Burundi/Zaire			Zambia			Total	%‡
	Exports	Imports	Total	Exports	Imports†	Total		
1965	53	39	91	–	–	–	91	9.9
1966	60	46	105	39	59	97	203	14.6
1967	65	46	110	189	77	266	276	14.5
1968	60	47	107	225	76	301	408	19.1
1969	98	45	142	221	107	328	571	26.3
1970	128	59	187	237	154	391	578	23.5
1971	88	67	155	218	186	404	559	20.0
1972	115	57	172	203	95	298	469	15.0
1973	103	63	165	271	211	483	648	20.2
1974	117	72	189	240	295	535	724	19.6
1975	66	62	128	368	434	802	930	23.9
1976	111	69	180	700	558	1,259	1,439	33.7
1977	145	22	167	675	681	1,356	1,523	34.0
1978	133	37	170	610	406	1,016	1,186	28.6
1979	51	54	104	450	469	919	1,023	30.4
1980	61	60	120	424	438	862	982	26.1
1981	80	49	129	414	352	766	895	26.6

(*Sources*: East African Harbours Corporation [for 1965–74], and Tanzania Harbours Authority [for 1975–81].)

* '000 dwt.
† Excluding bulk oils.
‡ Total non-Tanzanian cargo throughput as a percentage of total (Tanzanian and non-Tanzanian) cargo throughput.

ance has been very substantially increased by the inclusion of Zambian traffic. Since 1966 substantial exports of Zambian copper have been directed through the port and, apart from oil imports, copper exports now constitute the principal commodity handled. The impact of this abrupt, politically stimulated change in the structure of port traffic at Dar es Salaam has been considerable, both in terms of the expansion of port facilities, the increased problems of port operation, and the improvements in hinterland transport. Prior to the rise of Zambian copper exports, cotton and sisal were the two outstanding export commodities at Dar es Salaam. For many years sisal was the leading export item, and during the period 1959-64 over 100,000 tons a year were shipped – over one-third of the total volume of exports passing through the port. In the later 1960s and 1970s the volume of sisal exports through the port declined considerably, as a result of the fluctuating fortunes of hard fibres on the international market and consequent efforts to increase internal sisal consumption. Cotton exports, however, have continued to increase; there was a rapid increase in cotton exports during the 1950s, largely attributable to increased acreage under the crop in the lake zone of Tanzania and to the stimulation provided by high cotton prices maintained by the Tanzanian government by means of a price stabilization fund. Market conditions in the Far East and in Europe are good, and there is likely to be a continued increase in cotton exports through Dar es Salaam, although this may be achieved by the continued expansion of acreage rather than by the achievement of higher yields in areas already under the crop. Increases in raw cotton exports have been parallelled by increases in shipments of oil seeds. Exports of coffee through Dar es Salaam are relatively slight and variable in quantity compared with those moving through Mombasa; this results from the fluctuating quantities exported through Tanzania from Burundi, Zaire and Rwanda, and from the fact that most of the coffee crop from northern Tanzania passes through Tanga. Other important and regular export commodities at Dar es Salaam include tea, tobacco and twine.

Export Cargo Throughput at Tanga

At Tanga export cargo throughput attains only a modest level, and is described in outline in Tables 6.9 and 6.10. The main feature of the export traffic of the port throughout the 1960s, and for many years previously, was that only one major commodity was involved. Exports of sisal, which rose to a record level of 235,000 tonnes in 1970, generally formed about three-quarters of the total volume of exports handled at the port and about half the total cargo throughput. The predominance of sisal exports at Tanga, and their important role in the pattern of export traffic at Dar es Salaam, reflected the fact that sisal production constitutes a very important agricultural industry in Tanzania, particularly in the hinterland of

TABLE 6.9
CARGO THROUGHPUT AT TANGA, 1976–81*

	1976	1977	1978	1979	1980	1981
Exports						
Dry general cargo	175	139	166	192	144	156
Imports						
Dry general cargo	89	111	166	113	147	85
Bulk fertilizer	65	49	45	33	72	60
Bulk liquids	23	23	26	22	23	18
Total	176	183	236	168	241	163
Total throughput+	351	321	403	360	385	321

(*Source*: Tanzania Harbours Authority.)

* '000 dwt.
\+ Including transhipment.

TABLE 6.10
PRINCIPAL COMMODITIES* EXPORTED THROUGH TANGA, 1976–81+

	1976	1977	1978	1979	1980	1981
Sisal	95	76	84	67	53	55
Coffee	64	49	49	58	49	68
Twine	33	30	34	54	43	14
Beans, peas and pulses	13	10	11	13	20	22
Tea	11	13	16	14	8	5

(*Source*: Tanzania Harbours Authority.)

* '000 harbour tonnes.
\+ This table includes all individual commodities exports of which exceeded 5,000 harbour tonnes in one or more of the years 1976–81.

Tanga. Exports of sisal increased gradually from modest beginnings in the early years of the century; in the mid-1960s over 200,000 harbour tonnes a year were exported through Tanga, and sisal exports contributed nearly 25 per cent of the volume of all export cargo throughput at Tanzanian seaports. This situation reflected a reasonably high level of demand for sisal on the world market, where relatively high prices were obtainable, and to some extent high sisal export figures in the early 1960s represented a policy of cutting and selling in a favourable but vulnerable market situation. The later 1960s and early 1970s witnessed a sharp decline in the world demand for natural fibres, largely as a result of successful competition from artificial substitutes, and although exports through Tanga did not fall sharply in the early 1970s the world price decline in hard fibres meant that the Tanzanian sisal industry was much less profitable than previously. Whilst the rapid general rise in world commodity prices in the 1970s affected sisal favourably, the industry remains essentially vulnerable. Sisal exports through Tanga declined to about 50,000 tonnes in 1980 and in the following year lost their pre-eminent place in the export traffic structure of the port. In common with many other less-developed countries, Tanzania pursues a policy of agricultural and industrial diversification in order to reduce dependence upon a very limited range of primary produce; attempts have been made to increase domestic consumption of sisal in the manufacture of paper and twine. Exports of twine are now important at Tanga, and coffee exports from northern Tanzania have also increased substantially as a result of the Tanzanian government's policy of directing traffic through the national port system rather than using the facilities at Mombasa in neighbouring Kenya.

Export Cargo Throughput at Mtwara

Mtwara remains the smallest of the four East African mainland seaports, and traffic levels there have not increased substantially in recent years. Table 6.11 shows the general pattern of port throughput, and Table 6.12 the principal commodities exported, for the years 1976-81. The most important export item passing through Mtwara from the mid-1950s to the later 1970s was cashew nuts. Exports of this commodity rose from a modest level of three or four thousand tonnes a year, in the period immediately following the opening of Mtwara as a deep-water port in 1954,

PLATE 6.5. The lighterage process at Tanga: cargo being loaded on board a vessel anchored in midstream. (*Source*: Tanzania Harbours Authority, Dar es Salaam.)

to over 40,000 tonnes in 1962 and over 80,000 tonnes in 1972. To some extent therefore cashew nuts may be said to have taken the place which it was originally expected that groundnuts would occupy in the structure of port traffic at Mtwara, although the volume of cashew nuts exported has by no means equalled the anticipated level of groundnut traffic which was scheduled to rise to 600,000 tonnes a year by 1950-51 (see Chapter 4). It is arguable that the presence of Mtwara as a deep-water port has done something to encourage the development of cashew nuts as a cash crop, although considerable quantities of cashew nuts continued to move through the older port of Lindi (1955-59: 7,000-11,000 tonnes annually)

TABLE 6.11
CARGO THROUGHPUT AT MTWARA, 1976–81*

	1976	1977	1978	1979	1980	1981
Exports						
Dry general cargo	80	85	105	66	38	51
Imports						
Dry general cargo	62	58	42	36	59	41
Bulk oils	24	21	17	10	21	23
Total	86	80	60	45	80	64
Total throughput+	166	165	166	111	118	115

(*Source*: Tanzania Harbours Authority.)

* '000 dwt.
\+ Including transhipment.

TABLE 6.12
PRINCIPAL COMMODITIES* EXPORTED THROUGH MTWARA, 1976–81+

	1976	1977	1978	1979	1980	1981
Cashew nuts	50	63	47	32	17	37
Cassava	16	21	32	23	17	3
Sisal	6	4	4	5	3	–
Tobacco	3	–	–	–	–	–
Timber	–	–	1	2	–	–

Source: Tanzania Harbours Authority.

* This table includes all individual commodities exports of which exceeded 1,000 harbour tonnes in one or more of the years 1976–81.
\+ '000 harbour tonnes.

until deep-sea ships ceased to use that port in 1962. More important factors in stimulating production, however, were the suitability of large areas of southern Tanzania for cashew nut cultivation, which does not require good soil and can tolerate dry conditions; and the rising demand for cashew nut products on the world market in the 1960s and early 1970s. In the later 1970s, however, the export of cashew nuts declined as a result of reduced crop yields, falling overseas demand and the development of local processing. Some revival of exports was experienced in 1981 due to increased yields, however.

The only other export commodity of significance at Mtwara is cassava; shipments rose to a record level of 34,942 harbour tonnes in 1968, but have since declined. Sisal was exported through Mtwara during the *primitive* era in the development of the port (see Chapter 4), and production from local estates is still of some importance. A total of 18,651 tonnes of sisal was exported in 1963, a figure not subsequently equalled. The volume of groundnuts exported has never risen above two or three thousand tonnes a year, and exports of timber (which in the 1950s usually stood at about 10,000 tonnes a year) declined by the early 1960s to the level of groundnuts. In 1962-63 a total of 9,927 tonnes of railway material was shipped from Mtwara, consisting of lines, sleepers etc. from the Southern Province Railway which ceased to operate in July 1962; most of the material was sent to Mombasa for use on the railway extensions in northern Uganda which were under construction at that time. In the early 1970s there were low-level increases in the quantities of tobacco, sim sim and coffee exported through the port; but at the end of the decade the range of export commodities handled appeared very limited and the prospects of development towards a higher level of port activity seemed equally restricted.

Seasonal Variations in Export Cargo Throughput

Seasonal variations in the volume of the principal commodities exported through each of the four seaports are important, especially because exports (with the notable exception of Zambian copper flows through Dar es Salaam) consist primarily of agricultural products, the cultivation of which is closely related to climatic conditions. Some crops are of course less dependent than others upon rainfall and temperature variations; stocks of some export commodities are sometimes held by producers or marketing organisations for considerable periods; and exports fundamentally reflect overseas market demand rather than production patterns. In spite of these factors, however, the seaward flow of agricultural exports tends to vary substantially from one season of the year to another, and this can cause considerable problems in terms of transport and port working. If the exporting seasons of several commodities coincide pressure upon port capacity may occur temporarily, whereas at other seasons of the year port facilities may be underworked. At Mombasa there is theoretically a double peak in coffee exports in March-April and September-November. The crop has traditionally been exported through Mombasa from four major areas each with a different peak exporting season. The bulk of the Uganda crop normally passes through the port in January-April, and this overlaps with the slightly later Kenya crop which is shipped chiefly between February and May. Coffee from Rwanda (and traditionally from northern Tanzania) is exported chiefly towards the end of the year. There is some degree of overlap, therefore, between coffee-exporting seasons in different parts of East Africa; but in fact exports from Mombasa do not often fall below about 20,000 tonnes in any one month. Variations in monthly tonnages of cotton exported through Mombasa normally reflect the Uganda cotton exporting season which runs from January to May. Sisal exports through Tanga and Dar es Salaam do not show variations that are significant in the same respect; changes are more directly attributable to market conditions and are less closely related to circumstances of production. The degree of concentration in particular seasons of the exports of coffee and cotton is, however, more marked at Dar es Salaam than at Mombasa; coffee exports rise sharply in June and continue at a fairly high level until October, and within this midyear period coffee is exported both from Tanzania and from Zaire. Exports of cotton through Dar es Salaam chiefly take place in the period September-January, so that there is an important overlap in September-October as cotton exports rise rapidly before the shipping of the coffee crop is completed. At Mtwara a concentration of cashew nut exports in the period November-January in certain years overlaps with the main cassava exporting season which extends from August to December. During these peak periods port facilities at Mtwara may operate under some pressure; but during the rest of the year the volume of traffic handled is comparatively slight.

Import Cargo Throughput at the Mainland Seaports

As an element within the structure of the total cargo throughput at a group of seaports in the less-developed world, the pattern of import cargo traffic is relevant to two main broad considerations: the general level of the economy of the hinterland, chiefly in terms of the purchasing power of the population, and the general nature of the resources of the hinterland, in terms of the degree of dependence upon overseas sources of essential goods. The economies of the East African countries, like those of many other parts of the less-developed world, are essentially based upon the production for export of a fairly narrow range of primary products, almost all agricultural. Local resources for the development of manufacturing industry are relatively limited, in spite of the considerable progress made in this sector in recent years. In these circumstances the basic pattern of import cargo throughput at East African seaports comprises four main elements: fuel and power supplies, industrial products (machinery and other goods based on advanced technology), manufactured products for the consumer market, and supplementary foodstuffs.

Bulk oils represent by far the most important item in the structure of import cargo throughput at Mombasa, Dar es Salaam and Mtwara; at Tanga, bulk fertilizer imports are more important than bulk oil imports. East Africa seems unfortunately to be completely devoid of significant domestic crude oil resources, and such coal reserves as are known (in south-western Tanzania, for example) remain unexploited. The hydroelectric power potential of all three East African countries has been partially exploited, but the area as a whole remains heavily dependent upon imported oil. Since the mid-1960s, when oil refineries were opened at Mombasa (1963) and Dar es Salaam (1966), crude oil has formed a high proportion of all oil imports at both ports; previously a wide range of oil products had been imported in large quantities, and to some extent this still continues since the refineries are not yet equipped to produce all the petroleum products for which a demand exists. At Mombasa and Dar es Salaam the tonnage of bulk oils imported comprises a very high proportion (about 65 per cent at Mombasa, and about 60 per cent at Dar es Salaam) of all goods imported. At the two smaller seaports, where there are no oil refining facilities and oil imports therefore consist entirely of refined oil products, the tonnage of bulk oils imported comprises a much lower proportion of total imports: less than 30 per cent at Mtwara, and less than 15 per cent at Tanga. These points reflect the general level and range of cargo throughput at each seaport, and may be correlated with the individual character of their respective hinterlands.

Apart from the variations noted above in the relative predominance of bulk oils, no very clear pattern emerges in the structure of import cargo flows through East African ports. It is, in fact, the characteristically wide variety of relatively small consignments that has frequently created problems in terms of port operation, especially at the two larger ports where the total volume of imports is considerable; at the smaller ports only relatively small quantities of break-bulk import cargoes are handled, but the introduction of bulk fertiliser imports at Tanga in 1972 represented an important new departure. At all four ports, break-bulk import cargoes comprise primarily foodstuffs, manufactured goods, consumer goods and machinery. Railway materials are imported at Mombasa and Dar es Salaam, and some coal is imported at Mombasa.

Cargo Throughput at Zanzibar

The general pattern of port throughput at Zanzibar is broadly similar in some respects to that associated with the mainland seaports of East Africa; the marked concentration of the export trade upon a single primary commodity suggests, particularly, a close parallel with Tanga and Mtwara. The number and net registered tonnage of ocean-going vessels entering the port of Zanzibar stood in the mid-1960s at around 450 vessels and just over 2 million tonnes. A considerable number of coastal vessels continue to visit the port, but in recent years the Arab dhow trade has ceased and Indian dhow traffic has declined almost to negligible proportions. Detailed information on recent trends in port throughput at Zanzibar is not available, and it is possible only to describe in general terms the trade patterns characteristic of the immediate pre-revolutionary era together with comments on more recent developments.

The products of the clove and coconut trees have provided for many years a very high proportion (often over 95 per cent) of the value of the domestic exports of Zanzibar. The clove is the more important of the two, and the reliance which Zanzibar has traditionally placed upon this single predominant item is clearly unhealthy from an economic standpoint. The high value of cloves per unit of weight largely explains the fact that the volume of exports is generally lower than the volume of imports at Zanzibar. Clove plants were probably first introduced into Zanzibar from Mauritius in 1818; on the orders of Seyyid Said much of the best land of Zanzibar and Pemba was planted with cloves, and by the middle of the nineteenth century the industry had become well established. The initial success of the crop was partly due to the use of slave labour, and following the final abolition of slavery in Zanzibar in 1897 a decline in the standard of cultivation took place in the early years of the present century. Between the two World Wars the Government of Zanzibar took an increasing share in the organisation and marketing of the crop, and in 1927 the formation of the Clove Growers' Association (which was incorporated within the Zanzibar State Trading Corporation in 1964) introduced a measure of price control. A characteristic feature of the clove industry is the very wide variation in production from one seasonal year to another; in a good year the crop may exceed 20,000 tonnes and in a bad year may fall below 3,000 tonnes. This does not, however, directly affect the pattern of exports since cloves may be stored for long periods without loss of quality. Storage for several years may cause discoloration, but the oil content remains unimpaired. New cloves are therefore sold as spice, and old cloves on markets where the oil content is the main criterion. Exports do not therefore show such wide annual variations as do yields, and are more closely allied to market demand than to production. The value of clove exports on the world market has varied in the past between quite wide limits, and since 1968 has increased to unprecedented levels. During the 1950s the volume of clove exports fluctuated between 7,500 and 12,000 tonnes per annum, and the value between £2 million and £4 million, but the general trend at that time was towards decline. In 1950 the condition of the clove industry of Zanzibar was described as satisfactory in spite of the ravages of 'sudden death' disease on Zanzibar Island. In the later 1950s and early 1960s the industry suffered a relative recession, partly as a result of a declining demand for cloves in the main market areas, and more precisely as a result of the immediate aftermath of the 1964 revolution when many clove plantations formerly owned by Arabs were confiscated and, for a time, were not tended with sufficient care. The later 1960s, however, saw an unprecedented and very sharp rise in world clove prices, so that although the volume of exports has continued to vary between quite wide limits, the price per tonne and therefore the total value of clove exports has increased very substantially. The cloves boom started in 1968, continued through the 1970s, and led to a considerable accumulation of capital reserves which has allowed Zanzibar to accelerate her programme of economic diversification.

The coconut industry is the second most important activity in Zanzibar and coconut plantations occupy large areas of land much of which is unsuitable for cloves. The coconut has been described as 'the universal provider of the tropics,' and with good reason. The dried kernel produces copra, from which is extracted coconut oil for use as food and as a base for the manufacture of margarine and soap, and the residue is made into oil cake. The fibre of the coconut, coir, is exported both in its raw state and in the form and hand-manufactured ropes and matting. These, with other minor products of the coconut, constitute the only really significant exports from Zanzibar apart from cloves. Other commodities traditionally exported include marine shells, chillies, hides and skins, mangrove bark and seaweed, the latter exported mainly to Britain where it is used in the manufacture of ice cream and paint.

A traditionally important aspect of the structure of port traffic at Zanzibar is the re-export trade. This transit traffic has its origins in the nineteenth century when Zanzibar acted as a major emporium for the redistribution of mainland produce. Re-exports are not now of such relative importance as they were in the early years of the present century; in 1900 they constituted 79 per cent of the total export traffic (Bartlett, 1936, 17). In the 1950s, when re-exports formed about 40 per cent of total exports, the most important item involved was ivory from the East African mainland re-exported to India, Hong Kong and Japan. No reliable recent data on re-exports are available.

Imports have traditionally exceeded exports at Zanzibar in terms of volume and also (prior to the recent 'cloves boom') in terms of value. A wide range of foodstuffs and other consumer goods is involved. For many years rice – a staple foodstuff in the diet of the population of both Zanzibar and Pemba – was the most important single commodity imported, but the rapid recent expansion of domestic rice production has affected the situation considerably. Apart from food products, other major items imported include clothing and footwear, construction materials, machinery and equipment, and petroleum products. Traditionally the heavy emphasis on food imports reflected a basic orientation in the agricultural economy of Zanzibar towards cash crops; the success of commercial agriculture in the islands in the past encouraged the neglect of food crops. Recent trends have been in the reverse direction; in the early post-revolutionary years (1964-68), declining clove exports gave an added impetus to subsistence crop production; and in the post-1968 period when clove prices have been very high, the Zanzibar Government has made considerable efforts to achieve a greater degree of self-sufficiency in foodstuffs. Chinese assistance in the establishment of rice farms and sugar cultivation has helped to reduce Zanzibar's traditionally heavy dependence upon imports of these commodities. A programme of import-substitute industrialisation has also been important in this respect. Some of the policies pursued during the period 1964-72 by the Afro-Shirazi Party under Chairman Karume provoked considerable controversy, particularly when severe limitations upon the importation of essential foodstuffs were involved; since the assassination of Sheikh Karume in 1972 more flexible policies have been followed and the economic development of this part of Tanzania has accordingly shown considerable progress.

Container Traffic

The rapid recent development of seaborne container-carrying capacity on a global basis is well known. In the later 1960s and early 1970s the conversion of the Europe-Australia and Europe-Far East trades was a major factor in the rapid if somewhat unsteady growth of the world container transport network. As the major trades between advanced countries were containerised close to the limits of their potential, more rapid progress was made towards the containerisation of cargo throughputs at ports in less-developed countries. In the later 1970s the rates of increase in containerised throughputs at many ports in developing countries were unexpectedly high, and the view that container shipping services would develop rapidly only until trades between advanced countries were saturated with capacity is clearly now redundant. The world fleets of container ships and seaborne containers have continued to expand, and container traffic is increasingly penetrating routes serving the less-developed countries.

The potential for the development of container services in any area of the less-developed world is of course related to a wide variety of factors, but reflects most directly the volume and character of general-cargo

PLATE 6.6. East Africa's first container: unloading the first UK–East Africa container at Kilindini in 1968 – a consignment of medical supplies for Kampala, Uganda. (*Source:* Kenya Railways Corporation, Nairobi.)

throughput at the ports concerned. The extent to which this potential is realised depends in turn upon the development of shipping services and port installations designed to facilitate the operation of the system, and a lack of capacity in any specific part of the system can clearly limit the extent to which the system as a whole can be developed and can operate efficiently. The successful development of container-handling systems linked with the transport networks of the less-developed countries requires the cooperation of a wide range of organisations and the development of coordinated planning systems involving shippers, ship operators, land transport authorities, government departments, port and customs authorities and other interested organisations. In the early stages of the

PLATE 6.7. Container handling at Mombasa: container throughput at many ports in the less-developed countries increased sharply in the later 1970s. (*Source*: Kenya Ports Authority.)

development of container services within a less-developed country it is clearly advisable that a national coordinating and planning committee should be set up to represent the interests of all the organisations involved and to maximise as far as possible the efficiency and logical development of the operation as a whole.

While the character of general cargo trade and the pattern of shipping services are the principal determinants of the development of container traffic in a less-developed country, the inland transport network provides a major additional factor that conditions the way in which the container transport system operates. In order to work at maximum efficiency, container services are designed to link inland consignors with inland consignees; if inland transport systems in less-developed countries are unable adequately to handle container traffic, this factor alone can seriously affect the efficient operation of the system. Ideally, container terminals developed in the ports of the less-developed countries require not only efficient rail and road links but also a series of efficiently operated inland container depots located at carefully selected points within the space economy of the hinterlands.

These points apply to the development of container terminals in any part of the less-developed world, and may be illustrated with reference to the seaports of Kenya and Tanzania. Prior to 1975 relatively few containers were seen in East Africa, but since that date the growth of container traffic at the larger ports of Mombasa and Dar es Salaam has been remarkably rapid (Tables 6.13 and 6.14), and it is quite clear that East

TABLE 6.13
CONTAINER TRAFFIC AT MOMBASA, 1975–81

	1975	1976	1977	1978	1979	1980	1981
Number of containers handled*							
Imports	0.6	1.6	2.3	4.7	8.0	15.5	22.0
Exports	0.4	1.6	1.9	4.0	6.4	14.2	19.1
Total+	1.3	3.4	4.6	9.1	15.2	30.4	42.7
Number of TEUs	1.2	3.3	4.5	9.0	15.1	30.7	44.1

(*Source*: Kenya Ports Authority.)

* In '000.

\+ Including transhipment.

TABLE 6.14
CONTAINER TRAFFIC AT TANZANIAN SEAPORTS, 1975–81

	1975	1976	1977	1978	1979	1980	1981
Dar es Salaam							
Number of containers handled*							
Imports	0.2	0.3	0.8	1.1	2.4	4.7	4.3
Exports	–	–	–	–	1.9	4.5	8.2
Total+	0.2	0.3	0.8	1.1	4.3	9.3	12.6
Number of TEUs	0.1	0.2	0.6	1.0	4.4	9.3	12.6
Tanga							
Number of containers handled*							
Imports	–	–	–	0.2	0.2	0.2	0.8
Exports	–	–	–	–	–	0.3	0.7
Total+	–	–	–	0.2	0.2	0.5	1.5
Number of TEUs	–	–	–	0.2	0.2	0.5	1.5

(*Source*: Tanzania Harbours Authority.)
* In '000
\+ Including transhipment

Africa has crossed an important threshold in economic and technological terms. It is generally assumed, however, on the basis of recent experience in other less-developed areas such as West Africa, that high initial growth rates during the early years of the container era will be followed by lower growth rates as most of the containerisable cargo is absorbed into the new system and further expansion becomes a function of overall traffic growth. Several specific factors appear to have triggered the East African container era, and it is significant that they were related more closely to maritime and foreland conditions than to port or hinterland characteristics. Among these factors may be cited the availability of spare containers in South Africa for bulk loading to North American destinations, and the stringent enforcement of food and drugs legislation in the USA which virtually dictated that East African tea exports should be containerised to avoid contamination. The introduction of container services by one or two shipping lines inevitably leads to a bandwagon effect, and other lines participate in order to remain competitive. Some container movements through the ports are not directly related to cargo throughput, however, but involve the repositioning of containers (empty or loaded) in relation to the wider international maritime network which they serve.

East African seaports are linked by container services with a variety of European and North American ports, and also with destinations in Japan, South-east Asia, India and the Middle East. In the initial stages of the development of the system almost all containers handled at East African ports were stuffed and unstuffed in the ports themselves, but as the system has expanded it has become possible to handle an increasing proportion of container traffic at inland depots. In Kenya the most obvious location for the development of inland container depots is Nairobi, but other areas where traffic growth and concentration are likely to warrant the development of additional depots include western Kenya, southern Uganda, and Rwanda. No inland container depots have yet been developed in Tanzania, but container traffic through Dar es Salaam to extranational hinterlands in Zambia and Burundi has grown considerably. Most inland container depots in East Africa are rail-dependent, but the movement of containers by road transport is increasing.

Considerable progress has been made towards the shipping of a wide variety of East African export cargoes in containers, the most important individual commodities being tea, coffee and canned fruits. Containerisation does not seem to have an adverse effect on coffee consignments, as was feared; and virtually all tea exports to North American destinations are now containerised. Imported commodities are mainly unspecified in detail, but include large quantities of fertilisers and chemicals in bags and drums. The potential for the further development of containerisation at East African seaports is considerable: all the principal agricultural export commodities (coffee, tea, maize, cashew nuts, vegetables, fruit, cotton, sisal, sugar, etc.) are regarded as 100 per cent containerisable, as are most mineral and cement exports and a high proportion of import cargoes. Clearly, from the standpoint of the early 1980s, only a small proportion of the container potential at East African seaports has yet been realised.

As in all other respects there are major differences between the East African ocean ports in terms of their present levels and potential future development of container traffic. Mombasa was the first East African seaport to reach the takeoff point in terms of container throughput in 1975-76, when a number of general and specific factors combined to create circumstances favourable to the rapid expansion of container services there. The development of a well-equipped container terminal, and a series of inland container depots within the economically buoyant hinterlands of the port, provide a technologically adequate infrastructure;

the efficiency with which this infrastructure is utilised is enhanced by a national container committee designed to coordinate the operations of the various organisations involved. Many of the external factors involved in the growth of container traffic at Mombasa also apply to Dar es Salaam, although internally the relatively depressed economy of the national hinterland provided only limited encouragement for the introduction of new technologies, and the initial expansion of container throughputs at Dar es Salaam was not therefore as rapid as at Mombasa. Nevertheless, the transition to containerisation is well advanced and has been much more rapid than was envisaged in the mid-1970s, encouraged not only by shipping lines and overseas freight forwarding companies but also by trading companies and government organisations in Zambia and Burundi. At the smaller Tanzanian seaports containers are handled in much smaller numbers: at Tanga, container traffic is expected to increase in spite of the difficulty of handling containers at the lighterage quays; but at Mtwara it is considered that the very low general throughput levels at the port are unlikely to attract specialised unitised cargo services in the foreseeable future.

Passenger Traffic

Emphasis on the structure of cargo traffic flows should not be allowed to mask the fact that at most seaports passenger traffic is of some significance. The varying amounts of passenger traffic handled re-emphasize the pattern of quantitative relationships between the various terminals already illustrated in other respects. Passenger traffic data for the years 1976-81 at East African ports are given in Table 6.15. The number of passengers using the port of Mombasa in recent years had declined sharply from over 70,000 passenger movements in the early 1960s to very low figures in the later 1970s; at Dar es Salaam, conversely, the records show a rise in total passenger movements from 28,000 in 1963 to over 62,000 in 1973; more recent data reveal a varying but substantial total passenger throughput. Passenger traffic at the smaller ports of Tanga and Mtwara, although never entirely absent, is comparatively slight; only a handful of passengers use Tanga, but at Mtwara there has been a considerable increase in passenger movements in recent years. Factors involved in the situation represented by these figures include the decline in the number of passenger sailings

TABLE 6.15
PASSENGER TRAFFIC AT EAST AFRICAN SEAPORTS, 1976–81

	1976	1977	1978	1979	1980	1981
Mombasa						
Disembarked	2,010	367	477	66	178	285
Embarked	1,616	481	579	8	4	76
Dar es Salaam						
Disembarked	17,949	23,581	13,859	14,030	17,036	36,558
Embarked	21,497	22,691	14,489	11,568	12,187	30,966
Tanga						
Disembarked	242	1,890	104	–	100	8,534
Embarked	373	1,847	172	227	45	8,438
Mtwara						
Disembarked	9,797	6,112	4,140	6,331	7,054	9,709
Embarked	7,816	5,068	3,781	8,856	7,300	8,208
Total						
Disembarked	29,998	31,950	18,580	20,427	24,368	55,086
Embarked	31,302	30,087	19,021	20,659	19,536	47,688

(*Sources*: Kenya Ports Authority, Tanzania Harbours Authority.)

between East African and European seaports; an increase in the Chinese shipping at Dar es Salaam in the early 1970s; the importance of services between the Tanzanian mainland and the offshore islands of Zanzibar, Pemba and Mafia; and the inadequacy of road transport services in southern Tanzania. The introduction of a coastal passenger steamer service between Dar es Salaam and Mtwara in 1972, established with Norwegian financial and technical assistance, greatly increased the accessibility of southern Tanzania. The passenger and cargo services are operated by the Tanzania Coastal Shipping Line, and serve not only Dar es Salaam and Mtwara but also the intermediate ports of Mafia, Kilwa and Lindi (Foss and Hiorth, 1969).

REFERENCES

Bartlett, C.A. (1936), *Statistics of the Zanzibar Protectorate, 1895-1935* (Zanzibar, Government Printer).

Bird, J.H. (1971), *Seaports and seaport terminals* (London, Hutchinson).

Britton, J.N.H. (1965), 'The external relations of seaports: some new considerations,' *Tijdschrift voor Economische en Sociale Geografie* 56, 109-112.

East African Harbours Corporation (1970), *Annual report and accounts for the period 1 June to 31 December 1969* (Dar es Salaam).

East African Harbours Corporation, *Annual report and accounts for the year ended 31 December 1970, et seq.* (Dar es Salaam, annually to 1974).

Economist Intelligence Unit (1981), *Traffic survey and forecast 1980-2000, prepared for the Kenya Ports Authority, final report* (London).

Foss, B. and O.C. Hiorth (1969), *Coastal shipping services Dar es Salaam – Mtwara: a feasibility report* (Oslo, Norwegian Agency for International Development).

Hirschmann, A.O. (1945), *National power and the structure of foreign trade* (University of California Press).

Kenya Ports Authority, *Annual bulletin of port statistics, 1978, et seq.* (Mombasa, annually).

Kenya Ports Authority, *Annual report and accounts for the period 1 January to 31 December 1978, et seq.* (Mombasa, annually).

Ogundana, B. (1970), 'Patterns and problems of seaport evolution in Nigeria,' in B.S. Hoyle and D. Hilling (eds.), *Seaports and development in tropical Africa* (London, Macmillan), 167-182.

Ogundana, B. (1971), 'The location factor in changing seaport significance in Nigeria,' *Nigerian Geographical Journal* 14, 71-88.

7 Hinterlands and Forelands

The Concept of the Hinterland

A study of the economic geography of the hinterland is an essential component of any survey of a seaport or seaport complex. Any discussion of a port without reference to the hinterland offers only a partial and truncated view of reality; for a port cannot exist in geographical isolation since its *raison d'être* is to link together land and sea transport systems. The broad concept of the hinterland, the land area behind the port which is served by it, has long been familiar, and many attempts have been made to define the term with some precision in order to avoid "the fiction of a continuous isotropic area served by a port" (Bird, 1971, 125). A simple parcelling out of the land area served by a port complex is clearly an inadequate interpretation of the concept of the hinterland; a more realistic approach involves a recognition of the point pattern of cargo origins and destinations, and an appreciation of the variety of individual commodity hinterlands that comprise the composite hinterland of a port.

Three main factors may be said to influence, in different ways, the hinterland of a port: first, the pattern and the nature of export cargo generation and of import cargo demand within the hinterland; second, the installations of a port which control the level and variety of cargo throughput that a port can handle; and third, the extent, density and efficiency of the surface transport network in the hinterland area. A distinction may be suggested between 'simple' hinterlands linked only with one port, and 'complex' hinterlands where an inland area enjoys access to two or more ports and where interregional traffic movements and overlapping of hinterlands both occur. Within a 'complex' hinterland it is often possible to differentiate a 'primary' area firmly within the sphere of influence of a single port, and a 'secondary' area tributary to two or more ports. Where hinterland overlapping occurs in such a 'secondary' area, there may be active competition between two or more ports, producing a 'competitive' hinterland within all or part of the 'secondary' area; in addition, overlapping or competition may occur only in respect of certain specific commodities or commodity groups. The hinterland transport system introduces a further variation, in the sense that hinterlands may be defined in terms of the method of inland transport used: rail and road transport hinterlands may represent contrasted patterns and areas, and the question of intermodal competition may be an important factor. Beyond this, port geographers have suggested a wide variety of terms by which hinterlands may be further defined and the concept clarified, although frequently the use of specialised terms may contribute to the analysis of individual hinterlands rather than to the refinement of a universal theory. The complexities of hinterland typology have been discussed by various writers (Morgan, 1958; Weigend, 1956 and 1958; Mikolajski, 1964; Bird, 1971); all agree that port hinterlands may be defined in a great variety of ways according to the criteria used, the objectives of the analysis and the degree of detail required.

The present discussion of the hinterlands of the seaports of East Africa is thus based upon a recognition of the fact that a port possesses not a single uniform hinterland but a complex multiple pattern of hinterlands open to definition in both spatial and typological terms. For each individual commodity that a port exports or imports a distinctive commodity hinterland may be identified, given adequate statistical resources; the correlation of a range of commodity hinterlands representative of the total throughput of a port permits the delineation of the composite hinterland with a reasonable degree of accuracy. The statistical records maintained by the Kenya Ports Authority, the Kenya Railways Corporation, the Tanzania Harbours Authority and the Tanzania Railways Corporation allow at least a partial understanding of this aspect of port throughput and hinterland traffic flow. Rail transport movements are recorded in terms of individual commodity consignments despatched from or to each railway station within the system. Data on the precise origin and destination of road traffic movements to and from the ports are less readily available, and sometimes unobtainable; this is unfortunate in view of the importance of road transport in relation to port throughput. An additional factor which is especially relevant at Mombasa is that significant volumes of traffic are railed to and from warehouses in the urban areas of the East African cityports, but are transported between these warehouses and the ports by local road services. No data are available on the inland origins or detinations or on the volume of these cargo flows, and these patterns of cargo movement naturally tend to affect the usefulness and interpretation of any available data on road and rail transport to and from the ports.

At Mombasa the importance of the railway has declined considerably during the 1970s, and a very high proportion of the break-bulk exports are now brought to the port by road; similarly, the proportion of break-bulk imports moved by road transport is very high, but the railway remains the preferred mode for the movement of container traffic and for bulk traffic other than oil imports transported by pipeline. At Dar es Salaam a very high proportion of imported break-bulk goods are transported from the port by road, but almost half the break-bulk export cargo throughput is brought to the port by rail; this reflects the importance of Zambian copper exports via the Tanzania-Zambia railway, for almost all other break-bulk exports are delivered to the port by road. Road services dominate the pattern of break-bulk cargo movements at Tanga, whilst the port of Mtwara is of course served only by road transport.

The question of the relative efficiency of the two principal modes of hinterland transport, and the related question of intermodal competition, have been discussed elsewhere (Hazlewood, 1964; Prest, 1969; Hay, 1973) and lie beyond the scope of this study. The relative general importance of rail and road transport in terms of the movement to the ports of major export commodities underlines the reduced overall importance of rail transport and the increased importance of road transport for a high proportion of long-distance agricultural consignments. In 1972, 60 per cent of break-bulk exports through the port of Mombasa were delivered to the port by rail, and 40 per cent by road; in terms of commodity movements, the railway system carried almost all the coffee, cotton and oilseed cake consignments, and approximately half the tea and sisal exports. At Dar es Salaam the overwhelming importance of Zambian copper, brought to the port entirely by road in the early 1970s, tended to distort the picture; cotton, sisal and oilseed cake exports were transported to the port almost exclusively by rail, as were most coffee consignments and about half of the tea exports through the port. At Tanga a high proportion of the relatively small quantities of coffee exported in the early 1970s reached the port by rail, but three-quarters of the sisal exports and virtually all the tea passing through the port were normally transported by road.

By the early 1980s this pattern of inland transport modes had been substantially modified. At Mombasa the proportion of break-bulk export commodities despatched to the port by road in 1980 was over 85 per cent, and less than 15 per cent were delivered by rail. As explained earlier, however, these figures disregard consignments railed from inland locations to Mombasa warehouses and subsequently moved by road into the port. A considerable proportion of many agricultural exports, including coffee, continue to reach Mombasa by rail. At Dar es Salaam copper exports from Zambia are now transported by rail, as are sisal and most cotton consignments. Sisal consignments for export also reach Tanga by rail, but most other export commodities passing through the port are moved by road.

Export Hinterlands

Some attention is now given to the hinterlands associated with the major export commodities handled at each port. In view of the difficulty of obtaining comprehensive reliable statistical data on hinterland traffic flows, and the uncertain situation at the time of writing with regard to the Kenya-Tanzania border and the economic condition and prospects of Uganda, no attempt is made to present a detailed statistical analysis. Sufficient information is available, however, to give a reasonably clear overview of individual commodity hinterlands from which the composite hinterlands of the ports may be derived. All export hinterlands consist essentially of areas within which there is a varying spatial distribution of points of cargo origin; in most cases these points are numerous, but in a few cases certain export commodities occupying an important place in the traffic structure of East African seaports (e.g. soda ash and cement exports passing through Mombasa) are derived from a single source in the hinterland.

Coffee was for many years the leading commodity exported through the port of Mombasa, but although the volume of both petroleum products and cement exported through the port now exceed coffee exports by a considerable margin, coffee remains the principal agricultural export handled. Coffee has attained this position partly because it is the only major cash crop produced for export in all of three particularly important areas that have traditionally been included within the hinterland of Mombasa: Uganda, the highlands of Kenya, and northern Tanzania. Three major coffee collection points – Kampala, Nairobi and Moshi – were for many years important elements within the coffee hinterland of Mombasa. Kampala emerged in the 1950s and 1960s as the most important single cargo generation point within the coffee hinterland of Mombasa; the city acted as the sole collecting centre for Uganda dry Robusta coffee, brought into the Coffee Marketing Board by road from a wide area of southern Uganda. Arabica coffee grown in West Nile, Toro, Ankole and Kigezi was also collected by the Board, but Arabica coffee grown in the Bugisu District of eastern Uganda was collected by the Bugisu Cooperative Union on behalf of the Board. The total amount of coffee despatched from Kampala normally made up over half the total exported from Mombasa. Coffee was also despatched coastwards from stations in Uganda – chiefly between Kampala and Tororo – without passing through the capital centre, but on the whole the degree of centralisation was very strong. The extent to which the reconstruction of the Ugandan economy in the post-Amin period will involve a reestablishment of these patterns is an unknown and unpredictable factor. Coffee has traditionally been Uganda's primary export commodity, and the restoration of previous levels of production is likely to be a major objective during the reconstruction period. In a situation of political instability such as has existed in Uganda since the late 1960s coffee yields have declined and much land previously used for coffee cultivation has been used for subsistence crop production.

The relative importance of Nairobi as a coffee collecting centre is greater than that of Kampala, although the total volume handled is normally considerably less. Coffee from both African growers and from estates reaches the Nairobi market almost exclusively by road, and few other railway stations enter into the picture to give a clearer impression of the precise extent of the coffee-growing areas of Kenya. The same is true of Moshi, which acts as the principal collecting and despatching centre for the coffee-producing areas of northern Tanzania. The fact that the Moshi area, and the Bukoba area west of Lake Victoria, both lay for many years within the coffee hinterland of Mombasa rather than those of Tanzanian ports, is significant; it reflected in part, in the case of Bukoba, the greater convenience of transport via the lake and the Mombasa railway than via Mwanza to Dar es Salaam, and in the case of Moshi the utilization of a modern deep-water port in preference to a small lighterage port. The physical expansion of the port of Dar es Salaam, together with political factors and the increasing unreliability of inland water transport, led the

Government of Tanzania to direct traffic to and from the Bukoba, Musoma and Arusha-Moshi areas through Tanzanian national seaports from 1974. Coffee from western Tanzania, as well as from Burundi and eastern Zaire, passes through Dar es Salaam; and the coffee-producing areas of northern Tanzania now lie within the exclusive hinterland of Tanga, where rising coffee throughput has to some extent counterbalanced declining exports of sisal.

Hinterland sources of tea exports through Mombasa are less numerous and less widely distributed than those of coffee, although the volume of tea exported and the geographical extent of the port's tea hinterland have both increased in recent years. Both road and rail transport are extensively used for the transport of tea exports from Kenya and Uganda to Mombasa, and some tea is air freighted to the port from Rwanda. Tea production in East Africa was for many years concentrated in the Kericho district, where conditions of altitude, temperature and rainfall encouraged the early establishment of large-scale tea cultivation on an estate basis; production

PLATE 7.1 Tea picking, Uganda: the expansion of tea cultivation in many parts of highland East Africa in recent years has been reflected in increased export throughput at the seaports. (*Source:* Kenya Railways Corporation, Nairobi.)

on a smallholder basis is now widespread in many parts of highland Kenya, and in some years is a more important source of tea exports than estate production. In Uganda several tea estates are located in the southern parts of West and East Mengo Districts, and production in western Uganda increased considerably in the later 1960s and early 1970s. Environmental conditions would permit the further expansion of tea production in both Uganda (Hanna, 1974) and Kenya, and in present economic circumstances the crop can easily bear the cost of long-distance rail or road transport to the coast. Some tea from the southern highlands of Tanzania, and from Burundi and eastern Zaire, is exported through Dar es Salaam, but that exported through Tanga is grown locally in the Usambara mountains. Further increases in tea production in various parts of the hinterlands are likely as schemes sponsored by the Kenya Tea Development Authority come to fruition, as political stability in Uganda is gradually restored, and as the Tanzanian government continues to promote policies of economic diversification in the agricultural sector.

The cotton hinterlands of the East African seaports are less widespread than the coffee hinterlands; although all three East African countries are represented, the degree of concentration of production in north-western Tanzania, western Kenya and (in normal circumstances) in Uganda is very marked. Cotton has long been an important element in the hinterlands of Mombasa and Dar es Salaam, but its overall importance has declined due to the political disruption of the Ugandan economy during the 1970s and to the development of cotton processing and textile industries which absorb a considerable proportion of domestic production in all three countries. The core area of the cotton hinterland of Dar es Salaam lies in Sukumaland – in Shinyanga, Mwanza and Mara Regions – and the crop is also grown around the south-western coastlands of Lake Victoria, in the Morogoro and Arusha-Moshi areas, and in the Indian Ocean coastlands between Tanga and the Rufiji river. Cotton is the most important agricultural export commodity handled at Dar es Salaam. Only very limited quantities of cotton are exported through Tanga. Exports of Kenyan cotton through Mombasa are derived from the Western Region, around the shores of Kavirondo Gulf, and a small amount is grown in the dry eastern areas in the vicinity of Kibwezi. Cotton production in the Ugandan part of Mombasa's hinterland declined sharply during the 1970s and exports through the port reached a very low level. As with coffee and tea, however, rehabilitation of cotton production could be achieved quite rapidly in conditions of relative stability. In normal times cotton is a major export crop in Uganda, and production is widespread in the eastern and northern parts of the country. Some expansion took place in the 1960s (as coffee output increased in the south-central areas) and the opening of the northern railway line beyond Soroti to Lira (1962), Gulu (1963) and Pakwach (1964) was principally significant as a more satisfactory means of transporting the cotton crop of northern Uganda towards the coast than the earlier lake steamer services. The environmental conditions and transport infrastructure of Uganda provide a sound basis for the restoration of cotton exports at a higher level.

Of the various cash crop hinterlands of the seaports of East Africa, the sisal hinterland of Tanga is one of the most restricted in the sense that it is confined to an area within relatively close proximity to the coast; although other cash crop hinterlands are areally restricted, in most cases they lie some considerable distance inland. Sisal was for many years the only agricultural commodity handled in large quantities at Tanga, and the sisal hinterland may be taken to represent at least the core area of the hinterland of the port as a whole. The sisal hinterland of Tanga is fairly precisely confined to the area served by the Tanga railway which extends as far as Arusha; the hinterland does not extend outside Tanzania, and production is fairly evenly distributed through this zone. Sisal is also an important export commodity at Dar es Salaam, although tonnages have generally been far smaller than at Tanga. Exports of sisal through all East African ports declined during the 1960s and 1970s as a result of generally adverse world market conditions and, in contrast to the other agricultural export commodities discussed above, there is no prospect that sisal exports will revive to any significant extent.

The hinterland source areas of sisal exported through Tanga and Dar es Salaam are generally located within 300 km of the coast and normally within a relatively short distance of railway services. This is not so much a reflection of the particular suitability of this zone for sisal cultivation, for the crop requirements of sisal are minimal and are fulfilled over a wide area of East Africa, but rather of the bulky nature of the crop which encouraged cultivation as near as possible to the exporting ports so as to reduce heavy transport costs. Large amounts of capital were required to establish the industry on an economic footing, and this encouraged concentration of production on an estate basis rather than its dispersal amongst individual farmers. The core area of the sisal hinterland of Dar es

PLATE 7.2. A sisal plantation at the foot of Kilimanjaro, near Moshi, Tanzania. (*Source:* Kenya Railways Corporation, Nairobi.)

Salaam does not extend far beyond Kilosa, and lies close to the main railway line serving the port; a high proportion of sisal consignments to Dar es Salaam is despatched by rail. The progressive decline of sisal exports from Tanzania in recent years, and the parallel efforts to establish domestic industries designed to absorb surplus sisal output, have substantially affected the pattern of the sisal hinterlands of the Tanzanian seaports. At Mombasa, sisal continues to rank amongst the principal cash crop exports passing through the port, and the sisal hinterland reveals an interesting pattern that contrasts forcibly with the patterns established for coffee and cotton. Since sisal is a crop characteristically associated with the drier parts of East Africa, its cultivation is very limited in Uganda, which is in any case rather too far from the coast to permit the economic exportation of so heavy a crop. Production is, however, significant in several parts of Kenya, notably in the dry zone between Nairobi and Mombasa.

Export commodity throughput at Mtwara is restricted both in range and volume; cashew nuts and cassava are the only major items. Although cashew nuts are grown quite extensively northwards along the coast, the main focus of cultivation lies in the Newala area, on the main Mtwara-Masasi road near to the Mozambique border. Beyond Masasi and Nachingwea the incidence of cashew markets is notably less marked, although cultivation continues sporadically even beyond Tunduru. The relationship of the cashew nut hinterland of Mtwara to the road network of the area is important in other ways. The road system within the hinterland is generally inadequate, although funds have been made available for improvements and extensions to potentially productive but previously virtually inaccessible areas. In the past a heavy strain was placed on the road system when record crops of cashew nuts were shipped, particularly if unusually heavy rains occurred in November; to some extent this is still true today. Before 1949, the marketing pattern of cashew and other export crops in the area had traditionally been closely geared to the road system and to the lighterage port of Lindi, so that the impact of the new facilities provided by the railway in 1949-62 was comparatively slight. The opening of the railway coincided with a period of road improvement, and road transport for both exports and imports through Mtwara was generally more convenient and sometimes cheaper than rail. The poverty of the hinterland of Mtwara has long been considered a problem, and "there is reason to suppose that a more fundamental cause of the lack of develop-

PLATE 7.3. Sun-dried sisal on an estate near Tanga. (*Source*: Kenya Railways Corporation, Nairobi.)

ment around the railway is the fact that it did not offer any real attraction to agricultural or business enterprise, and that no development was likely unless the government took action to exploit the opportunities it provided. Inadequate transport facilities may not in fact be the main problem in this area, and if this is the case their improvement could not be expected to stimulate new development" (O'Connor, 1965b, 25). Cashew nut production increased considerably in southern Tanzania in the later 1960s and early 1970s, as overseas demand expanded, and exports through Mtwara (and other Tanzanian seaports) correspondingly rose; in the early 1960s the cashew nut crop was of relatively minor significance (Northwood, 1962) providing an export throughput of about 40,000 tonnes a year. By the early 1970s these export figures had more than doubled, and Tanzania was producing more than 25 per cent of the world cashew crop most of which is grown in or imported by India; in a context of rising output, Tanzania established a Cashew Nut Authority (CATA) in 1973 and facilities were established to process an increasing proportion of the crop before export. In the later 1970s, however, Indian demand for Tanzanian cashew declined rapidly, and in the absence of alternative export markets production of cashew nuts in the hinterland of Mtwara has accordingly been very substantially reduced.

Import Hinterlands

In Chapter 6 attention was drawn to the importance of export throughputs at East African seaports in terms of bulk and break-bulk cargo flows and in relation to imports. The varying importance of the different categories of exports and imports within the port hierarchy, and at individual ports, illustrates in some detail the complexity of relationships with the hinterlands; for each commodity imported or exported through a port there exists a specific hinterland the character of which is dependent upon a wide range of factors of production and consumption. However, exports constitute, in general terms, the key to the hinterlands, partly because they are sometimes more important than imports (if oil and oil products are excepted), but mainly because it is chiefly to the source areas of the main exports that most of the import commodities are directed. An important distinction between imports and exports is, however, that whereas exports originate largely from a series of core areas that are to a considerable extent mutually exclusive, as has been shown, a representative proportion of many of the imported commodities is distributed to almost all populated parts of the hinterland of each port, the proportion varying with the density and purchasing power of the population of each region, and with spatial variations in the level and variety of economic activity.

The pattern of distribution of imported commodities may be briefly illustrated by reference to certain selected items known to be characterized by wide dispersion throughout East Africa. Of these commodities the various types of oil products are the most important, and the largest up-country movements consist of petrol, kerosene, and gas and diesel oils. Oil products derived from the crude oil imported and refined at Mombasa and Dar es Salaam are received in all parts of the hinterlands where motor vehicles and machinery are found and, indeed, in almost all areas where population is present since kerosene is still widely used for cooking and lighting. Oil products are thus despatched to a high proportion of all stations on the East African railway system, and transport by road tanker and by pipeline (Mombasa-Nairobi) is also important. The main concentrations of consumption of oil products are found in the larger towns from which secondary distribution is affected both by road and rail. Nairobi and Kampala, amongst the inland towns, stand out as major consuming areas for oil products of all kinds. The extranational hinterlands of Mombasa and Dar es Salaam in Rwanda, Burundi and Zaire are also supplied with oil products; and, of course, the Zambian INDECO oil refinery at Ndola is supplied by pipeline with crude oil imported at Dar es Salaam.

A variety of other major imported goods are distributed very widely throughout the hinterlands. These include fertilisers, salt, ironware, foodstuffs (chiefly wheat, maize and rice) and motor vehicles (together with tyres and spare parts). Railway materials are also an important category of imports, distributed as required to stations throughout the system; and some coal is imported at Mombasa, mainly for the use of the Bamburi Portland Cement Company. The development of domestic industries has reduced imports of some commodities, notably gunny bags and paper. Certain other categories of imports are of interest in that their inland distribution pattern does not parallel closely the distribution of population but reflects the influence of other factors. One such category is comprised by machinery, agricultural and dairy implements, and tractors. Although the main markets for machinery are naturally found in the towns – the chief industrial centres, apart from the ports themselves, being Nairobi, Jinja and Kampala – the consuming areas for agricultural machinery and tractors are concentrated in the core areas of production of some of the principal export crops. The cultivation of sisal and grain crops, and the processing of coffee, cotton, sisal and tea, all require a considerable degree of mechanization and this is concentrated in the main producing areas.

Composite Hinterlands

Some of the main elements that comprise the economic geography of the composite hinterlands of the seaports of East Africa are indicated in Figure 7.1, which shows the core areas of the cash crop hinterlands of each port together with the major sources of industrial exports. The interest of the composite hinterland of a port lies in its internal structure and pattern, and in the character of the dynamic development surface thus represented. The outer limits of the composite hinterlands of the East African seaport complex lie well beyond the political boundaries of the East African countries; Zambia is served by Dar es Salaam; traffic to and from Uganda, and occasionally southern Sudan and southern Ethiopia, passes through Mombasa; and both the major ports handle cargoes originating in or destined for Rwanda, Burundi and eastern Zaire. Within East Africa the boundary between the hinterland of Mombasa and those of the Tanzanian seaports is now defined by the political boundary between the two countries, which at the time of writing remains closed to normal commercial traffic; prior to 1977, when the border was closed, the hinterland of Mombasa extended into northern Tanzania and overlapped in several areas with those of the Tanzanian ports.

The pattern of core areas within the hinterland of Mombasa is clearly far denser than in the case of any of the other three seaports. The hinterland of Mombasa contains core areas for the production of coffee, cotton, sisal and tea, together with several sources of minerals, oil products and cement that are exported in quantity by surface transport. In terms of area there is a strong emphasis on Uganda; but production of cash crops in the highlands of Kenya is intensive and it is mainly from this area that a wide variety of other export commodities is obtained, although none is so outstandingly significant as to compare with those included on the map. At both Mombasa and Dar es Salaam the cityport area is itself a major

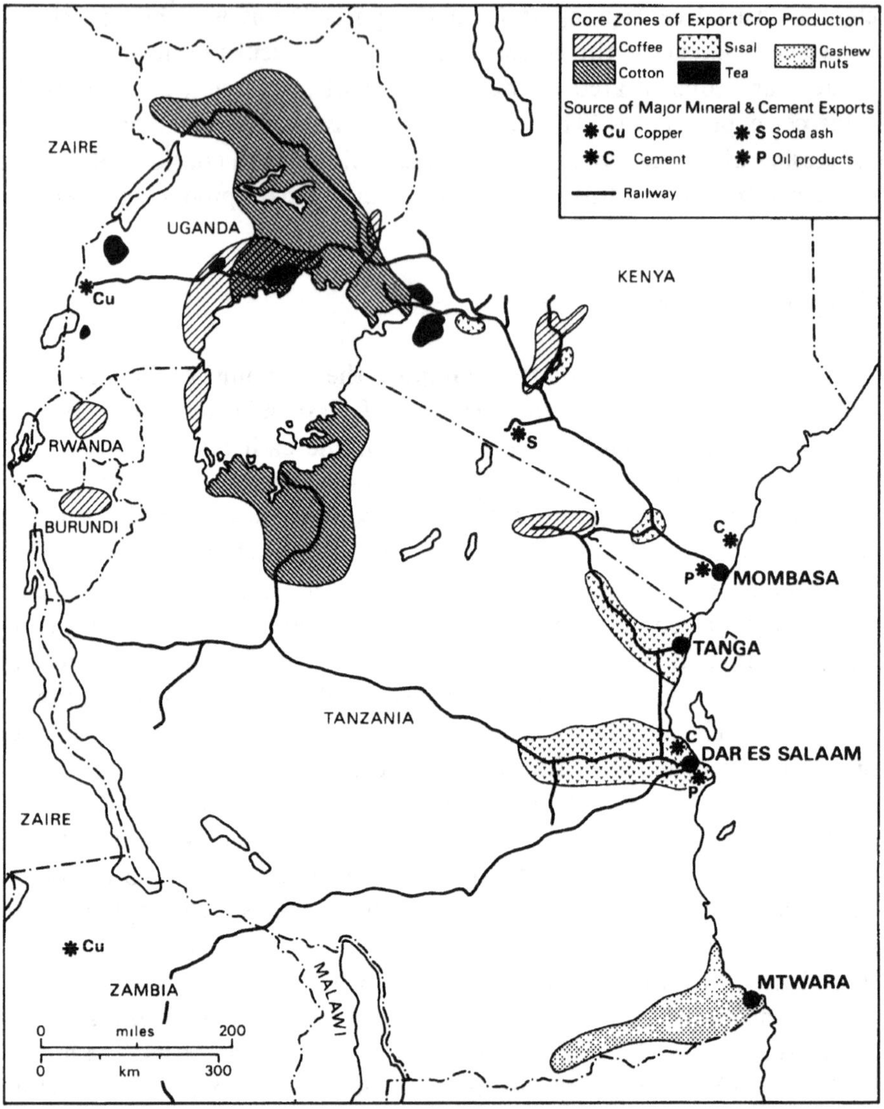

FIGURE 7.1. Some aspects of the economic geography of the hinterlands of East African seaports.

source of export cargoes, especially oil products and cement. The Tanzanian hinterland of Dar es Salaam affords a striking contrast with that of Mombasa, since it contains only two core areas: sisal in the Dar es Salaam-

PLATE 7.4. Mombasa: cement exports from the immediate hinterland of the port: bagged cement from Bamburi being offloaded from a lorry at berth 13, Kipevu. (*Source:* Kenya Ports Authority.)

Kilosa zone and cotton in the Mwanza area. Also, in contrast to the Uganda section of Mombasa's hinterland, the East African hinterland of Dar es Salaam affords no major examples of the overlapping of core areas. In the case of Tanga the core area of sisal production close to the port is very significant; and Tanga is now the principal port serving the coffee core area of the Moshi-Arusha zone. The hinterland of Mtwara compares in size with that of Tanga, but the cashew nut core area is somewhat larger than the sisal core area of Tanga; the contrast in the traffic levels between the two ports reflects the greater weight of the sisal crop and also a variation in the intensity of production as between the two core areas.

No definitive boundary delimits the hinterlands of the East African port group as a whole. Nevertheless, in northern and western Uganda, and in western Tanzania, the political boundaries of these countries set a general limit across which only small amounts of traffic reach the ports at irregular intervals. Very little traffic of any description passes between Mombasa and the southern Sudan, for example; north-eastern Kenya generates relatively little traffic, and Somalia has its own primate port at Mogadishu. For many years the most important element in the extra-national hinterlands of the East African seaports undoubtedly comprised traffic to and from Zaire, Rwanda and Burundi; this continues to form a significant element in port throughput at Dar es Salaam, and occasionally at Mombasa. A considerable area of eastern Zaire lies well within the hinterlands of the East African ports, at least in a potential sense; both the two major East African ports possess rail links penetrating almost to the interstate boundary with Zaire which is crossed by several road links with Uganda and Tanzania. Traffic on these routes has fluctuated considerably in recent years. Traffic across the Tanzania-Zambia boundary, which was relatively slight in the early 1960s, increased sharply as a result of Rhodesia's unilateral declaration of independence in 1965 and Zambia's subsequent search for alternative transport outlets. The improvement of the pre-existing road through the southern highlands of Tanzania to Zambia, and the introduction of important new modes of transport along the same axis (the TAZAMA pipeline in 1968 and the TAZARA railway in 1975), have permitted a greatly increased flow of Zambian traffic through the port of Dar es Salaam. In 1980 Zambian cargoes accounted for 23 per cent of total cargo throughput at Dar es Salaam; copper exports, sent to the port by rail, and crude oil imports, despatched to Zambia by pipeline, are the main items of trade involved.

Within East Africa the southern boundary of the hinterland of Dar es Salaam is partly defined by the extent of the hinterland of Mtwara. In the north there exists a broad zone stretching over north-eastern Uganda and northern and eastern Kenya which is the source and destination of only negligible traffic movements and so hardly qualifies for inclusion within the hinterland of Mombasa as properly defined. The most interesting part of the hinterland lies in the central area where a degree of complexity has arisen in the past as a result of hinterland overlapping. The hinterland of Mombasa has traditionally extended into the northern part of Tanzania, and in two areas this has resulted in a degree of overlap with

PLATE 7.5. Dar es Salaam: Zambian copper exports. (*Source*: Tanzania Harbours Authority, Dar es Salaam.)

the hinterlands of Tanzanian ports. There are three areas of special interest in this central zone. First, the north-western corner of Tanzania, lying between the western shores of Lake Victoria and the Rwanda border, is an important coffee-producing area and has sometimes been within the hinterland of Mombasa by reason of the convenience of transporting coffee exports through the port of Bukoba, across the lake to Kisumu and thence to Mombasa, rather than via Mwanza to Dar es Salaam as is done today. Second, part of the cotton crop from the south-eastern coastlands of Lake Victoria has traditionally been exported via Kisumu and Mombasa rather than via Dar es Salaam; in the past this was largely a reflection of the shortage of railway rolling stock on the central Tanzania line during the main cotton exporting season, and the opening of the Mnyusi-Ruvu link in 1963 was partly designed to alleviate this difficulty. Third, the Moshi-Arusha area of north-eastern Tanzania retained for many years its traditional orientation in transport terms towards the primate East African port of Mombasa as well as towards the regional northern Tanzanian port of Tanga. One of the principal objectives and implications of the closure of the Kenya-Tanzania border in 1977 was the direction of all port traffic originating in or destined for northern Tanzania through Tanga rather than through Mombasa. The main effect of this policy, in terms of port throughput and hinterland traffic flows, has been to increase coffee exports through Tanga at the expense of those through Mombasa.

A point that is sometimes overlooked in the context of the composite hinterlands of the seaports of East Africa is that the two larger ports of Mombasa and Dar es Salaam, together with the intermediate port of Tanga, are situated relatively close together; as a result, their hinterlands are quite narrow at the coast but broaden out considerably inland. Hinterland overlapping has occurred partly for this reason – indeed, it is perhaps surprising that the phenomenon is so limited – but a more important cause of the southward penetration of the hinterland of Mombasa into three important areas of northern Tanzania in the recent past was the existence of superior facilities at the port of Mombasa which traditionally outranked those of the Tanzanian ports, and which in turn reflected the more advanced level of economic development in Kenya than in Tanzania. With the possible exception of Mtwara, none of the major seaports of mainland East Africa can claim an exclusive hinterland, with no overlapping at any time, although the greater part of East Africa may be said with some justification to lie within the exclusive hinterland of one of the four chief port outlets.

The Hinterland of the Port of Zanzibar

The concept of the hinterland of a port is expressed in its most simple form by an island served by a single ocean terminal. There is no question of hinterland overlapping, which occurs in some measure in the case of almost all ports serving parts of larger land masses and in cases where small islands are served by several ports. Furthermore, where the traffic of an island port is small, the range of individual commodity hinterlands is accordingly likely to be rather narrow. The interest of this peculiarly simple form of hinterland thus lies largely in the degree of internal differentiation that can be distinguished within the tributary area, and in the nature of the transit traffic handled.

The hinterland of the port of Zanzibar consists simply of the islands of Zanzibar and Pemba; and, since none of the minor ports of these islands engages in overseas trade, the hinterland is exclusively that of the principal port. Geographical variations within the hinterland may, however, be distinguished in terms of the two major export crops, although this can only be done in general terms. The bulk of the clove exports are derived from Pemba Island rather than from Zanzibar Island; the average share of the total output provided by Pemba has normally exceeded 75 per cent, and that of Zanzibar Island has correspondingly normally been less than 25 per cent. This imbalance within the hinterland is a major factor in the proposals to develop modern port facilities on Pemba Island.

Within the two islands specific areas within which clove production is concentrated are well defined, and correspond to the core areas of export crop production discussed above in relation to the mainland ports. The clove belts are largely confined to the areas underlain by Lower Miocene sedimentary rocks, and avoid the areas of Pliocene and Pleistocene reefal limestone. The *Changa* soils, associated with the Lower Miocene Masingini beds in western Zanzibar, and the corresponding *Utasi* soils of north-central Pemba, are fertile sandy loams particularly suitable for clove growing, whereas the coral areas of the eastern parts of both islands yield thin stony soils unsuitable for intensive cultivation of any kind. The predominance of Pemba in terms of clove production is directly related to the much greater extent of the Lower Miocene sedimentary rocks and associated soils in that island as compared to their much more restricted occurrence in Zanzibar. There is also a relationship with the pattern of communications; within both islands the zones of most intensive production tend to lie close to the main roads linking the rural areas to the ports, and the concentration of production in western Pemba may perhaps be related to the location on the western coast of the island of the three small ports of Wete, Chake Chake and Mkoani through which the clove production of Pemba has traditionally been shipped in small coastal vessels to Zanzibar prior to its exportation overseas.

Although the coconut also grows best on sandy soils it is more tolerant of poorer soils than the clove tree and its distribution is thus much more widespread in both Zanzibar and Pemba Islands than that of cloves. The pattern of coconut distribution is in fact the converse of that of clove distribution: whereas Pemba is dominant in terms of clove production, Zanzibar leads in terms of coconut output. This reflects the general pattern of land utilization whereby the best, most suitable soils are devoted to the production of the most lucrative crop, whilst coconuts are widely grown on a variety of soils that are largely unsuitable for cloves. Outside the clove areas of the two islands coconuts are widely and fairly evenly distributed, and their cultivation is also important within the clove zones. A certain amount of local specialisation was formerly important and may occur in respect of the varied products of the coconut tree; the production of coir fibre, by the method of burying the coconut husks in the sands of the seashore for five months, was traditionally concentrated in the villages of the east coast of Zanzibar Island, particularly Makunduchi, although most of the present-day output comes from small factories in Zanzibar town.

The pattern of clove and coconut production remains the basic key to the economic geography of the hinterland of the port of Zanzibar. Together these products provide over 90 per cent of domestic exports; and the clove belts contain the main concentrations of rural population and therefore tend to be the chief source areas of minor exports (excluding marine produce) and the chief import-consuming areas. In this context the importance of Zanzibar town, as a major element within the hinterland, should not be overlooked; containing about 20 per cent of the total population of Zanzibar and Pemba Islands, the town is the most important market in the islands both for domestic and imported produce. Traditional urban industries include the production of copra and coir fibre, and the distillation of clove oil and coconut oil.

Forelands

The term 'foreland' is a useful one, although not so widely accepted as the term 'hinterland'; it is used here, following Weigend (1958,195) to indicate "the land areas which lie on the seaward side of a port, beyond maritime space, and with which the port is connected by ocean carriers." The concept of the maritime foreland is thus complementary to that of the hinterland; and the seaports, together with their hinterlands and forelands, are economically the pacemakers for ocean carrier developments – "an interesting reversal of the relationship between ports and ships when technical developments are in question" (Bird, 1971, 126). The balance between hinterland and foreland factors in port development is always delicate; in East Africa, the primary stimulus for the initial development of major seaports in both medieval and modern times came from overseas areas, but the present-day patterns of the port complex principally reflect the economic geography of the hinterlands.

As in other parts of the world, the absence of available data on a port-to-port basis prevents a thorough examination of the forelands of East African seaports. Theoretically, just as each port may be said to have an individual hinterland for each commodity imported or exported, so there exists also an individual foreland for each commodity, represented by those ports with which trade is carried on. The seaports of East Africa, like major seaports elsewhere, naturally maintain transport links with many of the large ports of the world; in theory it should be possible to distinguish those ports which are particularly important in relation to the movement of particular commodities through East African seaports in either direction. For example, the coffee hinterland of Mombasa and the movement of coffee through the port need to be related to the coffee foreland of the port; conversely, the petroleum foreland of Dar es Salaam amplifies the pattern of commodity movement partially revealed by a study of the import traffic in petroleum at that port and of the subsequent distribution of petroleum products throught the hinterland. In practice, however, it is not possible to construct an accurate analysis of the various forelands of the seaports of East Africa, even for the major commodities involved; adequate data are not available, since the interests of the Kenyan and Tanzanian railway and port authorities do not extend, as far as official records are concerned, beyond the handling and movement of goods by means of their own respective railway and port systems. No composite data are recorded by the port authorities to cover the destination of exports or the provenance of imports, in terms of port-to-port traffic, and no other source of detailed information is available on this basis. A complete analysis of all shipping manifests, of which there are several thousands each year, would partially reveal the foreland pattern; but even this laborious method would present problems since there exists in respect of certain major commodities exported a system of optional cargo discharge whereby the choice of destination ports is made at a late stage during a voyage. These freighting arrangements, which apply particularly to coffee consignments to Europe and the USA, entirely rule out the possibility of a completely accurate analysis of the forelands in terms of port-to-port consignments. Customs and excise authorities in Kenya and Tanzania provide, however, detailed records of commodity movements on a country-to-country basis, although the data are not related to the individual seaports through which the commodities pass, either in East Africa or elsewhere.

A high proportion (75 per cent in 1980) of the total volume of East African coffee exports pass through Mombasa, which serves in this context the major coffee-producing zones of Kenya, Uganda and Rwanda. The remainder of the coffee export flow is distributed between the three Tanzanian mainland seaports, with Tanga handling coffee consignments from the Moshi-Arusha zone. The USA is the principal customer for East African coffees; in normal times, exports of robusta coffee from Uganda to the USA are particularly important. In contrast, exports to West Germany consist primarily of arabica coffee from Kenya. Coffee exports to the UK have normally followed the American pattern with a strong emphasis on Ugandan robustas. Other major customers include Sweden, the Netherlands, and Japan.

The pattern of the cotton foreland of the seaports of East Africa is rather different. Kenya exports very little cotton, and export traffic is therefore mainly a matter of the Ugandan crop passing through Mombasa and the Tanzanian crop through Dar es Salaam. In 1963 the People's Republic of China appeared for the first time at the head of the list of East Africa's cotton customers, purchasing roughly equal amounts from Uganda and from Tanzania. Hong Kong, India and Japan also import large quantities of East African cotton and together Asian countries now provide a market for a high proportion of the total exports of cotton from

East Africa. West Germany is the principal European customer for cotton.

The sisal foreland again presents a different pattern. Because of the heavy weight of sisal in relation to its value, very little is exported from Uganda. Sisal throughput at the ports thus involves Kenyan exports through Mombasa, and exports through the three Tanzanian ports derived largely from their more immediate hinterlands. Tanga, traditionally the main sisal-exporting port of East Africa, handled in 1980 over 67 per cent of the total Tanzanian sisal export throughput, and 46 per cent of the East African total. In 1963 East African sisal exports totalled 279,000 tonnes, a figure reduced to 114,000 tonnes in 1980. In spite of marketing problems, however, Tanzania and Kenya remain major exporters of sisal fibre, and a wide variety of countries is represented in the sisal forelands. The United Kingdom remains the leading importer; Belgium, West Germany, Japan and Australia are traditionally important customers; and in recent years Asian markets have increased in relative importance whilst those in North America have declined.

Exports of tea through East African seaports have increased considerably in volume and value since the early 1960s, and as the search for new markets has progressed the tea forelands have become more diversified. All three East African mainland countries produce tea, and all the mainland ocean terminals export tea overseas; the bulk of the East African tea crop is grown in Kenya and is exported through Mombasa. As in the case of sisal the United Kingdom is clearly the principal customer, and large quantities of East African tea are despatched to the USA, Canada, and several West European countries. Asian markets, naturally enough, do not figure in the tea forelands of East African ports, but small amounts are despatched to neighbouring African countries. The cashew nut foreland has almost disappeared; the crop was exported predominantly through Mtwara and almost all consignments went to India.

In addition to the five main cash-crop forelands of the four mainland seaports of East Africa brief reference may be made to the forelands associated with three other major exports: copper, soda ash and cement. Copper, mined at Kilembe in western Uganda and smelted in Jinja, was exported principally to Europe during the 1950s and 1960s, but by 1972 Japan had emerged as the predominant market area, taking over 70 per cent of the Ugandan output in that year. Owing to the cessation of copper mining and smelting in Uganda from the mid-1970s, the copper foreland of Mombasa is now virtually nonexistent; given the existence of further reserves of copper at Kilembe, and overseas demand, Mombasa's copper foreland may become reestablished in the future in a context of technological recovery and political stability in Uganda. The copper foreland of Dar es Salaam, dependent upon Zambian resources, touches a very wide variety of ports and industrial areas throughout the world.

There are several major centres of cement production in East Africa – at Tororo and Kasese (Uganda), Athi River (Nairobi), Bamburi (Mombasa), and at Dar es Salaam. All serve different parts of the East African market, and because of the low value of cement per unit of weight exports take place principally from the Mombasa plant, and to a smaller extent from Dar es Salaam. There are small-scale overland exports to Rwanda and Burundi, and the cement foreland of the ports is restricted to destinations in the western Indian Ocean and the Persian Gulf. Mauritius has been the chief customer for many years, followed by Réunion and the Seychelles.

The soda ash foreland, which links the single hinterland source at Magadi with overseas markets, is slightly more extensive. In 1963 South Africa purchased 58 per cent of the total exports of soda ash, which of course pass exclusively through Mombasa, but in 1964 this proportion was reduced to nil as a result of the severance of trade relations between Kenya and South Africa. Soda ash is able to withstand transport costs more readily than cement, and is despatched in significant quantities to countries as far away as Thailand and New Zealand. Nevertheless, countries within the Indian Ocean and its borderlands receive a major share of the total volume of soda ash exported from Mombasa.

Exports of grains, which are important at Mombasa and Dar es Salaam in certain years, chiefly take the form of maize consignments. These are sometimes despatched in quantity to the United Kingdom and other European markets (e.g. Italy, Netherlands), and to Japan. West Germany is also an important maize buyer. In other years comparatively little maize export takes place. Exports of millet and wheat flour have occurred during recent years. Exports of frozen and canned meat take place mainly through Mombasa. Quite a wide variety of destinations are involved, and canned beef shipments to the United Kingdom are particularly important. Hides and skins are exported through all East African ocean ports, and are sent chiefly to the United Kingdom and to Italy.

The pattern of the external trade relations of Zanzibar is somewhat different from that which a superficial examination of the geography of the area might suggest. Although trade with the East African mainland is important, it has traditionally ranked lower than trade with a number of more distant areas. During the 1960s Indonesia and India were consistently Zanzibar's principal customers for cloves, and they have remained the primary export markets although sales to a wide variety of other countries have reduced the relative importance of the traditional market areas. The emphasis upon Asian destinations is important, since it represents a modern perpetuation of Zanzibar's historic trade relations within an Indian Ocean context. Asian countries are also very important as sources of imports at Zanzibar; the United Kingdom, relatively unimportant as a market for Zanzibar's exports, was the principal source of imports in the pre-revolutionary period, but alternative trade links with China, the USSR, the German Democratic Republic and other countries have increased considerably in importance since 1964. The destination of clove exports from Zanzibar, the most important single item in the overseas trade of the islands, is naturally a subject of particular interest. The main feature is the concentration of the market in a restricted area, re-emphasizing the vulnerability of Zanzibar's economic preoccupation with a very limited range of produce. Indonesia, where cloves are used in cigarette manufacture, is traditionally the main market, generally taking over half the total exports. Singapore, Pakistan and India constitute important secondary markets; and the remainder of the crop is widely spread in small consignments to many countries, mainly Asian and European.

In general terms, the changing forelands of the East African seaports reflect the changing economic and political conditions that affect their throughputs. During the colonial period a high proportion of the overseas trade of the East African countries was with the United Kingdom, and as late as 1962 the UK was the destination and source of about 30 per cent of East African exports and imports. While trade with the UK, with other EEC countries and with the USA and Canada all remain important, the growth and diversification of the economies of the East African countries, especially that of Kenya, have involved parallel diversification of the forelands of the East African ports. Thus the share of Asian countries has risen very substantially: the importance of Japan and China as markets for East African exports is now considerable; trade with Middle Eastern countries, India and the USSR is also important. Similarly, although the UK and West Germany remain major sources of imported goods, Japan and China now also occupy high places in the list of East African forelands.

REFERENCES

Bird, J.H. (1971), *Seaports and seaport terminals* (London, Hutchinson).

Hance, W.A., V. Kotschar and R.J. Peterec (1961), 'Source areas of export production in tropical Africa,' *Geographical Review* 51, 487-499.

Hanna, L.W. (1974), 'Bioclimatology and land evaluation in Uganda,' in B.S. Hoyle (ed.) *Spatial aspects of development* (London, Wiley), 75-94.

Hay, A. (1973), *Transport for the space economy* (London, Macmillan).

Hazlewood, A. (1964), *Rail and road in East Africa: transport coordination in underdeveloped countries* (Oxford, Blackwell).

Hofmeier, R. (1973), *Transport and economic development in Tanzania* (Munich, Afrika-Studien series 78).

Mikolajski, J. (1964), 'Polish seaports, their hinterlands and forelands,' *Geographia Polonica* 2, 221-229.

Morgan, F.W. (1958), *Ports and harbours* (London, Hutchinson, 2nd edn.).

Northwood, P.J. (1962), 'Cashew production in the southern province of Tanganyika,' *East African Agriculture and Forestry Journal* 28, 35-39.

O'Connor, A.M. (1965a), 'The geography of tea and sugar in Uganda: some comparisions and contrasts,' *East African Geographical Review* 3, 27-36.

O'Connor, A.M. (1965b), 'New railway construction and the pattern of economic development in East Africa,' *Transactions of the Institute of British Geographers* 36, 21-30.

O'Connor, A.M. (1971a), *The geography of tropical African development* (Oxford, Pergamon).

O'Connor, A.M. (1971b), *An economic geography of East Africa* (London, Bell, 2nd edn.).

Prest, A.R. (1969), *Transport economics in developing countries* (London, Weidenfeld and Nicholson).

Weigend, G.C. (1956) 'The problem of hinterland and foreland as illustrated by the port of Hamburg,' *Economic Geography* 32, 1-16.

Weigend, G.C. (1958), 'Some elements in the study of port geography,' *Geographical Review* 48, 185-200.

8 Seaports and the Development Process

The progress of the less-developed countries towards a more advanced level of economic and social activity involves a very large number of problems and is dependent upon a wide range of factors and influences. The process of development, furthermore, is open to a variety of interpretations based upon economic, political, social or spatial viewpoints (Keeble, 1968; Hoyle, 1974; Mabogunje, 1980). Whatever perspective on the development process is paramount, it is commonly accepted that a modern transport infrastructure, designed both to integrate the constituent parts of an area and to link that area with other overland and overseas areas, is an essential prerequisite of modern economic growth and social progress. In this context a transport infrastructure may operate as an elementary permissive factor, allowing economic interchange to expand and intensify; within such a system the seaport occupies a strategic place, for its essential function is to integrate land and sea transport networks. In less-developed countries this role is particularly important since the modern economies of such countries tend to be predominantly oriented towards distant overseas markets; in this context the capacity of seaports acts as a useful indicator of the relative prosperity of the area served, and may also directly affect economic growth by facilitating or hindering increased port throughput. The development of seaports and overseas trade is a vital factor in the emergence and growth of the money economy, in the expansion of urban populations, and in the growth of market systems; increased trade also helps to create conditions favourable to the development of modern agricultural systems and to the establishment and expansion of modern industry. There is thus a close relationship between seaports and the development process; for Africa, it has been claimed that "the provision of port facilities has been a necessary precondition of modern economic growth," and that "today, the stage of economic development reached in a given part of the continent is in considerable measure a function of the capacity and degree of sophistication of the port facilities available" (Hilling and Hoyle, 1970, 2). Yet ports exist to serve their customers, and the character of a seaport inevitably reflects the demands made upon its services from a wide variety of sources in the hinterlands and on the maritime side; those demands are, in turn, an expression of the development process, and it is essential that a port should respond with flexibility and efficiency.

The location, development, operation and influence of any individual seaport are all affected by a multitude of largely interdependent factors, and the problems of analysis become increasingly complex when the horizon is widened to include a group of seaports in terms of their spatial and temporal development and in the context of their hinterland and foreland relationships. To attempt a comprehensive survey of a port complex in this way would require several volumes each far longer than the present work, and would involve the discussion of much material peripheral to the geographical perspective presented here. A wide range of technical, practical and financial questions, together with a number of social and political issues, all of prime concern to those whose responsibility it is to ensure the smooth working of the ports, have been excluded from detailed consideration in this book; but the broader discussion presented may provide a useful framework within which those who are concerned with specific aspects of port development or who are intimately involved in the minutiae of day-to-day port operation may perceive new interrelationships or fresh viewpoints on familiar scenes.

In general terms the seaports of the less-developed world are obviously playing a fundamental and extensive role in the economic development of the areas they serve. Unfortunately this role is too often taken for granted, and its importance insufficiently appreciated. The writers of the report of the East Africa Royal Commission, 1953-55, a most important general survey of East African conditions and problems at the time, paid no attention to port matters and discussed East African transport solely in terms of roads and railways. Thirty years later it is not uncommon to hear repeated demands for new or extended railways or for major road development programmes, in East Africa and in other developing areas, based on the false assumption that surface transport elaboration automatically and inevitably promotes economic development; but public attention seems to be devoted to seaports only at times when severe congestion causes widespread inconvenience. Even the national development plans outlined in recent years for Kenya (Republic of Kenya, 1969, 1974 and 1979) and for Tanzania (United Republic of Tanzania, 1969 and 1974) pay relatively little attention to port problems. The development and maintenance of an adequate range of port facilities is, however, vital to any area engaging in external trade, and this is particularly the case in areas where the economic structure is still essentially based upon exports of primary produce and imports of manufactured goods. Seaports constitute a series of vital nodes in a transport system which is one of the principal elements by means of which this economic structure has been developed and is maintained. The continuing, but varied, dependence upon exports of primary produce draws attention to the fact that agricultural developments in the developing countries are often impeded by inadequate and unreliable rainfall, by soil deficiencies and by pests and diseases. Export crop production is usually concentrated in a number of limited core areas, which are to a certain extent coincident with core areas of population concentration and import consumption. These general considerations relate to the Third World in general, and they have a close bearing upon seaports and upon the problems with which this book is concerned. But it is not enough to say that seaports are vital to a less-developed area or country as a whole; it must also be appreciated that they are far more important in relation to certain parts of such an area or country – to those relatively restricted, favoured areas of population concentration and export production – than they are to those vast intervening spaces basically characterized by low population densities and subsistence economies. Undoubtedly there is enormous scope for expansion of economic activity in developing countries, and much expansion is likely to re-emphasize existing core areas rather than to initiate major new growth centres. The growth of the economies of the less-developed countries implies increasing external trade, and the question arises as to whether the seaports serving these countries, now and in the future, will be able to cope with traffic increases without suffering serious congestion.

Environmental Constraints

These general points are amply illustrated by the seaports of Kenya and Tanzania discussed in this book in relation to the developing economies of the areas they serve. In more specific terms, however, the role of seaports in the development process is conditioned by a series of factors which to some extent control or inhibit the extent to which seaports can fulfill their development functions and which affect the character of the relationship between seaports and development. One of the most potent of these factors is undoubtedly the physical environment, discussed in Chapter 2 where it was shown that environmental conditions affecting the development of the East African port complex are generally advantageous, and that site conditions at individual seaports do not present any insuperable obstacles to physical expansion, in the context of the functional framework within which each port now operates and is likely to operate in the foreseeable future. The conditions of land and water situation which now favour the growth of the seaports have largely arisen during the last hundred years; previously East African seaports lay between an undeveloped potential hinterland and a maritime trade system largely controlled in physical terms by the wind regime of the Indian Ocean and with few direct links outside that ocean. Developments on both the landward and seaward sides have now intensified and enormously widened the significance and relationships of the seaports, so that they no longer lie in a backwater but maintain links with major seaports in all the inhabited continents. In comparison with many other less-developed areas of the world, the East African coast is particularly fortunate in being equipped with several good natural harbours, where adequate shelter and deep water close inshore reduce that dependence upon tidal fluctuations which so frequently restricts shipping manoeuvres in many other countries. Mombasa, particularly, has been fortunate in its possession of two harbours, one suited to medieval conditions and one to modern circumstances. The potentialities of the harbour at Dar es Salaam, which were not appreciated until the era of steam navigation was well established, clearly illustrate how harbour utilization is partly a function of navigational conditions and techniques as well as a reflection of the conditions of land and water situation. Although the shallowness of the harbour at Tanga is one of several factors that have prevented the development of deep-water facilities there, it is at Dar es Salaam that site conditions are proving most problematical and restrictive in relation to present and future port developments in East Africa. The port of Mtwara, in spite of its possession of one of the best natural harbours on the East African coast, has seen comparatively little development as a result of adverse circumstances in terms of the land situation. At Zanzibar, circumstances of situation and site are the least encouraging amongst East African seaports; an offshore island, an indifferent site and a minute hinterland are not likely to stimulate increased traffic flow in modern conditions. In various ways, therefore, the seaports of Kenya and Tanzania provide a useful variety of illustrations of the relationships between land and maritime factors, between harbours and ports, and between situation and site, all of which deeply affect the pattern and level of port development throughout the modern world.

The Emergence of a Modern Port System

While the environmental conditions within which port activity takes place provide one set of conditioning factors in a spatial dimension, the role of ports in the development process must also be viewed over time. In this context, the seaports of the East African coast provide an excellent illustration of the concept of changing port hierarchies and, in more general terms, of the vital role performed by ports in the initiation and diffusion of development throughout the area served. The medieval trading settlements (Chapter 3) which were the precursors of the modern ocean ports along the coasts of Kenya and Tanzania were important points of contact on the fringes of the early trading circulations of the Indian Ocean. A variety of goods, people and ideas were introduced into East Africa by this means; but although the medieval ports and cities of the East African coast have provided a rich field for archaeological investigation, the overall impact of pre-twentieth century penetration and settlement in East Africa through the coastal ports was negative. The rising tide of Arab-controlled slave trading in nineteenth-century East Africa severely disrupted the social fabric of the area, although numerous innovations in terms of items of trade became increasingly widespread during this period. The importance of Zanzibar as a nineteenth-century centre of innovation in East Africa deserves emphasis, although, as has been shown, the port is of only local significance today.

The emergence of a modern hierarchy of seaports in any part of the less-developed world has inevitably been associated with a variety of technological, economic and political innovations. The re-entry of Europeans on the East African scene in the later nineteenth century coincided with a number of important technological changes: the opening of the Suez Canal, the change from sail to steam as a means of propulsion of vessels, the rapidly increasing size of ships, and the growing importance of railways. A combined result of these innovations was that in early colonial East Africa arterial railways were built inland from port sites selected for their ability to accommodate large steamers in a context of increasing East African trade with Europe via the new Suez route. The traditionally fluid port pattern in East Africa was thus crystallised as more capacious, sheltered, deep-water harbours replaced the minor inlets and open shorelines previously used by smaller sailing ships. The intention to build railways – themselves powerful agents of innovation – was the immediate cause of concentration of interest and activity on the modern seaports, and the subsequent extension and elaboration of the rail and road feeder systems has served to consolidate the importance of the seaports as gateways to and from East African hinterlands.

A temporary colonial political relationship with Europe was instrumental in the emergence of modern seaport hierarchies in many parts of the less-developed world, and in the establishment of the detailed internal structure of Third World transport systems. Subsequent changes within those structures, reflected in the comparative range and level of installations at the ports, have themselves reflected the varied economic and political fortunes of different parts of the Third World during colonial and postcolonial times. Today, the installations available at ports in the less-developed countries, as the case of the East African ports (Chapter 5) demonstrates, cannot normally be regarded as more than barely adequate in the context of present-day needs, and productivity levels achieved are frequently unsatisfactory. In the context of likely future traffic increases, therefore, close attention is given by port authorities to the extent and form which the expansion or rehabilitation of port installations should take, and to methods of improving productivity and management in the port industry. In some parts of the less-developed world there is still, unfortunately, a tendency on the part of many authorities not directly connected with ports and shipping to take port facilities for granted, and to assume that they are adequate until increasingly frequent congestion and public outcry prove otherwise. Too often port expansion has appeared to be a move made in desperation in the face of intolerable pressure upon existing facilities; it should, of course, be undertaken as part of a broad, flexible plan designed not only to serve present needs but also as an investment for the future. Wherever possible port capacity should always be slightly ahead of present throughput, so that increases can be absorbed without undue congestion. Whilst the dangers of overcapitalisation and resultant heavy interest charges must be avoided wherever possible, the cost of making available a reasonable margin of spare capacity should be compared with the cost to the less-developed economy as a whole of the delays, frustrations and traffic losses which inevitably result if serious congestion is allowed to occur. Naturally, such an ideal pattern of development is rarely carried out, chiefly because financial provision for port expansion is not normally made available until the need for it is extremely pressing, and because varying traffic demands (the problem of 'peaking') rule out any possibility of the total elimination of congestion.

Problems and Opportunities

There is usually, of course, a full and detailed awareness of these issues at senior port management levels throughout the developing countries, but concern for the full range of problems involved is apparently not always shared by those supranational organisations through which provision for port expansion might be made. An illustration of this problem arose in Kenya in the early 1960s. Commenting on an EARH forecast of capital expenditure on port development for the period 1963-67 (which amounted to £5.56 million), a World Bank economic survey mission commented that "We think that a critical review looking to a downward revision of the programme should be undertaken. Capital expenditure on East African harbours should be limited for the next few years to that required for safe operation, to complete projects already carried to a point where failure to complete would cause serious loss of funds already spent, or to prevent excessive delays in traffic under normal conditions" (IBRD, 1962, 138). This policy had certain immediate advantages in terms of financial expediency, but it assumed by implication that a degree of congestion is to be expected at all times and that severe congestion is to be tolerated when conditions vary from 'normal.' In the long run such a policy might well prove disastrous; since it must be assumed that traffic flow will continue to increase in volume, at least at larger seaports, and that this increase will probably be gradual but may involve sharp rises, provision must also be made for a gradual expansion of facilities to keep ahead of traffic requirements. Otherwise, if facilities are allowed to fall seriously behind traffic levels, an extremely difficult situation might build up which would have far-reaching implications for economic development from which ports would find it very difficult to recover.

In recent years there has been ample evidence from many parts of the less-developed world, including East Africa, that governments and port authorities have taken important steps, with the support of the World Bank and other international organisations, to alleviate congestion and to facilitate port throughput by the implementation of major physical expansion programmes. These developments have clearly illustrated, once again, the interplay of economic, political and technological factors in port development; and have demonstrated that, in the final analysis, there is no permanent escape from port congestion. At many seaports throughout the developing world, including those of Kenya and Tanzania, the perennial problem of congestion at the quayside and in the transit sheds and storage areas arises mainly from delays and difficulties involved in handling imported cargoes. Congestion is expressed in terms of a queue of ships waiting for berths, or in terms of inadequate coordination between ship operators, port authorities and land transport systems. In East Africa, congestion has at times been serious at Mombasa and at Dar es Salaam, which contrast strikingly with the underworked minor ports in Tanzania in this respect. The problem of 'peaking' in the context of cargo flows is common to ports everywhere, and has arisen in East Africa both in the context of overlapping export-crop seasons and in terms of variations in import throughput. At Mombasa, congestion reached a critical level in 1965-66 and again in 1973-74; the exceptional pressures at the port of Dar es Salaam throughout the 1970s also resulted in an unprecedented degree of congestion. At all East African seaports, imports present a greater problem than exports because of the nature of the goods handled; problems attached to working export cargo are comparatively simple because relatively few commodities are involved, quantities are often relatively large, and mechanization can therefore be employed to the full. Imports, in contrast, have traditionally consisted of a much wider range of goods in smaller consignments of very varied shape and size. The administrative problem involved in handling import cargo is also generally greater, and mechanization cannot normally be employed to the same extent. The increasing use of containers at the seaports of East Africa and in other less-developed areas of the world is likely in the longer term substantially to alleviate these problems.

The range of problems and opportunities that characterise the seaports of the less-developed countries in terms of port expansion schemes are well illustrated by the case of East Africa. As has been discussed in Chapter 5, there are ample opportunities within the natural harbours of Mombasa and Mtwara for extensive further development of deep-water port facilities; in the case of Mombasa, it is anticipated that such expansion might form the basis of a major maritime industrial development area with significant long-term implications for the space economy of Kenya as a whole; in the case of Mtwara, in spite of the development opportunities that are available in physical terms, it seems very unlikely that any significant expansion will take place in the foreseeable future. Dar es Salaam and Tanga present problems of a rather different nature in terms of the expansion of port facilities, and in both cases it is likely that new deep-water installations will eventually be constructed outside the confines of the natural harbour. In each individual case, as at all ports throughout the world, the extent and general character of port expansion is chiefly determined by traffic demand, derived largely from the hinterlands, whereas the detailed character and layout of facilities are conditioned by maritime factors in the form of the design of shipping and the methods of cargo transport by sea. Port expansion schemes designed by engineers are essentially the waterfront expression of the combined effect of these numerous influences, and in many locations have relatively little to do with the natural conditions of harbours which appear merely as one set of factors among many that affect port design and layout.

New Port Developments in Kenya

The further development of port facilities in a developing country is not necessarily confined to the existing port hierarchy, which is itself a dynamic phenomenon and may of course gain or lose constituent elements in the course of time. New ports of various kinds have been established in several African countries in recent years, usually in the context of a major regional development programme (Hoyle, 1981). In West Africa the port of Tema (Ghana) has emerged as a critical element in the Volta River regional development scheme; and in Ivory Coast a development programme for the south-western part of the country involves the new port of

San Pedro. In East Africa, Mombasa is the only major modern port with deep historic roots; the ports of Zanzibar, Tanga and Dar es Salaam represent nineteenth-century innovations, and Mtwara is a 'new' port of the 1950s. Today there is no serious prospect of developing additional new seaports in Tanzania, given that several existing ports are underutilised and a range of possibilities exists for expansion in the future at or near existing port sites. In Kenya, however, the possibility of establishing a second deep-water port as a basis for a new urban and industrial growth pole has been discussed for several years. The virtually complete dependence of Kenya and Uganda upon the port of Mombasa is a sensitive issue in political and strategic terms, and the creation of alternative coastal growth centres would accord with the Kenya government's broad development strategy. Consideration was initially given to three possible port sites north of Mombasa: Kilifi Creek, Malindi and Manda Bay. Factors affecting the choice of Manda Bay for further investigation included favourable conditions of land and water site, the likely impact on the development of the hinterland, and relationships with local and national transport systems.

Manda Bay is a large area of water 5 km wide and 10 km long, located about 10 km north-east of the historic island port of Lamu. It is connected to the open sea by a 19-km channel more than 18 m deep, which would require relatively little dredging. The land site offers extensive areas of flat land available for industrial development. Apart from Lamu (population c.6000) the area around Manda Bay has a very low population density; construction workers and port labour would therefore have to be imported and suitable infrastructures provided. Road and rail links could be routed from Manda Bay through Kitui to Nairobi (510 km), and in the longer term road links with Somalia and Ethiopia might be envisaged. From an engineering standpoint, the cost per berth of development at Manda Bay would be lower than elsewhere on the Kenya coast, since dredging would be minimal and no breakwaters would be needed. In some respects Malindi might provide a more suitable location, but sociopolitical and strategic considerations favour the north-eastern coastal zone, a very underdeveloped area in comparison either with the Mombasa-Nairobi-Kisumu axis or with the southern coastal area between Mombasa and Malindi. A new port at Manda Bay, equipped with adequate communications with the national as well as the local hinterland, would provide an adequate basis for a new industrial growth pole of considerable long-term potential. The immediate hinterland of Manda Bay includes part of the

Tana river valley and displays considerable economic potential for traffic generation. Existing road communications are poor, and there is no railway; the most immediate necessity, therefore, is the improvement of a road which would bring the lower Tana valley within the hinterland of the new port. The potential for agricultural and livestock development in this area is considerable; cotton production and the cultivation of mangoes and citrus fruits are well established and could be expanded considerably for export. The Tana River Development Authority, set up in 1972, has designed numerous irrigation schemes, but water is scarce and the demands of irrigation and hydroelectric power production require careful integration. The development of a fishing industry, livestock ranching and industrial projects such as meat canning and fertilizer production present considerable possibilities as yet untouched; a sizeable export throughput based on cotton, livestock products and fruit would result from such developments, and imports would be dominated by construction materials, fertilizers and machinery. The prospect of extending the hinterland of the new port to include parts of the Kenyan economic core zone centred upon Nairobi seems less favourable in the immediate future because of the very high cost of long-distance communications by road and/or by rail.

Part of the argument for a new cityport and growth centre in north-east Kenya rests ostensibly on the history of congestion in the primate port of Mombasa. These problems would not be significantly reduced, however, by the creation of a second deepwater port, since their root causes lie in the difficulties and inefficiencies of the land transport systems serving the port, and to a certain extent within the port itself, rather than in under-provision of berthing or cargo-handling facilities. Although a point has been reached where there is no longer any further obvious direction for port expansion at Mombasa, throughput, capacity and efficiency could be improved considerably; and the Kenya Government announced in 1979 that substantial further investments are to be made in the port of Mombasa. To this extent, therefore, the case for Manda Bay as a major national cityport and growth pole is at least temporarily weakened.

A master plan for the proposed new cityport (Republic of Kenya, 1977) outlines a port equipped to handle general-cargo vessels of 20,000 tonnes using conventional handling methods at two 180-m deepwater quays. Container traffic would be minimal, at least initially, and lighterage would be avoided. The plan outlines an industrial zone to the north of the main urban area. Traffic forecasting is always a hazy science, but in the context of regional development Manda Bay might expect to handle a total throughput approaching 250,000 tonnes by the 1990s. In the absence of substantial oil traffic (although imports of oil products would doubtless be important) the port would initially develop mainly as an exporting port. If some Mombasa traffic were to be diverted through Manda Bay, in a context of improved communications, total throughput might rise to over 500,000 tonnes within the first decade of the operation of the new port. These figures are relatively modest in relation to current throughput totals at Mombasa, where cargo handled in 1981 totalled 8.4 million tonnes (including 3.6 million tonnes of oil imports).

The possibility of a new seaport at Manda Bay developing as an industrial growth pole in the reasonably near future does not on present evidence seem very likely. There are no known major mineral deposits within the immediate hinterland, and the search for oil reserves has so far proved unsuccessful. The construction of the Mombasa-Nairobi oil-products pipeline, linked to the Mombasa refinery, largely pre-empts the position with regard to petrochemical industries. Similarly, fertiliser and cement industries which might have been located at Manda Bay are currently being developed in the Mombasa area, so increasing the dominance of the primate port in this respect. In the absence of any large-scale industrial traffic generator, it seems likely therefore that the industrial horizons of the new cityport would initially be strictly limited. In this context the proposed port contrasts with most other new cityport growth poles in modern Africa, where a specific industrial *raison d'être* has provided an essential stimulus for port development. The processing of iron ore at Saldanha Bay (South Africa), Nouadhibou (Mauritania) and Buchanan (Liberia), the treatment of timber at San Pedro (Ivory Coast), the aluminium industry at Tema (Ghana) and the phosphate developments at Lomé (Togo) all provide examples of motivating industries without parallel in the Kenya case. There is therefore an inherent danger that a new port at Manda Bay might become, in East African terms, nothing more than the Mtwara of the north. The arguments in favour of Manda Bay rest primarily on the socioeconomic and strategic desirability of developing a neglected corner of the national territory – an area of considerable long-term potential but limited resource endowment – and also to a certain extent on the need to provide solutions to the actual and potential problems associated with cityport congestion at Mombasa as Kenya's maritime industrial development area continues to expand.

Transition problems in Tanzania

The primate Tanzanian seaport of Dar es Salaam has presented for some considerable time the most acute problems in terms of development within the existing East African port system. With the present Main Quay was completed at Dar es Salaam in 1956 it was assumed that no further major expansion would be necessary at that port for some time to come. This view was quickly overtaken by events in the early 1960s, however, and although congestion was not often a serious problem at Dar es Salaam in the mid-1960s it quickly became so before further physical expansion at the port could be completed. Thus there has been a marked acceleration in the rate of port expansion at Dar es Salaam, largely as a direct result of the problem of finding politically acceptable outlets for the trade of land-locked Zambia. After the dissolution of the Central African Federation in 1963, and the subsequent hardening of southern Africa's colour curtain along the middle Zambezi as a result of Rhodesia's unilateral declaration of independence in 1965, Zambia sought increasingly close economic and political ties with East Africa (especially with Tanzania) and became an applicant member of the East African Community. These developments in one sense turned upon the ability of the port of Dar es Salaam to handle an increasing volume of Zambian trade – notably copper exports and oil imports – and the port became a centre of innovation in a political and technological as well as an economic sense. Plans were already well advanced for an international rail link between the Zambian copperbelt and Dar es Salaam before 1965, and the completion of the line in 1975 considerably strengthened the position of the port in relation to the Zambian hinterland, a position consolidated by the improvement of road conditions and the introduction and expansion of oil pipeline services along the same axis. Zambian developments thus considerably accelerated the rate of physical port expansion at Dar es Salaam, and in view of the restrictions imposed by the configuration of the harbour attention has been directed to the possibility of initiating a new phase of port development outside the harbour entrance. A very important factor affecting the further development of Dar es Salaam is, however, the extent to which Zambia will continue to use the Tanzanian port in the context of an independent Zimbabwe (1980) and the reopening of transport links with ports in Mozambique and South Africa. From October 1978, when Zambia reopened its border with Rhodesia and began to use South African ports again, the position of Dar es Salaam once more became competitive in relation to other ports in eastern and southern Africa, and the proportion of Zambian external trade passing through the port began slightly to decline.

Problems associated with port installations at the three smaller Tanzanian seaports are much less severe than at Mombasa and Dar es Salaam; but whereas the growth of the larger ports turns essentially on the twin problems of physical expansion and improved productivity, the difficulties of the smaller ports are in some respects of a different nature. Tanga remains predominantly a lighterage port, although the question of deep-water quay development is frequently discussed and presents no insurmountable physical obstacles. As a result of its geographical situation between, and relatively close to, the two larger seaports, and in the context of an inferior harbour and a hinterland restricted in both area and resources, Tanga has never attained in the past a sufficient throughput to justify expenditure on deep-water installations. Although a specialised deep-water jetty has been added, the case for developing a deep-water quay for break-bulk cargoes at Tanga still seems weak; the increased use of Tanga for Zambian exports, or for a higher proportion of Tanzanian imports, might create in the future a situation in which the prospect of Tanga as a deep-water port would seem to be more realistic. Mtwara, unlike Tanga, is equipped with an excellent deep-water harbour and a deep-water quay. Port installations are, however, greatly underused. Trading activity at Mtwara has hitherto fallen far short of the expectations of the port's founders, and in the decade prior to the political independence of Mozambique in 1975 the port suffered as a result of its proximity to the sensitive Tanzania/Mozambique border along the Rovuma river. On several occasions the possibility has been discussed of using some of the spare capacity that is available at Mtwara for Zambian traffic, but land transport routes are currently inadequate and new ones would be expensive and difficult to construct. In general the economic prospects for the port and its hinterland do not seem at present to be very encouraging; and, although the two cases are not strictly comparable, the experience of Mtwara does not give any support to those seeking to promote the idea of a second deep-water port in northern Kenya.

At the port of Zanzibar there is also some spare capacity, since the level of throughput attained has never effectively overstretched the installations provided in 1929. In one sense, therefore, there is little need to expand port installations, although in terms of the range of available equipment many improvements are necessary. For some years the most urgent need has been the replacement of outdated and outworn equipment; in the context of the government of Zanzibar's economic diversification policies, new port developments are included as a major element in infrastructural expansion. The economic revolution that has taken place in Zanzibar since the political revolution of 1964 has had some important effects on the structure and the pattern of the economy of the islands. In the early 1960s the classic overdependence upon an extremely restricted range of export crops was parallelled by a narrow range of overseas trading links, a heavy dependence upon imported foodstuffs, a virtually complete absence of modern industry and a very low average purchasing power amongst the population. Much of this situation has been modified in the later 1960s and 1970s, with Chinese assistance and in the context of the 'cloves boom.' Agricultural diversification – including rice and sugar schemes – is aimed primarily at a reduction in dependence upon imported foodstuffs. New cash crops include tobacco and chillies, and Chinese-aided industrial developments include a tobacco factory and a shoe factory; the former processes imported tobacco, the latter uses local hides. The modest industrial base of the islands, which includes numerous small plants processing coconut products together with furniture manufacture and fruit processing, is in process of expansion; current projects include light engineering, fish processing and fruit canning. The tourist industry, hitherto neglected, has considerable potential, and new hotels and transport facilities have been developed for this purpose. Some of the proceeds of clove exports have been utilised for airport extensions on both Zanzibar and Pemba Islands; for an ambitious road improvement programme; for new port facilities near Chake Chake on Pemba Island; and for an extensive housing redevelopment scheme based upon voluntary labour and local materials – a focus for self-help development at various points on the islands. In the Zanzibar of the 1980s, therefore, "the old values . . . have given way to a new era; and if the grey concrete blocks of workers' flats and factories make for a less picturesque Zanzibar, they certainly make for a more practical one" (Martin, 1973, 9).

The Response to Containerisation

Questions concerning port development and operation in East Africa, as elsewhere, are inevitably linked with major changes in cargo handling methods that have become increasingly widespread in recent years. The rising importance of bulk handling installations at East African ports reflects economic pressures and technological trends towards the further refinement and increased efficiency of the processes involved at the quayside, the crucial land-sea cargo transfer point. More generally, however, the use of standard-sized containers as a basis for unitised transport linking inland terminals through ocean ports and sealanes became the dominant trend in the 1960s and effectively revolutionised cargo-handling techniques in the seaports of all advanced countries. During the 1960s and early 1970s a high proportion of break-bulk ocean cargoes were unitised, port operation became increasingly automated and the overall efficiency of the world shipping industry was improved. An interesting problem during this period was the extent to which less-developed countries would find it in their interests to adapt their port systems to the 'container revolution.' The main arguments for increased containerisation of cargoes are that the pace is forced by the developed countries where the automation of cargo-handling processes has gone forward rapidly; and that shipowners and others involved in sea transport to and from developing countries require that port facilities in those countries match up to facilities in industrialised lands, or at least to a rising world minimum level. Against this view there is the point that containerised transport systems are most economic when used to facilitate the multidirectional flow of high-value goods in quantity between advanced countries; the incorporation of less-developed countries within this system presents a range of economic and technical problems, but there is no basic reason why these should not be overcome in circumstances where participation in the global container network is seen as clearly advantageous. During the 1970s Mombasa and Dar es Salaam both experienced the transforming influence of containerisation; deep-water berths built in anticipation of a gradual increase in container throughput were rapidly adapted as container terminals. At these major East African seaports the further development of container facilities and the growth of container throughput is likely to increase rather than reduce the degree of concentration of traffic within the East African seaport hierarchy at the major terminals. In this context the East African experience is representative of a much broader canvas: only a selected number of economically important or strategically located Third World seaports have to date been able to become fully involved in the new world maritime transport system based on the through transport concept; and containerisation, like all earlier technological innovations in maritime transport, tends to operate selectively, to reduce the number and increase the relative importance of major ports, and to reduce the relative status of minor ports unable to attract traffic based upon the new technology.

Seaports and Regional Development

An analysis of seaports in the context of regional economic development requires an emphasis upon the interdependence of the character of port throughput and the character of port hinterlands, for throughput is basically a function of hinterland production and demand, and the economic geography of hinterlands provides an explanation of the structure and character of port throughputs. Although total cargo throughput at the seaports of East Africa as a whole increased substantially during the 1960s and 1970s, a very considerable part of this increase was accounted for by rising oil imports and by the increased use of Dar es Salaam for Zambian traffic. Exports of East African primary and semiprocessed products have varied and in some cases declined; the traditional association between ports and export-producing zones in the hinterland is being eroded as the economies of the hinterlands are diversified and as the functions of the ports become more complex. The seaports of East Africa, like those of any developing area of the modern world, handle a very high proportion of the external trade of the countries they serve, and in this sense their vital functional role is undeniable. Beyond this, however, the emergence of a highly differentiated hierarchy of seaports is intimately linked with the detailed pattern of economic development in the hinterlands. Many of the factors involved in the emergence of the modern seaports came from the maritime side, but the chief factor affecting the structure of port traffic today is the pattern of economic geography in the hinterlands and the relationships between this pattern and the level, range and spatial disposition of available transport facilities. The ports themselves have contributed to the emergence of this pattern; the introduction of sisal through

Tanga, cloves through Zanzibar, cotton and coffee through Mombasa, have contributed in varying degrees to the growth and spatial pattern of the cash crop economy of East Africa. Each port now includes within its composite hinterland a series of core areas of cash crop production, areas which in most instances now constitute 'islands' of relative economic advancement in terms of import consumption and population concentration as well as agricultural development. This pattern is, in a sense, the most obvious spatial expression of the dual economy, involving on the one hand "export enclaves dependent on the sale of raw materials to world markets and the import of manufactured goods in finished or semi-finished form primarily for the limited high-income groups in the export enclave markets"; and on the other hand "a hinterland characterised by low-productivity, low-income agriculture which (provides) low-cost labour for export enclave production" (Seidman, 1972, 30).

Seaport Gateways: Towards the Future

A wide variety of problems is thus raised by the role of seaports in a context of modern Third World development. The cost of overcoming the restrictive impact of distance is one of the basic factors affecting progress in all less-developed countries, and the promotion of increased mobility is everywhere a primary objective of development planning in the socio-economic sphere. The less-developed countries have progressed beyond a stage when almost any transport improvement seemed bound to bring economic benefit, to one in which the need is not just for more and better transport facilities but rather for a greater degree of precision in the introduction of transport innovations and in the establishment of transport policies in the light of an appreciation of what transport can and cannot be expected to do, and of what else must be done if transport investment returns are to be maximised. Transport innovation does not work miracles; integration of transport planning with other economic sectors is essential to development strategy. Integration within the transport sector too is important; at the grass roots level in the developing countries the most primitive transport modes – head porterage and canoes – still account for a high proportion of goods movements; in view of the great importance of such modes in the lives of millions of people today, a high priority of national-scale transport policies must continue to be the extension and improvement of low-cost rural road systems so as to bring at least one modern transport mode within reach of a much higher proportion of the population. In a social and political context it may be claimed that rural road systems constitute the highest transport priority; in economic terms their role can be invaluable as they help to extend the traditionally restricted 'islands' of the modern economy and perhaps to initiate new centres of growth. The transport problems of the less-developed countries should not, however, be viewed in isolation from one another or from the rest of the world system of which they form a part. Transport systems provide a framework for integration at local, regional, national and international levels; such systems are interdependent, and the power of transport innovation in any part of a system to facilitate development and to promote interregional and international understanding and cooperation should not be underestimated (Ogundana, 1974). Equally, the restrictive impact of substandard transport systems and facilities can seriously impair the economic progress and prospects of a region, state or community. It is in this context that the role of the seaport, as a node in a complex web of temporal and spatial interrelationships, is particularly crucial.

The ports of Mombasa and Dar es Salaam have developed, during the twentieth century, as the twin master gateways to and from East Africa, thus replacing the port of Zanzibar which fulfilled that role in the mid-nineteenth century. Their position has been stabilised by the provision of rail and road networks in the hinterlands, and by the pattern of modern East African economic development. They are likely not only to retain their predominant position but to consolidate it. The division of the greater part of East Africa between the hinterlands of these two ports stems from the partition of the area between 1886 and 1919 into two colonial dependencies administered respectively by Great Britain and Germany. These very temporary political circumstances, coinciding with the building of the initial arteries of rail communication, effectively ensured the continuing division of East Africa into two economic compartments, each with its own principal railway and port. Independent East Africa has perpetuated this division by the pursuit of divergent economic policies at the national level. The smaller mainland seaports of Tanga and Mtwara fulfil a more restricted and closely circumscribed role but remain integrated within the general pattern of mainland transport. Individually they present relatively few problems, in comparison with the two larger seaports. The position of the port of Zanzibar, however, is in many respects more difficult. Initially developed to fulfil a role now performed by the mainland port group, Zanzibar has declined into relative economic insignificance as its hinterland has been reduced to the offshore islands. Although Zanzibar has been a part of the United Republic of Tanzania since 1964, there is still relatively little sign of unity between the islands and the mainland in practical terms. No serious attempt has yet been made effectively to bring the port of Zanzibar within the jurisdiction of the port authorities of the mainland.

Looking towards the future, what major problems seem likely to confront East African port authorities? It cannot be assumed that the further economic development of the East African countries will necessarily take place within the established system – economic, political and spatial – that has been inherited from the colonial era and already substantially modified. The problem of restructuring the dual economy characteristic of East African and other less-developed countries involves not only the spatial and social diffusion of development, the emergence of new growth centres and more progressive industrial location policies, but also a reordering of the inherited institutional complex upon which the development process is founded and through which it operates (Seidman, 1972). In political terms the East African Community, which in many respects represented the most advanced form of interstate economic unity in modern Africa, was based historically upon a succession of increasingly close forms of functional cooperation between the three partner states, but made very limited progress and eventually collapsed. In a spatial context, as many writers have observed, variations in economic development as measured by interregional income inequality or development expenditure are often remarkably persistent; expansion and innovation often tend to be located in those areas already established as primary development zones (O'Connor, 1963; Williamson, 1965; Safier, 1969), in spite of government policies designed to counteract or counterbalance these trends. Although these broad problems far transcend the scope of the present discussion, their eventual solution will not leave the ports unaffected since the activity of the ports is predominantly a reflection of the activity of their hinterlands. Changes in the distribution and range of economic development, and changing political relationships between the various constituent elements of East African society, will undoubtedly continue to affect the operational patterns and functional structure of the contemporary port hierarchy. As in other developing countries, the main problems will not be the lack of an adequate number or range of ports, but will rather lie in the excessive development of those cityports where growth is already far advanced. Present tendencies throughout the less-developed world are towards a state of urban hypertrophy, and this is particularly important in the case of cityports. Many developing countries are not equipped with either an adequate urban hierarchy or a well-developed transport system, yet frequently possess cityport capitals which are primate several times over. The major cityports are thus already faced with the danger of producing a polarisation of economic and social activity which may not stimulate the wider diffusion of benefits necessary for a fuller realisation of economic potential. The tendency towards urban hypertrophy may be further accentuated in the future by the continued rapid growth of the cityports, uncompensated by the growth of urban industrial areas elsewhere. Whilst such a situation would undoubtedly bring many benefits, it might also lead to conurban problems on a scale as yet unknown in the Third World (Vennetier, 1969).

Fortunately these problems of urban and regional balance have long been given a considerable measure of attention in East Africa. The Kenya Government's policy of growth centre diffusion (Taylor, 1974), and the Tanzania Government's policy of rural development, both illustrate in different ways a strong concern for interregional balance in levels of investment and economic development. Moreover, the decision to remove the capital function from the Tanzanian primate cityport of Dar es Salaam and to develop a new administrative focus at Dodoma is aimed precisely at the problem of polarisation and ineffective distribution of development benefits which besets so many less-developed countries. This separation of functions between an inland capital city and a coastal port (sometimes primate in economic terms) is a situation that has existed in Kenya since 1907, when the capital of the British East Africa Protectorate was removed from Mombasa to Nairobi, but which characterises very few other tropical African states.

The emergence and continuing development of a port complex serving less-developed countries thus involves the interplay of a complex range of variables; factors involved may not themselves be geographical or economic, but may nevertheless have economic or spatial implications. Some factors may operate only on a very local scale, such as those associated with port sites; others, such as the distribution of rainfall or feeder road systems, indicate regional conditions within the hinterland; on a still broader canvas, continental or global factors represent involvement in far wider systems, circumstances and changes. Seaports do not grow in isolation but in response to changing opportunities and demands at different times, over different areas, on different scales and with different intensities. An appreciation of the dynamic elements in port development is therefore necessary, for seaports are continually changing; the East African port hierarchy of 2000 or 2150 will not be the same as that of 1980, itself substantially different from the patterns of 1850 or 1950. Today the major role which the seaports of Kenya and Tanzania are fulfilling affects in some measure the lives of all the people in the hinterland area, including of course the cityports themselves. The seaports are one set of instruments through which East African external relations are conducted; in trading terms, these relations still involve important links with those countries which were formerly colonial powers in the area – the United Kingdom and West Germany – together with the United States and India; but trade with European countries has declined in relative terms and that with Asian countries (especially China) has increased, a trend which is natural in the early postcolonial decades and which marks a partial return to a much older pattern of trade focused upon the Indian Ocean which persisted for more than a thousand years before the coming of the Europeans. In the context of their environment, their history, and their conditions of operation, the seaports of East Africa are generally fulfilling their varied roles with a high degree of efficiency; the first concern of all who are involved in port operation – whether in management, cargo handling, navigation or planning – should be the maintenance and improvement of efficiency, for the costs of inefficiency are widespread, long-lasting and serious.

REFERENCES

Clayton, A. (1981), *The Zanzibar revolution and its aftermath* (London, Hurst).

East Africa Royal Commission, 1953-55, *Report* (London, HMSO, Cmd. 9475).

Hilling, D. and B.S. Hoyle (1970), 'Seaports and the economic development of tropical Africa,' B.S. Hoyle and D. Hilling (eds.), *Seaports and development in tropical Africa* (London, Macmillan), 1-9.

Hoyle, B. S. (ed.) (1974), *Spatial aspects of development* (London, Wiley).

Hoyle, B. S. (1981), 'Cityport industrialization and regional development in less-developed countries: the tropical African experience,' B. S. Hoyle and D.A. Pinder (eds.), *Cityport industrialization and regional development: spatial analysis and planning strategies* (Oxford, Pergamon Press), 281-303.

International Bank for Reconstruction and Development (1962), *The economic development of Kenya: report of an economic survey mission* (Nairobi, Government Printer).

Keeble, D.E. (1968), 'Models of economic development,' R.J. Chorley and P. Haggett (eds.), *Socio-economic models in geography* (London, Methuen), 243-302.

Logan, M.I. (1977), 'The spatial system and planning strategies in developing countries,' *Geographical Review* 67, 229-244.

Mabogunje, A.L. (1980), *The development process: a spatial perspective* (London, Hutchinson).

Martin, D. (1973), 'After Karume, Zanzibar quietly changes course,' *African Development* 7 (1), 9-10.

Middleton, J. and J. Campbell (1965), *Zanzibar, its society and politics* (London, Oxford University Press for the Institute of Race Relations).

Ndegwa, P. (1968), *The Common Market and development in East Africa* (Nairobi, East African Publishing House, 2nd edn.).

O'Connor, A.M. (1963), 'Regional contrasts in economic development in Uganda,' *East African Geographical Review* 1, 33-43.

Ogundana, B. (1974), 'Seaport development: multinational cooperation in West Africa,' *Journal of modern African studies* 12, 395-408.

Republic of Kenya (1969), *Development plan 1970-74* (Nairobi, Government Printer).

Republic of Kenya (1974) *Development plan 1974-78* (Nairobi, Government Printer).

Republic of Kenya (1977), *Manda Bay port: feasibility study of Kenya's second port: report* (Nairobi, Renardet-Sauti for the Ministry of Power and Communications).

Republic of Kenya (1979), *Development plan, 1979-83* (Nairobi, Government Printer).

Safier, M. (1969), 'Towards the definition of patterns in the distribution of economic development over East Africa,' *East African Geographical Review* 7, 1-14.

Seidman, A. (1972), *Comparative development strategies in East Africa* (Nairobi, East African Publishing House).

Taylor, D.R.F. (1974), 'Spatial aspects of Kenya's rural development strategy,' B.S. Hoyle (ed.), *Spatial aspects of development* (London, Wiley), 167-187.

United Republic of Tanzania (1969), *Second five-year development plan, 1969-74* (Dar es Salaam, Government Printer).

United Republic of Tanzania (1974), *Third five-year development plan, 1975-79* (Dar es Salaam, Government Printer).

Vennetier, P. (1969), 'Le développement urbain en Afrique tropicale,' *Etudes de géographie tropicale*, 1 (Bordeaux, Centre d'Etudes de Géographie Tropicale).

Williamson, J.G. (1965), 'Regional inequality and the process of national development: a description of the patterns,' *Economic Development and Cultural Change* 13 (4), Part II, 84pp.

Glossary and Abbreviations

Sw. = Swahili

AMI	Agence Maritime Internationale
Andromache, HMS	a British warship which visited Mombasa in 1824, when the Mombasa Protectorate was governed by Lieutenant J.B. Emery.
Bahari (Sw.)	sea
Banadir (Sw.)	coastal zone and ports north of Mombasa
Bandari (Sw.)	harbour, roadstead, port
BPCC	Bamburi Portland Cement Company Ltd.
CGA	Clove Growers' Association
dwt	deadweight tonne(s)
EAC	East African Community (1967-76)
EACHS	East African Cargo Handling Services Ltd. (1964-76)
EACSO	East African Common Services Organisation (1964-67)
EAHC	East Africa High Commission (1948-64)
EAHC	East African Harbours Corporation (1969-76)
EAOR	East African Oil Refineries Ltd.
EARC	East African Railways Corporation (1967-76)
EARHA	East African Railways and Harbours Administration (1948-67)
Foreland	the land areas which lie on the seaward side of a port, with which the port is connected by ocean carriers.
Forodhani (Sw.)	a place where goods are landed and shipped (from *Forodha*, a customs house)
Hamali (Sw.)	a cart drawn by men; a porter
Funguni (Sw.)	sandbank, spit
Harbour tonne	either 1,000 kilogrammes or one cubic metre, whichever unit is used for raising port charges.
IBRD	International Bank for Reconstruction and Development (World Bank)
ICD	inland container depot
ICHCA	International Cargo Handling Coordination Association
Kaskazi (Sw.)	the north-east monsoon
KCHS	Kenya Cargo Handling Services Ltd. (1976-)
Kilele (Sw.)	point, pointed end (nb *Kelele*, shouting, uproar, noise)

Kilindini (Sw.)	a place of deep water , a deep channel
KPA	Kenya Ports Authority (1976-)
KRC	Kenya Railways Corporation (1976-)
Kusi (Sw.)	the south-west monsoon
Leven, HMS	in 1822-23 Captain W.F.W. Owen made a hydrographic survey of the East African coast in HMS *Leven.*
manifest	list of a ship's cargo, for the use of customs officials
Mchanga (Sw.)	sand
Mji (Sw.)	town, village, settlement
Mrima (Sw.)	the East African coast between the Kenya/Tanzania border and the Rufiji delta
Mto (Sw.)	creek, estuary, inlet, arm of the sea; stream, river
Mvita (Sw.)	the island and town of Mombasa
Mwamba (Sw.)	reef, rock
Mwera (Sw.)	the coast of Tanzania south of the Rufiji delta
Ngalawa (Sw.)	outrigger canoe
Ng'ambo (Sw.)	the other side (e.g. of a creek or river)
Nyika (Sw.)	semiarid wasteland; zone parallel to the Kenya coast, a few miles inland; also the Nyika people of this area
Ras (Sw.)	cape, headland, promontory
Reitz, Port	Lieutenant J.J. Reitz, commander of the HMS *Leven*, was the first Governor of the Mombasa Protectorate in 1824.
Ria	a coastal indentation formed by submergence as a result of a relative rise in sealevel
RO/RO	Roll on/Roll off
Sawahil (Sw.)	coast, littoral
Sawahila (Sw.)	coastal inhabitants, the Swahili
SBM	single buoy mooring
Shangani (Sw.)	v. *mchanga, ushanga*
Tanga (Sw.)	sail (of a vessel); to go to and fro, to loiter
TAZAMA	Tanzania-Zambia Pipelines Ltd.
TAZARA	Tanzania-Zambia Railway Authority
TEU	Twenty-foot equivalent units
THA	Tanzania Harbours Authority (1976-)
TIPER	Tanzanian and Italian Petroleum Company Ltd.
Tonne	metric ton (1,000 kilogrammes)
TRC	Tanzania Railways Corporation (1976-)
UNDP	United Nations Development Programme
Unguja (Sw.)	Zanzibar Island and town
Ushanga (Sw.)	bead
VLCC	very large crude carrier
Wa-Changamwe (Sw.)	one of the twelve tribes of the Swahili of Mombasa
Wa-Kilindini (Sw.)	one of the twelve tribes of the Swahili of Mombasa
Wali (Sw.)	an appointed headman in a Moslem community
ZSTC	Zanzibar State Trading Corporation

Index

www.ingramcontent.com/pod-product-compliance
Lightning Source LLC
LaVergne TN
LVHW011120300926
849160LV00008B/458
9780415850506